T0329481

# BODIES IN BEDS

# Bodies In Beds

## Why Business Should Stay Out of Prisons

Sue Binder

Algora Publishing
New York

Library of Congress Cataloging-in-Publication Data —

Names: Binder, Sue, 1943- author.
Title: Bodies in beds: why business should stay out of prisons / Sue Binder.
Description: New York: Algora Publishing, [2017] | Includes bibliographical
    references.
Identifiers: LCCN 2017001375 (print) | LCCN 2017008923 (ebook) | ISBN
    9781628942644 (soft cover: alk. paper) | ISBN 9781628942651 (hard cover:
    alk. paper) | ISBN 9781628942668 (pdf)
Subjects: LCSH: Prisons—United States. | Privatization—United States. |
    Corrections—Contracting out—United States.
Classification: LCC HV9471 .B52 2017 (print) | LCC HV9471 (ebook) | DDC
    338.4/736573—dc23
LC record available at https://lccn.loc.gov/2017001375

Printed in the United States

This book is dedicated with much love and appreciation to my four children: Carl, Pam, Angie, and Kris.

# Table of Contents

# ACKNOWLEDGMENTS

First and foremost I must acknowledge my editor and agent, Alice Heiserman. This book would never have been completed without her wise red ink and editorial comments. Just when I was ready to throw up my hands in defeat, she would send another email and spur me on to action. You are one awesome lady, Alice!

Alex Friedmann, Associate Director, Human Rights Defense Center, Managing Editor of *Prison Legal News*, and a former CCA prisoner, has been instrumental in providing support and encouragement. Special thank you, Alex for linking me with my attorney and providing the wonderful Introduction to my book.

Bob Cumbow, Attorney and Partner with Miller Nash, Graham & Dunn, has graciously reviewed the manuscript and given advice. I would still be wandering in the dark without his assistance.

Algora Publishing and my editors, Martin DeMers and Andrea Secara, supported this project and gave constructive suggestions. Without their sharp eyes and vision, the manuscript would still be on my desk.

I also thank all the folks who have provided research and contributed to this manuscript, even though I may not have directly spoken to them. These include American Civil Liberties Union (ACLU); Bob Libal at Grassroots Leadership; Shane Bauer of *Mother Jones*; the writers and workers at Human Rights Watch, Human Rights Defense Center, Source Watch and the Sentencing Project, and numerous others who have provided inspiration to pursue this project.

# FOREWORD

*Bodies in Beds* exposes the realities behind the rhetoric of prison privatization, and provides an inside look at what happens when a prison is run by a private corporation that cares more about profit than the people in its correctional facilities—both offenders and employees.

The author examines understaffing and other endemic problems in privately operated prisons, where the corporate goal of maximizing revenue eclipses the societal goals of ensuring humane conditions of confinement and rehabilitating prisoners—the vast majority of whom will one day return to our communities.

While this book may have resulted from the author's objections to CCA's business model, and moral conflicts regarding her employment with a company that puts profits over people, it is a greater reflection on CCA's own moral failings. Unfortunately some people need to be locked up to ensure public safety; that's the reality. Though they do not need to be held in prisons run by businesses that answer not to the public but to corporate shills and shareholders. That is also a reality that public officials need to acknowledge.

As with most companies, private prison firms have a need for constant expansion—which means more bodies in more beds. Ironically, crime does in fact pay if you're a CCA executive or shareholder.

Ours is a nation of mass incarceration, and what the author saw at the CCA-run Bent County Correctional Facility in Colorado is replicated in thousands of other prisons and jails across the United States, both public and private. While she has correctly identified the profit motive as one of the great evils in our criminal justice system—an evil that serves as the core business model for companies like CCA—the larger underlying issue of mass incarceration also must be addressed if we are to achieve any meaningful change.

While the author makes a number of useful suggestions for improvements based on her empirical experience as a former CCA employee, she omits the most obvious one: ban private, for-profit prisons. My only complaint with this well-written book is that the author should have resigned from her position with CCA and released this account much sooner.

Alex Friedmann
Associate Director, Human Rights Defense Center
Managing Editor, *Prison Legal News*
Former CCA prisoner

# Introduction

Writing this book has been a journey of conflict and of learning about the reasons privatization is so pernicious. I worked for the Corrections Corporation of America (CCA), now renamed CoreCivic, for more than twelve years as a mental health professional. During that time, I participated in and used their medical benefits program, added to my 401K, even held a minute piece of stock for a time, and happily collected my biweekly paychecks as well as bonuses. I am grateful for this and for having the opportunity to exercise my skills as a counselor and therapist.

On the other hand, as I will relate in the following chapters, I harbor a sense of having "sold out." Until my resignation, I continued to collect my paycheck and receive those fringe benefits (well, almost always—Chapter 19 details how CCA at the end cheated me out of my last paycheck, and I learned that this is not atypical of privatized facilities). Yet, my conscience was eating at me. As the years passed, the whispers in my mind grew louder. Soon, they increased to a mighty roar as my spirit protested. The work that I was doing—or failing to do— no longer corresponded to my moral code. I increasingly came to realize just how much my initial impressions of CCA had changed. As CCA has grown, so has the focus of the company, and therein lies the problem. Throughout my employment, I tried to tell myself that the significant changes were simply a matter of my own perceptions—that it was my viewpoint that had changed, colored by my own personal evolution. Certainly, some of that is true.

Yet, as I reviewed the increased challenges that resulted in staff resignations and my own sense of being overwhelmed, I became increasingly aware that most of the problems and issues related to one basic issue—understaffing.

Understaffing is at the heart of many problems throughout the private prison industry, as I learned in the course of my research. This is one reason that there are so many problems across the range of private prisons—both those run for the federal government and those run for state and local governments. The model of the private prison that puts profit ahead of rehabilitation and even safety is, by its very nature, untenable.

Understaffing is simply a symptom of the true problem. In the end, all decisions are driven by the need to show a profit, and this can translate into an inability to obtain needed supplies, lack of staff, or not being able to adequately perform one's job. It's okay for a company to make a reasonable profit, but not when that comes on the backs of the taxpayers, the company's staff, and the inmates. I contend that private prisons or privatized parts of prisons cannot do a responsible job of handling the mental health care needs of prisoners, and this book provides the proof.

Still, I faced a dilemma in writing this book. I have worked with good people, many of them talented and caring professionals, who have over the years kept me safe and watched my back. I care for them. I respect them. Yes, on many days, I abandoned the writing of this book because of the good people I had worked with, as well as the paycheck and benefits I had earned along the way. I also bore a sense of my own inadequacies in not being able to implement changes that might have led to greater benefit for the offenders, the facility I worked with, and the prison system as a whole.

Nevertheless, these factors were outweighed by my own indignation. I finally realized that I could no longer do the job I was trained to do as a therapist. I was no longer able to help offenders. Readers will note my frustrations primarily due to this factor. As a Licensed Professional Counselor (LPC) in the State of Colorado, my focus was on the issue of understaffing and the far-reaching implications primarily as related to the mental health field—providing appropriate care and services for offenders. Understaffing affects both staff and offenders. It also has major ramifications for the safety of staff and offenders within the facility.

I have worked with good, caring people, but the company I worked for, Corrections Corporation of America (CCA), did not and does not care. Discussions with staffers who work at other private prisons run by Management and Training Corporation or GEO, show that their experiences are similar, as are their disappointments with the ruling theme of their employers. Those working with juveniles at other privately-run facilities face similar issues, including the "Kids for Cash" episodes in Luzerne County, Pennsylvania.

This book will describe my experiences with one for-profit company and will show through specific incidents just how the profit motive (the resulting understaffing) has cheated inmates of what they had a right to expect—treatment for their mental health needs, has impacted staff morale, and has played a significant role in not satisfactorily fulfilling safety and security issues—concerns vital to prison welfare for both staff and inmates. This book describes my experiences within the Bent County Correctional Facility, which is owned and operated by the Corrections Corporation of America (CCA), a for-profit prison system. Many other staff who work at CCA and other privatized prisons throughout the country can tell the same story. My experience is not unique; it is emblematic of what other staffers in mental health and in other areas all face. This could have been written about any of the private prisons across the country.

As I further researched the way the profit motive affects the work of these companies, I learned that CCA, while the largest private prison system in America, is not the only private company that is reaping profits at the hands of its offenders and taxpayers. GEO Group and Management and Training Corporation have also been criticized for understaffing and cutting corners in order to assure profits and mega-salaries and benefits to their upper management.

Concerns about these prisons-for-profit splashed into headlines with the August 2016 announcement by the Justice Department that they would begin severing ties with both CCA and GEO, citing an audit which indicated that they are less efficient and more ineffective than government-run facilities. My experience verifies this finding. Privatized correctional facilities should be outlawed. Earning money from imprisonment or jailing is an anathema. It was a bad practice when the earliest jailers charged their "clients" for food and any conveniences including straw for sleeping. It is even worse today: companies that expect to earn profits have no reason to provide adequate services and help rehabilitate individuals. In fact, they have a disincentive to do so, since they are generally paid per capita. More expenses means less profit. More prisoners means more money, and more individuals who return to prison because they were not able to rejoin society means even more money.

To demonstrate the far-reaching consequences of the for-profit mentality, I have included incidents and experiences from other counselors and facilities as well as details on some congressional legislation, and the Justice Department's recent decision that might bring about some changes in the privatized operation of prisons. I show why these changes are imperative.

It is important to let the public understand what is happening to prisoners and to staff who work with them by exposing the problems of privatized prisons, particularly the failure to provide the mental health treatment prisoners need. Privatization of prisons causes many problems, but the lack of true mental health provisions for inmates shines a light on why legislators and other concerned citizens should be aware of the problems and lobby our legislators to abandon privatized prisons because in the end, the human costs they impose greatly outweigh any supposed cost savings they produce.

In the presidential debates of 2016, Hillary Clinton announced that she would do away with privatized prisons at the federal level and try to encourage this same thing at the state level. Having a president who is opposed to privatization in corrections would be a first step toward making major improvements to our correctional systems. This book will provide support for that position and show why such a change is necessary.

By exposing the issues and offering some suggestions and recommendations, I hope to spur some serious thinking about how we can provide incentive for change both by the political system and by the leadership and administration within the private prison system. Ultimately, this book may play a small part in bringing the private prison system to an end in the United States. Meanwhile,, those working behind the gates in private prisons may consider some of the suggestions in order to implement in-house and in-department changes which will assist them in preventing inmates returning to the system.

The very notion that released offenders often continue to commit more crimes and, as a result, circle back through the prison time and again, indicates that the system is not working. And when a large segment of those re-offending have been diagnosed with a mental health disorder that may contribute to their criminal behavior, that points even more accusingly toward a failure within the system. It screams for change. As a mental health clinician, I find this recycling of inmates intolerable. As a taxpayer, I am angry at the waste of my money because with proper treatment many of the people who return to prison could be productive citizens and not just warehoused entities. Over the long run, it is far cheaper to offer competent treatment than to let inmates linger without such treatment.

The next big frontier where legislation can make a difference is in the detention of immigrants. According to an August 2016 e-mail from the American Friends Service Committee: *"Nine out of the 10 largest immigrant detention centers are run by for-profit companies;* yet, Congress continues to approve a federal quota that mandates the federal government maintain 34,000 beds each day in these types of facilities, specifically for the mass detention of immigrants. The immigrant detention quota contributes to the inhumane detention of over 400,000 immigrants in a given year, to the tune of $2 billion in taxpayer money."[1]

We face a lack of treatment and concern for offenders due to the lust for profit. Privatized firms are in business to make profit—and to report such profit back to their owners/shareholders. This book will examine the myth that private prisons save money to taxpayers. Instead, they compete against public agencies by cutting services, paying less to their staff, and cutting corners whenever they can get away with it.

To protect privacy, all the names in this book have been changed and certain episodes were altered slightly to protect the identities of staff and offenders. However, all situations validly represent what I experienced or what other health professionals working in private facilities have undergone. My story is buttressed with findings from legislation and scholarly research.

# Chapter 1. "How Many Are Coming in Today?"

"How many are coming in today?" I heard the warden's question as I dumped my jacket and my shoes, along with my official Corrections Corporation of American (CCA) identity badge, into a plastic bucket to send them through the scanner. I watched as the conveyer belt grasped the white container and sucked the collection through to an officer waiting on the other side. No beeps, no stops. I passed the initial check. The machine and the attendant were now assured that I had not brought any weapons or drugs into the prison.

"A total of forty-eight—in and out," stated another officer, as he unclasped his utility belt, preparing to load his own personal effects into the next waiting container. Probably in stating the total, he may not have realized the full implications of the warden's question. Since Corrections Corporation of America (better known as CCA) is paid on a per capita basis, the more inmates coming in, the greater their revenue.

Unfortunately, I knew exactly how many inmates were coming in and going out. This was part of my job—I screened newly arrived inmates at Bent County Correctional Facility, just as I had for the last twelve years. Each move day, I prepared intake packets. I slapped each packet with labels with their names, Department of Corrections' identifying numbers, and noted the specialty codes on their initial screening form. These codes designated whether the offender needed mental health, substance abuse, anger management, or sex-offender treatment. Ironically, just because they "needed" such treatment did not mean that they would receive it, as we will see throughout this book. Because of this process, I knew exactly how many new arrivals were expected this date, so, naturally, I spoke out.

"Twenty-four in," I spoke up. "Twenty-four in and twenty-two out." I passed through the body scanner and picked up the container with my identity, shoes, and jacket. I slipped the identification badge over my neck, as I snagged my jacket and shoes. I dropped onto the blue metal bench to slip into my Dr. Scholl's gel-inserts to protect my knees and legs from the rigors of the concrete floors and staircases I had to traverse each day.

"Should be twenty-two out, thirty in," I heard the warden say. Those going out represented a loss of revenue. They might be leaving for parole or perhaps they had completed their prison sentences and would be discharged from the system altogether. Perhaps they were being transferred to another prison for a specific program or perhaps they needed a high level of treatment unavailable at Bent County. Whatever the reason, their departure meant a loss of dollars while More arrivals represented additional income.

Why was I not surprised at the warden's statement? The more inmates, the more reimbursement the facility received from the Colorado Department of Corrections. Simply put, payment to the private prison is based on the number of offenders housed in the facility. (And in one of the latest contracts with a private facility, the federal government guaranteed that the private company would receive a guaranteed amount even if the facility is empty or holds fewer than the maximum number of prisoners it was slated to hold.)

I shuddered a bit as I moved to the door and jabbed the access button so that I could gain entry into the next section of the prison, the area designated for administration. *Bodies in Beds*—that is what it is all about, I thought, as I realized that I would be dealing with those twenty-four inmates in another five or six hours. I would sit separately with each new offender and patiently conduct his intake. The intake required my completion of eight pages of information on each offender.

Bent County Correctional Facility held only male offenders who ranged in age from eighteen to perhaps eighty. We managed to acquire "kids" directly from youth offender programs, along with Department of Corrections "old-timers," or those who often had lengthy sentences, perhaps even "life sentences" due to their ages.

Intake required obtaining each inmate's signature for the Health Insurance Portability and Accountability Act (HIPAA), basically a confidentiality agreement. Their signatures also indicated that they understood the Prison Rape Enforcement Act (PREA), the policy relating to sexual contact, including rape, instituted by federal law. My duty also included explaining the suicide policy and process to each offender. In addition, I asked each offender a series of questions regarding mental health, medical issues, and about their general history. The process took five to ten minutes per offender.

I sighed outwardly as I paused before a metal lockbox containing keys. I had to punch in my secret code to obtain my office keys. In the beginning of my stay at Bent County, I carried "permanent issue" keys. They went with me everywhere, traveling between home and work. I hated those keys and lived in fear that I might lose them. After a few years, the lockbox arrived, further protecting staff against loss but also protecting us against inmates obtaining keys and constructing weapons with them or entering offices where they did not belong and procuring confidential or dangerous (to them and others) information. Lost keys meant a lockdown for the entire facility until the keys were located.

I reminded myself daily while working in the prison that lost keys and lockdowns were not my primary concern. The most important thing I could do and did do constantly was to keep a watchful eye out for myself and others. After all, our offenders' crimes ranged from what might be considered petty, such as theft or bad checks, to felonies such as murder or rape. These men were not choir boys. Thus, keeping a continual watchful eye was essential for my safety and that of my peers.

On the day when I overheard the warden's response, I must have given a bigger than usual sigh as well as made a noticeable frown. I was frustrated about the number of new inmates. I was the only mental health worker that day, which meant that with no setbacks, the process would take about two hours out of my already busy schedule. Of course, any setback, such as running into a lockdown, daily count time, or another emergency would mean that the process could take even longer.

Normally I had another mental health worker who shared the work with me. But, on this day, I was operating solo. My colleague's assignment on this day was to assist with the psychiatric clinic, referred to as *tele-psych*. This meant that she would sit with the inmate while the psychiatrist assessed his status over the television—much like Skype. I, too, had this duty, every other clinic. Because the activity included briefing the doctor on the inmate's current status, and answering any questions he might have related to the counseling or medications, the administration felt that having a mental health staffer do this work was a time-saving factor for the doctor. The process also required that the clinician make certain that the inmates arrived on time for their appointments. We would call their cell houses if they did not arrive when they were expected to be there.

Sometimes it meant insisting that Inmate Jones be roused out of bed and sent to clinic—over the protests of Correctional Officer Smith who was "too busy." Once the offender arrived, the clinician checked him in, got him to sign any necessary consent forms, documented his return time from the clinic, and noted any changed diagnoses in the computer to align with the doctor's current evaluation.

While much of this process could be allocated to a clerk, part of it required a licensed professional, so it was deemed more efficient for a clinician to do all of this. It was a time-consuming task, not a difficult one, and it required that one clinician was taken away from "active duty" once or twice per week. The management never considered what this meant in terms of completing other required duties or how well these other duties were completed.

My colleague's role was every bit as hectic as mine. Before the arrival of the twenty-four new inmates, I also had a full schedule: a morning full of appointments, one right after the other; clinical notes to write; and new appointments to be made. Then, there were the numerous interruptions to provide information to administration, staff, my supervisor, and to the Colorado Department of Corrections. All in all, it was just a typical day for the lead mental health coordinator. I was considered the lead because I had been there the longest, even though all coordinators had the same titles. This meant that I had the "good fortune" to be blessed with substantial administrative tasks.

As a result, even as I responded to the warden's inquiry, inwardly I was resentful. I swallowed my frustrations although I felt my stomach knot up and my throat tighten. These feelings were not new to me. The longer I worked at Bent County Correctional Facility, the greater my stress level. More frequently, I found myself just wanting to walk away from the job. But walking away from challenges was not in my nature.

When I wrote this section, the two of us worker bees, both Licensed Professional Counselors, with master's degrees, were serving more than 400 offenders, who had been diagnosed and/or coded as having mental health problems. That case load alone presented a formidable challenge, but those were not the only offender numbers we were responsible for.

The Colorado Department of Corrections asked us to monitor and screen about 700 sex offenders—approximately 50 percent of the Bent population. Of this group, about 180 lacked a specialized qualifying code to indicate their program-treatment level. Due to the lack of a proper code, we had to spend additional screening time to determine if they were amenable to sex-offender treatment.

The coding of sex offenders, along with the definition of what constitutes a sex offence in Colorado, meant that the mental health staff had to interview and process those inmates. Often that required consultation with the Department of Corrections' sex-offender team, all of which resulted in additional work hours for the mental health staff. Because of the number of sex offenders (more than 5,000 behind bars in 2014 in Colorado[1]) and because of a variety of offenses and sentences, some inmates may have life sentences, others only a few months. Treatment, therefore, becomes sporadic. Short or determinate sentences, such as those given to someone caught fondling, might mean that the inmates would never get to treatment due to the long wait lists for such treatment. They may end up in treatment *after* they got out of prison. Other sex offenders, who had lengthy sentences, may not receive treatment until they are closer to their parole eligibility date because those programs, too, have long wait lists. A KRDO-TV investigation indicated that 93 percent of the time, sex offenders were released with no treatment.[2]

This lack of treatment represented a real concern to mental health professionals. Those who had not received treatment would leave prison with no tools to combat their urges and triggers. Thus, they might be likely to victimize another human being. They were more likely to return to prison. Some sex offenders would be required to do sex-offender treatment, if placed on parole—but would they comply with the program?

With all of the screening and monitoring facing us, my colleague Christy, a true trooper, managed a smile and a positive attitude while I sometimes frowned and complained. Maybe she was so positive because she had only been at her job for about two and a half years. I had been doing this work for twelve years at that time, and the strain of it made me tired.

Over these twelve years, I had watched the number of inmates grow, but, more importantly, the number of those diagnosed or sometimes labeled as mentally ill had increased. At the same time, I had witnessed the reduction of services and programs, and of the lack of ability to reintegrate offenders back into the population. Yet, I had more paperwork to complete—much more, but with little or no clerical help. I had grown increasingly overwhelmed by the mountains of documents required by both CCA and the Colorado Department of Corrections—paperwork, which often served as band aids to stem the rising tide of litigation and which, oftentimes, was duplicative.

I was deeply frustrated at not being able to do the work that I had planned to do, that I was educated and trained to do. Years of education and supervised hours to obtain my master's degree and licensure—were those wasted? Perhaps as a clinician working in human services, I expected too much. I had previously been self-employed in my own counseling agency, and my goal had always been to provide therapy, counseling, group and individual services, as well as referrals for those who had needs that exceeded my ability to meet them. And during the first five to seven years of working at Bent County Correctional Facility, generally, I was able to continue that process.

Not anymore. I had not been true for about five years. When I looked back on the growth of CCA over my twelve years with them, and I reviewed some of the issues with the company that had arisen over the years, it sometimes appeared that my journey toward negativity had advanced at about the same rate as the company's expansion. Along the way, the company had lost its concern for its staff and "customers," that is, offenders. The company was now all about profit. While I am not necessarily opposed to profit, it should be earned for services that are provided, not for warehousing or storing inmates like bags of flour in a rat-infested warehouse.

I was ANGRY because the offenders were not getting their needs met. I was ANGRY because the motto of "Do More with Less" was taking hold. That meant fewer staff and fewer tools and materials to do the job. There also were fewer classes, fewer programs, and fewer jobs to help the offenders prepare for a return to the outside world. I was ANGRY because I saw young men who were being sent to prison in increasing numbers and who were learning to be better criminals, instead of gaining the skills to be successful when they were discharged. I saw that the majority of those incarcerated were of black or Hispanic origin.

Yet, practically all the individuals who were incarcerated would at some point be released. If they left the institution just as mentally unhealthy as when they entered, it would not surprise anyone that they returned because they did not have the skills or ability to live without resorting to criminal behavior—often brought about due to their mental health needs. The lack of programs to help them really mattered, to their own wellbeing and to the health of the population outside the prison when the inmates received their freedom.

This idea of locking people up for almost every conceivable reason, encompassing a wide variety of actions that constitute "crime," has made the United States the world leader in incarceration. We have a whopping 2.4 million people held in prisons, jails, juvenile facilities, Indian Country jails, military prisons, immigration prisons and jails, and in civil and U.S. territorial facilities. According to research conducted by *Prison Policy*, more than 636,000 people cycle through the system each year.[3]

Recognizing this fact, it would seem that the value of reintegration counseling and programs would be acknowledged. It is essential to provide tools to assist inmates in becoming successful members when released back into their communities. This is not the focus of CCA. Instead, the objective appears to be to garner more bodies in beds.

My anger, which fueled this book, included frustration at the direction that our society has taken with imprisoning more and more people for what appear, in my opinion, to be foolish uses of prison walls. Prison should be used to contain the dangerous elements of society, not young kids who stole watermelons from Farmer Jones' field (although there should, of course, be a consequence for that also). I was angry at CCA because their lobbyists and those in power (the Powers that Be) gave the implied assent to all of this, with the aim of making further company profits. For example, in 2013, CCA's revenue was nearly $1.7 billion with profits of $300 million.[4] At the same time CCA was making this profit, there was a history of lawsuits against them over everything from riots to poor conditions for offenders and a lack of appropriate supervision. All this further fueled my anger.

The other private prison companies face many of the same criticisms as CCA. The GEO Group, for example, has had its share of allegations of abuse and negligence of offenders, including sexual abuse, riots, deaths, and "deplorable conditions," with many also pointing at understaffing.[5] The Management and Training Corporation (MTC), too, has been involved in numerous controversies, including riots, smuggling of drugs, escapes, and even the loss of their Arizona contact.[6] Most of these allegations and lawsuits, whether they be for CCA or other private contenders, revolve around issues of safety and security.

And those of us worker bees who decided to remain employees had to contend with the safety and security issues, often the result of understaffing. In addition, this meant that a few of us had to do more work, handle more paper, attend more meetings, engage in more teaching, and more, more, more. At length, some of us opted out. Good, ethical employees burned out and moved on to other positions.

This book will document the issues arising from understaffing with an emphasis on the impact on the mental health treatment of offenders. I trace my own journey in these pages, indicating examples of issues with understaffing and failing to respond to the needs of staff and offenders. As many readers will note, when a tragic incident occurs, such as the murder of the Colorado Department of Corrections' Director Tom Clements, in March 2012, the media immediately challenges the role of the mental health department, and in particular the failure to provide for inmates in segregation. Thus, Colorado faced harsh criticism as a result of its treatment of mentally ill offenders.[7]

Such reactions are nothing new. Frequently, criticism occurs around the failure of the mental health segment to anticipate, to treat, or to prevent such tragedies. But when inmates with special needs are relegated to segregation, the hands of providers become even more restricted.

Offenders are placed in a small 8' x 10' cell with nothing but a hard metal bed attached to the wall, a mattress about two inches thick, a steel toilet attached to the floor and a steel sink attached to the wall. The door contains a window perhaps six inches wide and 20 inches tall plus a food/mail slot.

They must remain in the cell, often without an exterior window, for 23 hours out of 24 hours in a day.

They are taken out on a rotating schedule for showers and recreation time (which is spent in a large wire cage). They may have books and a pad and pen to write. Mostly, they sleep, and pace, and have far too much time to think. In most prisons, including Bent County Correctional Facility, they will not be able to attend any classes. They will see their case manager, who stops by maybe once a week, and the mental health clinician, who does rounds. The offender who has mental health problems is subject to the same rules as every other inmate and, thus, is just as likely to be sent to segregation. Depending upon the seriousness of his or her mental health condition, it may further deteriorate under segregation conditions.

Yet, the reality is that overpopulation of inmates, coupled with understaffing, increases the risk of such incidents. This is an issue within the prison system as a whole. I do recognize that I can address those problems mainly from my perspective and from the facility and company I was associated with, but friends and colleagues working in other systems also assure me that the issue is the same at their institutions. In addition, research into the controversies of the private prison systems reveal further evidence that the understaffing and safety issues are not simply my paranoia but reflect the reality of the for-profit prison systems.

This understaffing and overpopulation drives away good staff, leading to further understaffing, in an endless cycle. Caring and qualified mental health workers resign in frustration due to their inability to do the work they were trained to do. Entering the field of counseling, most workers want to help— yes, even with inmates. Mental health workers desire to provide therapy, counseling, intervention, and behavioral tools, which can assist offenders with their reintegration back into society.

I personally do not believe all offenders should be permitted to return to society. I am speaking here of murderers or serial killers and sex offenders who have been convicted of molesting children or raping children or adults. However, many offenders can be returned to their communities. They are not a danger to society. For example, those who might be safely returned to their communities include certain offenders caught with marijuana or other drugs, those selling drugs, committing robbery with no assaultive behavior, check forgers, or those engaging in other nonviolent crimes. This does not mean to condone their crimes. They have made mistakes and must shoulder the responsibility for their actions. Such offenders must have committed several misdemeanors and a more serious offense (a felony) to end up in prison.

Many of them need substance-abuse treatment. However, with no treatment and with no intervention or knowledge of how to manage their own behavior, including their anger, they most probably will not be successful when they return to their communities. Prison should offer them an opportunity to learn new skills and behavior so they are prepared to participate as responsible citizens, entering the workforce and caring for their families, financially and emotionally. If the intention is simply to get more bodies for beds, then doing what we are currently doing is the right path and the mental health of the inmates is not a concern. In fact, if they get well and do not return, there will be fewer bodies in beds.

Obviously, offenders make choices and engage in behaviors that are ultimately up to the offenders themselves. In other words, regardless of the tools provided, people remain responsible for their own choices. However, without guidance and treatment, their chances of success are minimized. They may even become institutionalized, so adapted to the prison way of life that they have no desire to leave or to remain free. This is where we, as mental health clinicians, can either help or fail them.

That is my beef. When our hands are tied and a facility is short staffed with no indication of help, when case loads continue to grow, then those of us who have a sense of morality and obligation are torn between our values and the need for a job. In truth, it is not we who fail the offenders, it is the system. It is the continual striving for profit that is at the heart of the private prison system that fails these offenders.

## Chapter 2. Prisons: The New Asylums

Another day, a typical Friday, I pushed the buzzer, which signaled master control. I was getting ready to conduct segregation rounds. Those inmates assigned to segregation had broken some rule or regulation of the Department of Corrections, and as a mental health professional, one of my roles was to monitor them. I glanced at the list of those I was expected to visit as I waited for a response from the door. It looked as if there were twenty-eight inmates to screen, including those housed in both the bottom and top tiers. My usual routine was to start with the bottom floor, the first cell on the list. I would then move from cell to cell, checking to see if the inmates were functioning well, spending a few extra minutes speaking to those who had mental health issues and those who were on psychotropic medications.

As I eye-balled the list, I realized it was probably not current. Sometimes, the actual numbers and names could vary because the person inputting the information into the computer had not received the latest update. This list showed Offender James Jones in the first cell. I knew he was to have been released that morning, upon my recommendation to the unit manager.

The unit manager's agreement to release James was an appropriate decision. James was a mental health priority for me. He had a history of prior suicide attempts, self-mutilation, depression, and anxiety. I had been worried about James ever since he arrived, but was extremely concerned when he was placed in segregation. Inmates who already have serious mental health issues have been known to deteriorate when placed in segregation.

This was a huge concern of Tom Clements, Colorado Department of Corrections' Director, when he first took his position. Unfortunately, he was murdered by a parole-released offender, Evan Ebel, on March 19, 2013. During his short time at the Department of Corrections, Clements noted that the average stay in administrative segregation was two years, and 47 percent of the inmates completed their time in lockdown, returning to the street with no preparation. During his two years, that 47 percent dropped by 50 percent, as well as a 50 percent drop in the recidivism rate. Before his death, he had ordered a review of inmates who were placed in administrative segregation for more than a year.[1]

As a follow-up to his efforts, his successor, Rick Raemisch, announced that the Colorado Department of Corrections has actively integrated reform with new practices. The goal was to phase out long-term isolation of inmates. A report, *Open the Door—Segregation Reforms in Colorado*, states that administration segregation had shrunk from 1,500 to 160. The average length of stay in restrictive housing was seven and a half months when the report was issued. Prior to that, some offenders had been housed in administrative segregation for more than twenty-four years. Fewer than 1 percent of the state's inmates were in restrictive housing, according to the report, compared with about 7 percent four years previously.[2]

It is important to recognize that there are different types of segregation. The report dealt with administrative segregation, usually when people are placed in restrictive housing due to safety reasons. Other types of segregation are used for institutional or disciplinary reasons or personal safety (protective custody). Understanding of this is important because even with progress made in administrative segregation regulations, facilities may still place offenders in institutional segregation or protective custody. The latter they usually deny, but it remains a reality, nevertheless.[3] Many studies have found that isolation or solitary confinement has caused severe mental decompression and is especially difficult on those who are already mentally compromised.[4] Even President Obama expressed concern for segregation, issuing an order to end solitary confinement for juveniles in federal prisons.[5]

Ironically, the offender who shot Clements when he opened his door for an unexpected pizza delivery, had spent all but a few months of his six-year sentence in segregation, living twenty-three hours out of twenty-four in an 8' x 10' cell. His father, Jack Ebel, who was friends with Governor Hickenlooper, later testified before the state legislature and described what he had observed as mental erosion of his son during his segregation stay. He told the lawmakers, "We are exacerbating mental illness."[6]

The American Psychiatric Association agrees with him. They note that 8 to 19 percent of prison inmates have psychiatric disorders that result in significant functional disabilities and another 15 to 20 percent require some form of psychiatric intervention during their incarceration. They state that "inmates with serious mental illness have more difficulty adapting to prison life than do inmates without a serious mental illness," adding that research shows that seriously mentally ill prisoners were less able to successfully negotiate the complexity of the prison environment, committing infractions at three times the rate of non-seriously mentally ill counterparts.[7] Other researchers and watchdogs make the same conclusions, providing further evidence of the impact of solitary confinement on those locked within prison walls.[8]

Because I understood the ramifications of a mentally-fragile inmate being in segregation, when I learned that James had been taken to segregation, I made a special trip to see him. I pushed through the steel door and crossed the dayroom until I reached his cell. Then, I peered at him through the oblong window. I spoke briefly with him through the food tray slot, bending over as I did so. I let him know that I was there to check on him. Thus, as soon as the officers had cuffed his hands behind his back and shackled him, I interviewed him in a small hearing room on the top level—that is, after he was led to the office, escorted by two officers, who wanted to remain with us. I denied their access. This was a confidential session. They complied, but stood outside the door. On this initial interview, James remained sad, despondent, his eyes cast downward, hesitant to talk. Yet, I managed to get enough information to realize that he did not belong in segregation. He was deteriorating rapidly. That was yesterday.

Now, as I entered the segregation unit, I looked at the large white board on the wall. James' name remained there.

"I thought James was to leave this morning," I ventured.

"No, not yet," the officer on duty informed me.

Puzzled, nevertheless, I traversed the room, heading straight toward James' cell. Perhaps he could tell me what had happened. Another charge? Had some emergency interfered with his release?

I stopped, dead still. "James!" I yelled. "James! Officer! NOW! Get here now. Hanging! Hanging!" I yelled at the top of my lungs.

My heart was throbbing, my hands shaking, as I continued to yell at the young man, who was buckled down on his knees, a sheet around his neck, a pillowcase over his head. Not a praying person, nevertheless, I thought to myself, *No, God, do not let this happen. He's just a boy.*

The officer was already on his radio. He was by my side so fast it seemed instantaneous; then another officer arrived, and, after what seemed an eternity, they opened the cell door. From a distance, like in a tunnel, I heard someone calling for medical help, and then an ambulance. Soon the room was abuzz with people, the investigator arrived, and pictures were taken. They were all doing their jobs, efficiently and following all the protocols.

Sometime during all the activity, I heard someone, I believe a nurse, state that James was not dead. Apparently, he had just begun the hanging procedure when I arrived. Later, I heard another person say that James heard me coming and staged the suicide attempt. I don't know the reality of that. If he did, it was certainly a cry for help.

As the ambulance crew completed their examination and the taking of vitals and lifted him onto the gurney for his trip to the hospital, I found my anger rising. I knew if I remained in the segregation unit any longer, I would say some things that I could not take back, and this was not the time.

I left to write my report of the incident. As I sat in my office, all I could think about was why this young man had not been removed from segregation that morning as I had been told he would be. I thought back on my visit with him the previous day and even a few days before, when we had reviewed his history and his mental health needs. The truth was he did not belong in segregation. He never should have been sent there in the first place.

I first met James when he arrived at Bent County Correctional Facility. Twenty-four years old, hands trembling, his legs shaking, and his eyes downcast, he was a recent addition to the inmate population. James was in prison for possessing drugs and assaulting someone. Apparently both incidents were serious enough to be classified as felonies.

As I introduced myself, he seemed to shy away, making few verbal comments. But I did notice something in his hands, something he seemed to be fiddling with. I caught a glimpse of a circular object, something seemingly delicate, almost lacey.

"That looks interesting...," I began.

He looked up, his eyes seemed to brighten. "I make them, but I can't tell you how or I'll get in trouble."

"I don't need to know, "I explained. "What is it?"

He held up the object. A circle about two inches around, but filled in with an intricate criss-crossing pattern of orange and green yarns, with more streams of yarn twisted together in hanging and knotted tendrils gracefully trailing at the bottom of the circle. I recognized the miniature construct.

"A dreamcatcher. Wow, that's beautiful!"

"Thanks," he acknowledged. "Just don't tell about the rings or I'll get a write-up."I was puzzled. "What for?" Perhaps I was having one of my naïve days, but I did not see how his constructing the tiny dream catchers would violate any rule. In fact, in my opinion, it was great therapy.

"Never mind. I don't want you to get in trouble either. But, if they took them away from me, I don't know what I would do," he explained. "They're mine. As long as I can make them and touch them, I don't feel so scared."

I spoke with him at length then, getting some background, trying to understand why this young man was *so scared.* During that half hour, he explained that he had no family left. He had been raised in foster care and then went to "juvie," as he called it. He was sent there for running away from foster care, and ended up on the street, and sold and traded drugs, and stole enough to eat. He slept with friends or under a park bench. He had been diagnosed with attention deficit hyperactivity disorder (ADHD), depressive disorder, adjustment disorder, and bipolar disorder, and maybe one or two other labels along the way.

Because of time constraints, I had to dismiss him that day, but I scheduled him back within the next week. By that time, I had had time to read his file. I learned some horrific things. As a toddler, he had been locked in a closet while his mother had sex with various men. He had been assaulted physically and, at some point, sexually as a child. He had been taken away from his mother. His father apparently was never in the picture. Off to foster care, one home after another, more physical and sexual abuse. More verbal and emotional abuse. Cases of abuse after abuse piled on top of each other. Confused, beaten back by people who should have taken care of him, he reacted as only a lost, throwaway child might.

He ran away, time and again. He stole, he did drugs. Occasionally, someone would try to get him into treatment, but it was short lived. He did not cooperate. Somewhere along the way, he had been so damaged that he had no clue how to rectify his life. He had no concept of what constituted a healthy, normal life. He'd tried suicide four times.

When I saw him again, he opened up even more. He explained that he had no one left. "Everything gets taken away," he said. "Everyone goes and everything I have ever had gets taken away."

I asked what he meant. He said that first he had no dad, then his mother left or he was taken from her. After that he went to foster homes and was passed around like a sack of groceries. He said, "Sometimes they'd even keep the clothes and toys they gave me."

And all the time he told me this, he rubbed the dreamcatcher he held in his left hand with the forefinger of his right hand.

Finally, the tears came, and we spent an hour talking about his losses. I conducted an exercise designed to help him find that lost boy inside him. At the end of the session, he took several deep breaths, steadying himself. He assured me he was all right and wanted to see me again soon. I agreed.

As he left and I searched for a time on my calendar, I cringed. Somehow I had to make time for this young man. He had obviously been traumatized, so much I wondered how we were going to break through all the layers of pain to get into the core of his trauma.

The next day I learned that he had been taken to segregation, and I stopped by and interviewed him. He told me that he had been written up for using the rings off the pop cans for his dream catchers. He said that he would retain them and smooth them taking out any rough edges. He knew it was against the rules, but it was important enough that he was willing to risk a write-up.

"They took them all from me," he sobbed. "And now I'm in seg."

I thought about the medications he had arrived with. Had he been taking them regularly? I wondered. I knew he hadn't had time to see the psychiatrist yet. But this was not the time to be concerned about his appointments and treatment planning. Right now, he just needed to talk, to rant, if need be.

I assured him I would talk with the unit manager about his case. Of course, I could not promise him anything, but I agreed to check it out. Later that day, I spoke with the unit manager who said he would be dismissing any charges and release him in the morning. Only, for whatever reason, that had never happened.

All I could think about was James' words to me the day before. "They took them all away from me." One more loss. And the dream catchers were all that seemed to be sustaining him, like a small thread still connecting him to life, to reality.

James was a mental health client. I spent a little more time with him than I did with some of the other mental health clients because of the necessity. I cringed because I did not have the staff or the time that these mental health inmates needed. I tried to make time when it was an emergency, when I saw a need. James was crying out for help. His help was not to be found in tossing him into segregation. That was the last thing that James needed, which is exactly why I recommended that he NOT be placed in segregation. I knew he would deteriorate even further. Jack Ebel was right about that.

If you or a loved one have a mental health diagnoses, my advice is simple. Do not break the law. Do not go to prison because in prison, you will not get decent treatment. Oh, you may be placed on medication, but you will not get the personal counseling and therapy that might actually assist you in getting back out and having a healthy, productive lifestyle.

Just how has the system arrived at this impasse—when prison has become the new mental asylum in America? It is almost as if we have gone back to the early nineteenth century when urbanization ushered in the asylums.[9] Here, in the twenty-first century, one would like to believe that our understanding of the mentally ill and our moral codes would mean that we provide ethical and effective care for those with mental health diagnoses. With exceptions, such as the rich and powerful, who can afford the best of care? Most Americans do not that have that option, and that option is certainly not happening to the extent needed in most of our correctional facilities. And if you are among the poor, and you belong to a minority population group, you are not as likely to be able to afford mental health treatment or medication. And even more frustrating, if you land in prison, you may discover that your resources have dried up even further.

The 2002 report from the Council of State Governments characterizes what is happening in the prison system as "criminalizing of the mentally ill." It discusses the overall lack of well-trained staff to evaluate, develop, and implement treatment plans and monitor them. The report states that many of those suffering from mental illness receive little more than medication and end up in a deteriorated condition.[10] This is still occurring today and the process is accelerated at private prisons.

Human Rights Watch reported in 2006 that the number of mentally ill in prisons in the United States had quadrupled over a period of six years, with 1.25 million in prison and jail. Those numbers are five times greater than the ratio of the mentally ill in the general population.[11]

In 2012, for example, there were 356,268 inmates with mental illness in prisons and jails in the United States. On the other hand, there were 35,000 in state hospitals. Dr. E. Fuller Torrey, founder of the Center, stated, "The lack of treatment for seriously ill inmates is inhumane and should not be allowed in a civilized society."[12] More recently, a 2014 report published by the Treatment Advocacy Center, a nonprofit advocacy organization dedicated to eliminating barriers to the timely and effective treatment of severe mental illness, states that there are ten times more mentally ill people in prisons and jails than in state hospitals.[13]

The mentally ill do not have the same capacity to deal with the rules as those without such conditions. This should be borne in mind when considering how to discipline these people. Yet, in the prison system, they are required to obey the same rules and follow all the same procedures as all the other inmates. The inmate who is actively schizophrenic, for example, may be hearing voices that make his compliance impossible or at least difficult. Many staff do not get proper training in how to deal with the mentally ill so when these mentally ill inmates do not follow the rules, they are punished, which often leads to greater mental illness.

I once worked with just such an offender, Joseph. Joseph's entire demeanor cried out "schizophrenic." He had a look to his face, the vacant eyes, and difficulty maintaining attention when you spoke with him. Joseph was taking monthly Haldol shots, which appeared to keep his condition "manageable." He was in prison for breaking and entering an apartment, which he said he mistook for his when coming home. When he discovered his mistake, he stole a computer. He already had several charges of stealing as well as possession of drugs (methamphetamines primarily) on his record. So, Joseph was sentenced to prison.

I was sitting in my office, waiting for Joseph to arrive for a session. I heard the officer call his name for his appointment. As I rose from the desk and entered the hallway, I overheard her chiding this inmate. "Why are you walking like that? Pay attention when I call you name! Hurry up. I haven't got all day!"

I stepped up to her. "Joseph just took his medications this morning, and he sometimes has a reaction."

I ushered him into my office. When our session was over, I spoke quietly to her. I explained that Joseph, like some other offenders, had a mental health diagnosis and that as a result, he sometimes had side effects of the medicine, as well as the disorder. He did not always respond quickly. She listened, but I had the feeling she couldn't care less. Joseph was, after all, an inmate, subject to following the procedures and the rules just like all the inmates.

To further explain to her without violating his confidentiality would be moot. To explain that he sometimes demonstrated the "schizophrenic shuffle" was unnecessary. After all, she was doing her job, hurrying the offenders in and out of medical. She barely had time to pat them all down, much less make allowances for their mental health symptoms. She was another person too busy due to the demands of the profit-making corporation to care for any inmates in a way that would make a difference in their treatment outcomes.

As pointed out by Jamie Fellner, a lawyer specializing in prison mental health issues for Human Rights Watch, in "A Corrections Quandry," prisons may be the largest mental health providers in the United States.[14] However, Fellner explains, they are not designed or equipped to handle the mentally ill. As a result, mentally ill offenders are often undertreated or mistreated.[15]

Some people will disagree with that statement and are quick to point out that offenders get "free" medical, dental, optometry, and mental health care. Don't even mention all the other freebees such as cable TV, clothes, food, and a bed—all at taxpayer expense. However, prisoners cannot get out to obtain their own medical and mental health care or fill other basic needs. Under the Eighth Amendment, they are entitled to decent medical and mental health care, and if they do not get it, they are seen as being subjected to "cruel and unusual punishment." While much debate exists over exactly how far this notion extends, the concept applies to both medical and mental health care in correctional facilities. Sharon Dolovich, Professor of Law at the University of California Los Angeles, writes that the state places offenders "in potentially dangerous conditions while depriving them of the capacity to provide for their own care and protection."[16]

Mental health care should be effective care—care, which, if conducted properly with the needed resources, can result in less recidivism within the prison system. Enormous numbers of prisoners could be treated more appropriately in other fashions, instead of being sent to prison. Not only would this help these individuals, but doing so would be cheaper than having them continuously recycle back into prison because they committed a criminal act due to their mental health problems. However, effectively treating individuals would diminish the numbers of bodies in beds, and the private prison companies would "lose business."

For example, several states, including Florida and California, as well as Colorado, have initiated mental health courts, which address the disproportionate number of people with mental illness locked in the judicial system. These courts also help to address the overcrowding, while providing more effective use of the system. [17] In addition, the use of drug courts also provides valid alternatives to prison. The National Association of Drug Court Professionals research states that drug courts work better than jail or prison and better than probation and treatment alone. In fact, they note that cost savings can range from $3,000 to $13,000 per client.[18]

While this option has been initiated in several states, the fact remains that the majority of those convicted of felonies will find themselves in prison, including those with mental illness. To make matters worse, many of these offenders have been poorly diagnosed before sentencing. They may arrive having had no treatment and no medication. And even if diagnosed, they are placed into facilities, including the private prison system, where they face understaffed conditions, with workers who have little knowledge of what constitutes mental illness. Staff who are trained only in incarceration tactics are in no position to recognize the need to refer these individuals to mental health. Their focus is on adherence to the rules. Thus, the rate of recidivism among the mentally ill soars.[19]

With approximately 2.3 million prisoners sitting behind bars in the United States, it is not profitable to advocate for less imprisonment—at least not to the private prisons. Between 1970 and 2005, the U.S. prison population increased 700 percent.[20]

If there is good news, it is that the prison population has been dropping and is now the smallest since 2005 for a total of 1,561,000 prisoners in the state and federal facilities. Of that number, 131,000 inmates are held in private prisons in 30 states and the Bureau of Prisoners (BOP). The number housed in private prisons grew from 69,000 in 1999 to 131,300 in 2014.[21]

Something is drastically wrong with this picture. What forces are driving these numbers? While there may be declines in certain areas, the message remains clear—the prison population in this country is alarming and the number of those locked up who have mental illness continues to rise. And to whose advantage is it to keep these numbers climbing?

How did the United States get to the point where prisons have taken the place of mental health facilities? Exactly what has happened in this country that the wellbeing of those with mental health issues has been relegated to correctional institutions? One could take the history of treatment of the "insane" back to the dark ages in an attempt to understand the process. However, for the focus of the current issue, let us just examine the problem from the beginning of this country.

During those early days, the care of the mentally ill basically followed standard procedures from our European forefathers. In reality, there was no care such as we know today. Instead, the mentally ill brother or parent was kept at home, out of sight, tolerated or not. That was fairly standard. For those who ended up homeless, out on the street, stealing for a living or just trying to get by, once they were apprehended, off they went to the "asylum." In a sense, it is not so very different from what we are doing today.[22]

In another sense, it is the age-old difference between those who have money to house their ill loved ones (out of sight usually) as opposed to the poor who are ostracized and left to fend for themselves. This is not so very different either from what occurs out there today.

The treatment of the mentally ill evolved in this county through various stages. From asylums in Colonial America, where people were locked away and were subject to ice baths and a variety of techniques to manage their symptoms or contain them to an institutional model circa 1960s. Along the way, the mentally ill were subject to procedures such as lobotomies (1930s) and electro-convulsive shock.[23]

This change resulted in people often being placed in a state, county, or local facilities where they could be "locked up" and supposedly monitored for safe-keeping. This "cuckoo's nest" environment did little to assist people in managing their symptoms. A breakthrough occurred in about 1964 under President Kennedy's administration with the passage of the Comprehensive Mental Health Bill, which created a community mental health movement. However, under the Nixon administration, with the 1966 advent of Medicare and Medicaid, a major reduction in the use of mental health hospitals occurred.[24]

In addition, the pharmaceutical companies had discovered psychotropic drugs. Beginning in 1951 with the first synthesis of chlorpromazine, known as Thorazine,[25] and in 1958 with the discovery of Haloperidal, known as Haldol,[26] the treatment of mental health disorders would never be the same again. As more and more medications developed, which act upon brain chemistry and appear to help with symptoms such as bipolar disorder, depression, and anxiety, the thinking of those who organized and operated mental health, as well as the politicians, of course, changed. The concept was that those with mental health disorders could be successfully managed through medication. Therefore, there was no need for the large and costly hospitals to maintain them. They could be moved to community facilities for monitoring of their drugs and symptoms

Except, that is not what happened. First of all, there were few community centers available at that time. Even fifty years later, community centers to assist the mentally ill are still woefully inadequate. At best, they provide medication, some counseling and little, if any, therapy. When this deinstitutionalization occurred, many of those clients were tossed out of the facilities and hit the streets, with little or no supervision.

One of the things we know now is that mentally ill clients are not particularly good at monitoring their own medications. And if they have no job, or no income, they have no funds to purchase medication. I have personally purchased medication for a former inmate, who did not even have a dollar for his co-pay.

So, we ended up in this country with vast numbers of our population who were homeless, who had mental conditions, and who had no funds or understanding of how to manage in society. They broke the rules. They might steal a loaf of bread and bologna, similar to the Victor Hugo character Jean Valjean in *Les Miserables*, who stole a loaf of bread to feed his sister's children.[27] Such homeless individuals also might seek out drugs to manage their symptoms and then steal or deal drugs to alleviate their symptoms. Suddenly, those with mental illness were placed in situations that appeared unmanageable.

Many reading this might say that the situation was brought on by their own failure to follow the rules, to take medications as ordered, and to avoid drugs and addiction. It might seem that way. The truth is that many of them—whether due to a birth injury or other injury to the brain, or a chemical imbalance—are not always able to follow rules or directions. Thus, have they been placed on the street and in precarious positions—which can lead them straight to prison.

As you can see, I have first-hand experience with the mentally ill. One time, during my workday, I met with a homeless man who had been in and out of mental health holdings at various hospitals and facilities; he had taken to drugs and alcohol in an attempt to manage his symptoms. I am amazed, but not surprised, that in a country with our capabilities and resources, this remains a continuing problem. However, alternative programs to incarceration are certainly not in the best interests of the private prisons, certainly not to CCA, which has expressed concerns for any threat of declining numbers on several occasions.

# CHAPTER 3. HOW DID WE GET HERE? A BRIEF HISTORY OF THE CCA'S RISE TO CONQUER

Historically, prisons were under the domain of the government. State and federal entities ran correctional facilities, implementing their own sets of rules and processes. Granted, as we look back at the history of prisons, not surprisingly, many of the rules were harsh by today's standards. Not so long ago, solitary confinement meant a prisoner was dropped into a hole in the ground, where he was literally fed only bread and water.[1]

Over the years, our sense of morality and humanity resulted in changing inhumane conditions. Granted, there have been and still remain, at times, corrupt officers who assault prisoners. Yet, with the growth of costly lawsuits, overall prisons have "cleaned up their act." Still, no one conceived that prisons could be run independently, privately, like your local bookstore or neighborhood bar. Until recently (1984), prisons were run by state and federal governments at the expense of the taxpayers.[2]

What happened is that in January 28, 1983, three men came together with a far-reaching idea—privatization. They formed the Corrections Corporation of America. Tom Beasley, Doctor (first name, not a title) Robert Crants and T. Don Hutto[3] began the process, which by 2012 has led to the management of more than sixty jail, prison, and detention facilities across twenty states and the District of Columbia owned or controlled by CCA. Of these facilities, forty-four are owned by CCA. CCA has a bed capacity of 80,000, it is the fifth largest correctional system in the United States. Its headquarters are in Nashville, Tennessee.[4]

A year after Hutto joined CCA, he became the head of the American Correctional Association, the largest prison association in the world, whose function is to accredit prisons. In addition, Beasley, former chairman of the Tennessee Republican Party, told Inc. magazine in 1988 that the business of private prisons was simple. "You just sell it like you were selling cars, or real estate, or hamburger."[5]

In 1984, CCA opened the Houston Processing Center, one of their first facilities built to house individuals awaiting a decision on their immigration case or repatriation.[6] As will be noted later, this interest in "immigration inmates" was to become an important source of revenue for CCA in their future business ventures with the government.

Also in 1984, CCA took over operations of the Tall Trees, a non-secure juvenile facility for the Juvenile Court of Memphis and Shelby counties. Two years later, CCA built the 200-bed Shelby Training Center in Memphis to house male juvenile offenders. Following that, in 1989, CCA opened the New Mexico Women's Correctional Facility in Grants, New Mexico. In 1990, they added the first medium-security privately operated prison, Winn Correctional Center in Winn Parish, Louisiana.[7] In 1992, CCA opened the Leavenworth Detention Center, operated for the U.S. Marshals Service, a 256-bed facility, the first maximum-security private prison under direct contract with a federal agency.[8]

Beginning with one facility, CCA quickly gained momentum until it became the largest private prison company in the country, owning and managing private prisons and detentions centers, while operating others on a concession basis. Interestingly, and with enormous impact, it was the first in the world to design and construct a private correctional company.[9]

Bent County Correctional Center began as a private county-operated facility in 1993, working with the State of Colorado to assist in the housing of offenders to offset any overflow from the state prison population. At that time, the facility held only a maximum of 350 offenders.[10] It had four cell houses, two with open floor plans. An officer sat on an elevated station, but, contrary to later cell houses, he was not enclosed by walls, windows, or other barriers. He overlooked the minimum risk offenders. The prisoners were housed in regular cells, although many lived "in the open." That is, their cots sat outside the cells and were back-to-back with one or more other inmates. This open concept apparently worked reasonably well with the lower-risk offenders. It remained in place when I came to Bent County in 2002.

CCA purchased the Bent County Prison in October 1996.[11] With an addition of two large cell houses, capacity increased to 720 inmates,[12] with the good news to the community that additional staff would be hired. This meant increased revenues, additional taxes, and increased payments for utilities for the city and county. And, of course, additional money would be spent in the community by workers, some of whom commuted distances from twenty to fifty miles for work. More money for the local cafes, the gas station, and the local motels, as those visiting their inmate loved ones might travel from Denver or the Western Slope and spend a night in the small rural town of Las Animas, Colorado, a community of about 2,410 residents.[13]

The belief is that locating a prison in a rural area can benefit the inmates while also offering something to communities that are desperate for economic development. A prison represents an environmentally clean industry that should not be affected by economic swings. However, there is a downside which often communities often do not see. Research completed in 2005–06 around Pennsylvania rural prisons indicated that it is harder to attract staff due to the lack of services and amenities in rural areas. In addition, locals who might seek employment are often not qualified for the positions, and still others commute from out of town. The positive effect on local businesses sometimes does not materialize or is marginal.[14]

When I first started work in 2002 at Bent County, during this developmental stage, it housed about 550–600 offenders. In terms of mental health services, this was a "doable" number of inmates for the staff who were there. Handling inmates with mental health issues is always a challenge, of course, but with the proper training and staffing, it can be safely managed. Yes, there were moments when I cringed at the expectations to handle this many inmates, and, of course, the accompanying paperwork. Yet, looking back, we clinicians were able to manage the workload with a minimum amount of frustration or friction.

At that stage, I could not imagine the future stressors that the huge growth of the population would bring nor the additional paperwork or other expected duties. In time, the increased numbers would incapacitate and sideline the entire mental health staff. Nor could I anticipate what would occur several years later with a growing lack of concern for the mental health needs of both inmates and staff.

In 2007 as the growth of the prison population continued, CCA decided that it would be in its best interest to increase the inmate capacity at Bent County. Once approved by the Colorado Department of Corrections, a third add-on occurred when the inmate capacity increased to 1,466.[15] At that time, the mental health department had two clinicians, but a third was added just before the completion of the new quarters. I thought that hopefully, the three of us would be able to accommodate the larger offender population.

I had concerns from the start. On two different occasions, I did a walk-through of the pending build-on, as well as reviewing the plans on paper. My primary concern was the allocated space for mental health. For example, the area consisted of one large corner room and one small adjacent office. The large room was to house two clinicians, along with two massive desks, a file cabinet, and bookcase, and a clerk. This meant that there was no provision for the required confidential sessions with the offenders. Somehow, we were to screen, evaluate, monitor, and conduct crises sessions in this cramped area with back-to-back desks and a clerk in the same room. Yet I knew that many organizations manage in cubicles with much less space. Nevertheless, under the Health Insurance Portability and Accountability Act of 1996, better known as HIPAA, mental health providers are required to ensure that all information gathered and all counseling sessions are to be held in the utmost confidential manner.[16]

The single room was to house the "lead" mental health clinician. It contained a mega-sized desk, a bookcase, and a file cabinet. Cramped to be sure, but at least it afforded the privacy necessary for counseling sessions. Normally, I would have had this office. However, the Colorado Department of Corrections asked me to work at their Ft. Lyon site, about six miles east of Bent County and much closer to my home. I explained the situation to my supervisor. This led her to feel that I would probably be leaving, so I was assigned to one of the monster desks in the large room.

Ultimately, I decided not to take the Department of Corrections' position. Thus, I settled into my desk in the mega-office, wondering if I should escort my clients to the safety cells in the rear corridor since I had no privacy for our sessions. Almost immediately the lead mental health person resigned and I was moved into her smaller office. I now had my own office, a location I maintained for the next five years. Another mental health person was hired, and, within a few weeks, both of the other two clinicians were moved out into an adjacent building, where offices were available in a corridor just off the two new cell houses. While the walk to the other building was not as handy for them, it did provide the required confidentiality. This was an appreciated and important start to managing the almost 1,400 offenders who now were part of the Bent County facility. Yet, with the increased duties and paperwork, our ability to safely and adequately monitor the increased inmate population went down.

And while all this was going on at Bent County, at approximately the same time CCA agreed to increase the inmate capacity at Bent's sister Colorado facility, Kit Carson Correctional Facility (KCCF). This addition represented another example of CCA's ongoing quest to expand their domination and profit in the prison system. Located in the northeast part of the state at Burlington, even before the approved add-on, Kit Carson Correctional Facility (KCCF) had struggled to maintain staff, largely due to its rural location. An acquaintance who worked there for several months told me that officers were drawn from Kansas, Limon, Colorado, and as far away as Lamar, Colorado, requiring extensive travel for staff. This region, the eastern plains, is notorious for treacherous winter storms. This deters many people from maintaining employment over the long haul. In fact, the wintery weather and icy roads were strong contributors to the death of an inmate and a staff person in December 2011 when a transport vehicle pulling a trailer slid off the highway.[17]

Both CCA and the State of Colorado agreed to expand the Kit Carson Correctional Facility along with that of Bent County, even though a more thorough investigation of inmate population projections would ultimately reveal that this expansion was untimely; the prison population was declining. But this did not deter CCA as we shall see.[18]

At that time, CCA also operated two other Colorado facilities. The first one, Crowley County Correctional Facility, was located about fifty miles west of Bent County. The other, Huerfano Correctional Facility, was located in the southern part of the state at Walsenburg—for a total of four CCA for-profit prisons in Colorado. At that time, it appeared that the prison population would continue to grow, providing even greater profits to the mother company and its stockholders.

Except the inmate population did not continue to increase; and the state had already recognized this trend. Since 2009 there had been a declining inmate population.[19] In 2010, the Huerfano prison was closed with a tremendous impact on the 4,000 person population of Walsenberg. Employing about 188 people, the prison had been the second-largest employer in the rural town.[20]

Interestingly, the state had negotiated with CCA behind closed doors to continue payment at the Walsenberg facility even after the pending closure was announced. According to Christie Donner, Executive Director of the Colorado Criminal Justice Reform Coalition, the state paid approximately $2 million in a deal behind closed doors to keep the private prisons operating.[21]

The deal, hashed out in meetings between the governor's office, CCA and its Colorado lobbyist, Mike Feeley, reportedly gave CCA a written promise of 3,300 prisoners at $20,000 each, according to Donner, in order to hold-off on the closing of Huerfano and other prisons until a study was conducted regarding the projected need for the prisons.[21] Spokesman for Governor John Hickenlooper, said "The General Assembly and the governor agreed to have a year where no other communities were affected by a prison closure" due to uncertainty about the number of prisoners and the impact of closing other prisons the previous year.[22]

Donner stated, "There was no (public) hearing on this whatsoever. I did not even find out about it until way after the fact..."[23]

When asked about how the governor could justify making such an important and expensive decision in secret, Hickenlooper's spokesman responded, "There is no way for the governor to send funds to a private company as a result of a backroom meeting" because the legislature makes all funding decisions.[24]

Really? *Colorado Public News* reported that office calendars for the governor, his chief of staff Roxane White, and his budget director Henry Sobanet showed a meeting with CCA executives and lobbyist Feeley in the governor's offices on the morning of March 28, 2012. That afternoon the budget committee began an unannounced discussion of the possible shutdown of CCA's prison in Burlington, if Colorado continued to reduce the number of inmates housed there.[25]

The budget committee effectively signed off on the deal when it later budgeted the extra CCA funds. The legislature then approved the budget that contained the payment.[26]

Representative Cheri Gerou, (R-Evergreen), who headed the legislature's Joint Budget Committee at the time, said the deal was negotiated in the governor's office. She stated that the legislators agreed with the plan because it delayed the threatened closure of private prisons by CCA and would have resulted in devastating job losses in several rural Colorado communities.[27]

As a result of the declining inmate population, one state facility at Ft. Lyon, Colorado, about seven miles east of Bent County, was closed in 2011.[28] The state also had built onto the Centennial Facility, a part of its Canon City complex. Known as CSP2 (Colorado State Penitentiary), it was designed to house 316 offenders, in what has been described as "high security beds." After reevaluating the state's needs for housing, CSP was closed in February 2014. Colorado stated that in closing the prison, it represented a $4.5 million savings to the state. In any event, there was a loss of 213 jobs. The state did report that employees would be reassigned, whenever possible.[29]

Again, the closing of two state facilities indicated that the prison population was not increasing as initially projected. Instead, at least in Colorado, it was decreasing, largely because the crime rate had dropped by a third in a decade, and the state had changed its sentencing structure, which allowed prisoners to earn more time off for good behavior. In the case of CSP2, it was reported that a secondary issue was that the state was relying less on the use of solitary confinement, and, therefore, did not need the additional high security level beds.[30] Yet, even with closing its own facilities, the state somehow managed to continue doing business with CCA, leaving the remaining three CCA facilities open.

However, CCA's Kit Carson facility found itself in trouble. Fewer Colorado inmates, but an expanded facility that would hold twice as many offenders, presented a troubling prospect to CCA, including a substantial expense and loss of income. Not to be thwarted, CCA found a solution. In 2012, CCA negotiated a contract with the state of Idaho for their inmate overflows.[31] As of December 1, 2015, the facility continued to house inmates from both states, with 228 Idaho offenders, although the contract allowed for up to 768 beds for Idaho beds.[32]

Kit Carson's efforts to maintain a profit for CCA ended on June 30, 2016. That morning the employees were notified that the closure would officially take place at the end of July. The Burlington facility has struggled almost from the beginning. While the facility has a capacity of 1,400 inmates, at the time of the announcement, it held only 400, since the prison populations have continued to decline. Previously, it had also held Idaho inmates, but they had been removed.[33]

This announcement meant a loss of 142 jobs to the small community of Burlington, along with a tremendous impact on its economy, where the prison paid $1.2 million in property taxes to fund schools, city and county. The prison has also been the town's largest customer of electricity, according to the *Denver Post*.[34]

CCA officials state that the 400 inmates will be divided between Crowley Country Correctional Facility and Bent County Correctional Facility. They also state that they will transfer workers to other facilities or help them find jobs in the area, according to spokesman Jonathan Burns.[35]

The Colorado legislature had budgeted $3 million extra for the next fiscal year, which began July 1 in an attempt to keep the facility open. This was the second bailout for CCA in recent years after lawmakers gave the company $9 million in 2012 to keep the Burlington facility open. [36]

Kathy Green, Governor Hickenlooper's spokeswoman, said the state had been trying to keep the prison open but both Colorado and out-of-state prison population had been declining. In addition, CCA wanted a guarantee of a minimum number of inmates and a higher daily rate per inmate than Colorado was willing to pay to keep the prison open. Initially CCA's contract with the prison was scheduled to expire the end of June, but was extended a month.[37]

Rol Hudler, Burlington Economic Development Director stated, "It wasn't a total surprise. There is no question it was unprofitable for them. It had to be."[38]

At one point, CCA assigned me to Kit Carson for a day to help with the intake of 130 Idaho offenders who had been flown to Denver and then bussed down to Kit Carson, located in Burlington, Colorado. With one other mental health clinician and two nurses, we spent the better part of a day assisting in the intake process, which I describe, hopefully, in a humorous and sarcastic style in my e-book *I'll Never Make Parole.*[39]

This experience reinforced the message that different states have different criteria and requirements. I especially noted this in the paperwork, which was much shorter and less intense than that required by Colorado. Fortunately, at that time, we had a third mental health provider, who oversaw the Bent facility in our absence in case of any emergencies. The good news was that I got paid for my mileage that day.

Bent County also received their share of out-of-state offenders. Wyoming inmates were brought in several years prior to the facility's last build-on. A lesson learned from this situation indicated that whenever inmates from different states are housed in the same facility, it creates more safety and aggression problems for staff. Different states have different rates of pay for care of inmates, as well as different rules regarding work and program requirements. This has resulted in conflict among the offenders. Therefore, increased aggressive incidents mean the facility is at greater risks for assault incidents or even the potential for riots. As mentioned in more detail elsewhere, Crowley County is an example of this, where the housing of Colorado and Washington inmates contributed to and resulted in a riot in 2004.

With the termination of the Wyoming contract, those offenders returned to their home state, and Bent County began seeing an influx of inmates only from Colorado. Much of this had to do with the contact negotiations. As mentioned earlier, once CCA has a hold in a state, they sometimes began insisting upon minimum bed requirements. As a result, over the past two-to-three years Bent County has remained relatively full, about 1,385 inmates out of a possible 1,400 bed capacity, as of the weekly reports in May 2015.

What this means is that if twenty-five inmates are shipped out of the facility for any reason, then the state will send about twenty-five other inmates to replace those taken. Offenders may be moved from Bent County because they were being paroled or sent to a community corrections or halfway house, or they may have completed their prison sentence and are actually headed home.

In addition, Bent County may not have been able to meet their needs. If they were suicidal, psychotic, or had aggressive behavior, or were being housed in segregation, they were not appropriate to remain at a private prison. In addition, they may have had conflicts with staff or other offenders, such as being in rival gangs, necessitating separation from certain specific enemies. Therefore, constant movement occurred among the various prisons within the state. But, despite the shifting of inmates among the various state prisons, the total number of inmates at Bent remained near the maximum allowable at all times.

Inmate moves occurred weekly between the Colorado Department of Corrections and the Bent County Correctional Facility. Of course, a few old-timers remained and served their entire sentence at Bent, but generally, there was a constant exchange of inmates providing a challenge to all staff, including mental health. This continual influx meant dollars to CCA, more bodies in beds. The fact that Colorado taxpayers were shuttering state prisons but continuing to shove dollars into the pockets of corporate bigwigs and stockholders only contributed to CCA profits.

This increased use of private prisons, such as CCA, often is based on the justification of cost-savings. A 2002 detailed research project regarding private prison and funding indicated that there is no legitimate data that using private prisons results in cost savings.[40] In fact, factoring in the then-average cost per inmate in a Level III facility and comparing the additional costs to Department of Corrections for services, such as administrative and medical, not included at private facilities, no real savings was reflected. At that time, the state-run facility cost $68.99 per diem. The private cost was $54.66 per diem. Sounds good.

However, when factoring in indirect costs to the Department of Corrections, the "real" per diem rate for the private facilities is $63.89, representing almost no savings.[41] The real cost of private prisons must include the contract monitoring and the treatment of all inmates—not just those cherry picked for private prisons. Much of the supposed cost savings from private prisons stems from the fact that they use nonunion workers who are paid much less than their unionized counterparts and there are fewer of them than in state or federal facilities.

Did the taxpayers get their money's worth? If one includes the understaffing and the associated issues of safety and security reported in private facilities, it certainly does not appear so. Yet, in the light of the "savings" propaganda that is thrown out to the politicians and public, the use of private prisons appears unstoppable. The major question to ask is the following: Is there any getting off of this privatization-profit merry-go-round? Don't be foolish.

Of course, CCA would be opposed to any change and would lobby hard to keep its current status or even expand it. After all, a decline of inmates and a change in criminal laws or regulations would affect the salaries and benefits of their corporate officers. According to 2014 records, CCA's President and CEO, Damon T. Hininger's salary was $3,666,117, while former Chief Financial Officer and Executive Vice President Todd J. Mullenger, made $1,786,375, with current Chief Financial Officer and Executive Vice President, David

M. Garfinkle pulling down $1,576,407, and the Chief Development Officer, Anthony L. Grande receiving $1, 740,115. Other executive compensation included Harley G. Lappin, Executive Vice President and Chief Corrections Office, $1,739,437, and Steven E. Groom, Executive vice President and General Counsel, $1,421,452. This entire package adds up to a whopping $ 11,929,903.[42] What incentive do any of these highly paid individuals have to alter or change any policy or procedure that would compromise their salaries or the bottom-line profit?

CCA revenue in 2012 was $1.77 billon, 100 percent of which comes from taxpayers through government contracts.[43] In 2013, CCA revenue was about $1.7 billion, a slight decline, but with profits of $300 million.[44]

With such revenues flowing in, what company would want to pay corporate taxes? As a result, in 2013, CCA was converted into a Real Estate Investment Trust (REIT), which helps the company avoid tens of millions of dollars in corporate taxes.[45] A REIT is a type of security that invests in real estate through property or mortgages and often trades on major exchanges. They typically provide investors with an extremely liquid stake in real estate. REITS must have at least 100 shareholders, but no five can hold more than 50 percent of shares between them. At least 75 percent of their assets must be invested in real estate, cash, or U.S. Treasuries. By law, they must maintain dividend payout ratios of at least 90 percent, making them a favorite for income-seeking investors. REITS can then deduct these dividends and avoid most or all tax liabilities, although investors still pay income tax on payouts they receive—not a bad deal for a major corporation or its shareholders.[46]

In July 2016, Senate Finance Committee Ranking Member Ron Wyden (D-Oregon) introduced legislation to limit the ability of private companies that operate prisons to take advantage of special tax rules for Real Estate Investment Trusts (REITS) — U.S. corporations that invest in real estate. The Ending Tax Breaks for Private Prisons Act of 2016 would significantly weaken the for-profit prison industry, and free up millions of dollars that could be reinvested in services that actually keep our communities safe.[47]

Wyden said: "I am very concerned that the U.S. prison system has become a way for private enterprises to turn an unfair profit. Our broken-down tax code has made this possible by allowing the private prison industry to take advantage of tax rules aimed at REITs. As part of rethinking our criminal justice system, particularly as it results in the mass incarceration of low-income and minority individuals, the tax rules for REITs must be changed so we are not encouraging companies to unjustly profit from prison detention services."[48]

In 2013, the IRS classified Corrections Corporation of America (CCA) and GEO Group as Real Estate Investments Trusts (REITs), based on the companies' claim that income received from local, state, and federal governments to incarcerate people was "real estate" income. The legislation introduced by Senator Wyden would clarify that much of this income is not in fact eligible for REIT status, as it goes towards operating costs like prison guards, healthcare, and food, not real estate.[49]

When I read the salaries and compensations of the top dogs at CCA, I was offended. I am reminded of my failed requests for a dozen composition books. As part of the therapeutic process, offenders are sometime given journaling assignments. This process of putting their feelings and activities on paper can provide some insight for both the offender and the clinician and can be a very useful tool. I had requested these books perhaps a dozen times over a period of two years, and had been successful only two or three times.

You see the problem lies within the budget. If I made a request when the department budget was tight, close to the end of the cut-off period, I was not going to get my request met. I was told: "They will be back-ordered." Usually, because I felt they were a valuable tool, I watched for the Walmart fifty-cent sales and purchased them myself. You might think I would get reimbursed. Don't be silly. I did not even ask.

A joke ran through the e-mail—at least I initially thought it was a joke. A clerk in another department sent out a plea for paper clips, as she was completely out. I soon learned that it was not a joke. She was out of this simple, needed, and relatively cheap tool.

At such times, I recalled how appalled I was when I first learned of the salaries and compensations of the CCA leaders. I then considered my struggles to maintain professional standards with sub-standard staff and often without necessary supplies. My blood pressure rose and my head throbbed with anger. I knew how to run a mental health program but due to budget constraints, I could not implement change in my department. At times, my anger escalated and I often wanted to walk out of the building. No notice. No resignation letter. Just go. Then, I had to consider my insurance and benefits, and logically, I knew that I could not resign at that time. Like so many other Bent County employees, I felt caught in a trap.

And somehow, it all went back to the profit motive. If I could not get notebooks, it was simply because the cost of those notebooks factored across seventy facilities just might bankrupt CCA! I jest, of course. But, such thoughts managed only to twist and influence my opinion and my relationship with CCA. The entire process, which defines my inability to function effectively as a mental health clinician, appeared to hinge on the profit margin of CCA.

Much concern has existed that with the emergence of the private prison system in the United States, there has been a significant impact on the prison population. CCA, of course, denies this, and states that it just meets the existing "demand" for prison beds and responds to market conditions. However, according to the Justice Policy Institute, "they have worked hard over the past decade to create markets for their product." [50]

CCA claims that it has not lobbied for bills that extend or increase sentences for prisoners; yet, for nearly two decades CCA has participated in and even led the task force of the American Legislative Exchange Council (ALEC) that pushed bills such as the so-called "truth-in-sentencing" and "three strikes' legislation as models for states to adopt across the nation. [48] Along with the National Rifle Association (NRA), CCA initiated a campaign to introduce two-pieces of the ALEC-inspired legislation at both the state and federal level. Truth-in-sentencing called for all violent offenders to serve 85 percent of their sentences before they would be eligible for release. Three strikes called for mandatory life imprisonment for a third felony conviction. [51]

As a result of this lobbying, by the end of 1998, twenty-seven states and the District of Columbia required violent offenders to serve at least 85 percent of their prison sentences. Another thirteen states adopted Truth-in-Sentencing Laws requiring violent offenders to serve substantial portions of their sentences before being eligible for release. With these restrictions, prisoners, especially those classified as violent, are spending more time behind bars and contributing to a growing prison population. [52] Not surprisingly, prison release rates also dropped. At the end of 1998, fourteen states had abolished parole boards. In addition, more prisoners were now serving their full sentences, thanks to the lobbying efforts of CCA, NRA, and other organizations affiliated with ALEC. [53]

More prisoners, held for longer periods of time, occurred directly as a result of the "get tough on crime" laws. More dollars for CCA. Even that was not enough. CCA also created a whole new market to ensure that there are sufficient Bodies in Beds. Following a massive increase in the number of illegal immigrant detentions in the wake of 9/11, [54] CCA got on the bandwagon. As the *Huffington Post* reported, immigrants are the third-highest category of offenders at 11 percent. [55] As of 2013, more than 60 percent of all federal criminal convictions have been for immigration-related crimes, according to federal data. [56]

In 2012, companies such as CCA, garnered a windfall of more than $546 million from federal contracts with the Bureau of Prisons and the U.S. Marshals Service. [57] Again, CCA has denied lobbying to influence immigration policy, but the evidence shows otherwise. The Associated Press in 2012 found that the three major private prison corporations, including CCA, spent roughly $45 million over the past decide on campaign donations and lobbyists. [58] The private prison corporations specifically targeted Republican legislators over immigration "reform."[59] Expanded details and explanations of the impact of the immigrant population on the private prison and CCA profit is detailed in a later chapter.

As of 2015, CCA reported more than sixty facilities with an inmate population of about 70,000 offenders employing about 17,000 individuals.[60] From its humble beginnings, the company has grown into the largest private prison corporation in the United States. Even with the decreasing prison population, CCA has managed to maintain its base in Colorado, still operating two facilities, and adding significantly to its coffers.

"Capital triumphs," said David Simon, producer of *The Wire* during an interview with Dan Rather in 2014, and this seemed to be true for CCA. As he stated, "Profit appears to be the answer to everything."[61]

# Chapter 4. My Journey to Awareness

I often wondered: How did I get myself involved with a company whose primary objective was profit at any cost? My initial hiring and early experience with CCA did not reveal the adverse effect that the profit motive would have on my ability to counsel or monitor offenders. While this may seem like a lame excuse, it was true. Perhaps I was genuinely naïve and, in seeking a steady income, I saw a seemingly solid company. Only when I was directly affected, did I begin to seriously question the true motives and values of CCA.

What I found made me realize that despite all my efforts, I could not do the job as a mental health provider to help inmates. My intentions were sidelined by the corporate culture of CCA, which put profit ahead of staff or inmates. At this point, I began to actively seek out the history of the now largest private prison conglomerate in the country. After struggling through a mountain of paperwork and working several years of long uncompensated hours, I realized that any actual counseling that I believed necessary to have an impact on the inmates and to contribute to their successful reintegration back into society was being thwarted by the very company that paid my salary. However, it was only in my later years with CCA that I began to feel the full impact of the profit motive and its accompanying component of understaffing on my ability to do the work I had been trained to do.

I thought back to my history with the company. Beginning in 2002, when I started working at Bent County Correctional Facility, the facility housed fewer than 600 inmates and was able to function reasonably well at least as far as the mental health department operation. I recalled being able to lead a variety of classes for inmates. I had time to conduct interviews and evaluations with offenders, while holding individual counseling sessions. Basically, I functioned in a positive and productive manner. My colleague and I kept busy and, yes, we might lag a few days behind at times. But, we were always able to catch up, while providing appropriate treatment, monitoring the offenders, and managing our case loads. Those were rewarding days.

FLASHBACK TO 2002. The classified ad read "Addictions Counselor." In a brief two-inch space, it provided a succinct description of the position along with contact information. I was in the job market. Armed with my credentials, known in Colorado as a Certified Addiction Counselor III (CACIII), I was well on my way to obtaining a license in the same field. I had been working part-time jobs in for several years including teaching journalism, English, and later psychology at Lamar Community College. I loved this position and I still miss interacting with the students, prepping for classes, and watching as one after another seemed to grasp the material. But the college did not hire full time professors, and I simply could not live on the meager income.

So, I diversified. Sometimes, I worked as a housekeeper, hiring myself out to local folks who lived in the elite section of town. I vacuumed, dusted, cleaned their toilets, and sometimes cooked, when needed—not a lot of motivation or enthusiasm on my part. After all, these were the very same duties I did at home. Still, I appreciated the work and the extra funds tucked into my purse.

On two separate occasions, I actually served as a stringer for a regional newspaper, the *Pueblo Chieftain*. My job consisted of covering a variety of meetings, such as city council, college advisory board, or political rallies (any newsworthy event, in other words), writing a concise article and forwarding it to the paper, and taking pictures, when appropriate to the story. My undergraduate degree had been in journalism and creative writing, so I fit well with this position and actually enjoyed the role, especially being able to write the articles in a readable and factual manner. However, this job paid very little, so much per column inch and so much per picture. Living in a small rural town, the news was meager, and there was no real chance to sign on with a major publisher. I needed a full-time salaried position. I also spent a couple years with the old *Lamar Daily News*, no longer in existence in that name or format. In that capacity, I wrote newspaper articles, covered meetings, took photos, and overall earned my journalistic wings. In fact, I progressed to the point that I served as news editor for a time.

Just to round things out in my eclectic background, at one time I embarked upon a sales career, hosting toy parties during the Christmas season. I traveled to homes throughout Lamar, demonstrating a variety of cheap gadgets for a meager commission. I marveled at the gadgets that people actually bought, sometimes feeling a twinge of guilt when I felt that some folks really could not afford the products they purchased.

Yet, all of these endeavors reflected my struggle to support myself and two of my children still remaining at home. While I don't begrudge truly needy individuals, especially those with children to support, I have always tried to manage without the help of government or others. Perhaps this philosophy spurred me on to obtain my degrees and licenses.

When I was teaching English and journalism at the local college, I was approached by the addictions' program supervisor to assist in writing the policies for the program so that they would concur with state requirements. I accepted this obligation, which eventually led me on a completely different path in my life. When the only counselor in the program resigned, I was asked to teach the Driving Under the Influence (DUI) class. Since I was already teaching, it was an easy step into the addictions arena. It was also the first step toward certification, which eventually would lead me to the Bent County Correctional Facility.

As I progressed in obtaining my credentials, that Certified Addiction Counselor I referred to earlier, I learned that a need also existed within the state for domestic violence providers. In 1994, Colorado had passed domestic violence legislation, putting teeth into what formerly had been vague rules. Previously, any alleged criminal actions associated with domestic violence had fallen primarily under the assault category, but was non-specific regarding domestic violence. Even after the passage of the domestic violence legislation, the cases still ran as an attachment or enhancer to another charge.

At the suggestions of a court official, I began exploring the possibility of becoming a domestic-violence-approved provider. Eventually, I obtained those credentials and opened my own office, New Lifestyles. At the time, I was also listed as an unlicensed mental health counselor but continued working my way toward licensure by taking the required classes, while obtaining the hours of experience required for certification. Although I remained in this part-time business for thirteen years, I struggled to survive. My obligations included a salary for a clerk and a second counselor, as well as such necessities as a telephone, utilities, supplies, and rent.

However, in my small town in rural Colorado, there was a limit to the number of clients who had the funds to pay for treatment. The regulations required a sliding-fee scale, which meant that most clients paid somewhere in the neighborhood of $10 a class. Therefore, I balanced several "jobs" over a period of about ten years just to make ends meet.

Even after obtaining a full-time position at the Bent County Correctional Facility, I kept New Lifestyles operating, taking money from my salary to fund the agency. A voice within me insisted I was doing the right thing, that I was helping clients. After completing a day's work at Bent, I would hustle to New Lifestyles, conducting an evening group. On Saturday, I held another group or individual sessions. Yet, the part-time agency was doomed, especially the last four years as modifications of sentencing reduced the requirements of thirty-six sessions down to twelve sessions of anger management. In addition, it appeared that less enforcement of strict domestic violence laws occurred. More "slap-on-the-hands" by the system meant that offenders were able to bargain their way out of treatment. This approach was largely the result of the local court system, which made the determination of whether a client should do the complete thirty-six-weeks of domestic violence treatment, which I understood was required by Colorado, or whether the offense was not so significant and required only a dozen anger management classes.

Furthermore, the requirements to retain approved status as an agency and individual became even more difficult to attain. For example, it was necessary that I have ongoing supervision, which I, of course, had to pay for, as well as traveling several hundred miles for reviews. In addition, I had to have approval through the local victims' agency and the local judicial district, submitting documentation for both. My own credentials had to be annually reviewed, and I had to take ongoing classes. Many of these requirements were appropriate enough. My problem was addressing all those issues with my time limitation, as well as financial limitations. At length, I decided that closure of New Lifestyles was unavoidable.

In the meantime, the position at Bent County Correctional Facility opened up. Because few full-time positions existed that fit with my degree, experience, and training, I felt that this was an omen. None of my part-time jobs had paid much nor could they provide the income I needed to meet my monthly living expenses. Certainly, the funds did not stretch far enough to repay my monstrous student loans. Thus, had I been searching for a position in which I could use my education, a master's in counseling psychology, and obtain additional hours toward my Licensed Professional Counselor designation. I had high hopes that I might attain a full-time position, one which would lead to a *career*, not just a job. Even New Lifestyles was not able to provide me with that satisfaction.

Thus, when I spotted the ad seeking an addiction counselor, even the brief description in the local newspaper, seemed to indicate that it just might meet my needs. At the bottom of the column, the invitation read "Bent County Correctional Facility, a CCA company." I had no knowledge of CCA. However, I had worked with court-ordered offenders for at least ten years, both in the alcohol and drug program, and in my own domestic violence treatment agency. My main concern was for a stable, full-time job with benefits.

The ad provided a phone number and an address. I updated my resume and placed a call. This was before e-mails, attachments, and on-line applications became prevalent. One phone call and a few keystrokes, and my journey through the private prison system began.

Looking back, I recognize that this was before the corporation assumed primary power over the screening and hiring of staff. I was brought in with an interview conducted by the then warden, the associate warden, and the lead addictions coordinator plus the mental health coordinator. I sat in the warden's office surrounded by these four friendly, professional faces, all encouraging me from the very beginning to take the position. Apparently, they were desperate for a body. Having reviewed my resume, they had a few brief questions for me, but, overall they urged me to take the job after perhaps only fifteen minutes. The idea was that I could divide my time—spending half with the addictions program and half with the mental health department, since I was still working on my hours to get my Licensed Professional Counselor (LPC) certification. At that time, Bent County's prison population was probably less than 600 inmates, which made splitting a position possible.

Looking back on this interview, I realized that I was basically hired on the spot, that I did not have to do any special computer application or go through a screening, which I would probably fail today. My understanding with the online procedure today is that it asks many questions that require a "yes" or "no," but do not provide for any explanations. My information comes from my acquaintances and relatives who have applied within the past five years, since I never applied in that manner. They have reported to me that the process appears to have grown more encumbered. Some have never passed the on-line computer test and have explained to me that it asks for items, such as "Have you ever known or do you now know someone who has smoked pot?" Comprised of several questions of such nature, I've been told that it make it very difficult for some applicants to get past this initial process. Fortunately, I never had to face that process.

In my opinion, as CCA has grown, with tremendous acceleration over the past twelve years, so have the processes, the paperwork, the complexity, and the difficulty of the hiring process. Part of the difficulty lies, especially with upper-level positions, in the job descriptions, which can prevent qualified people being hired, particularly in rural areas, where there are fewer people to apply. In the early years, it seemed to be easier to get hired and, as I soon learned, as an individual, I had a high degree of autonomy in managing my activities and in taking care of the offenders on my case load. That was then.

Of course, I took the job. My work station was with Michele, the mental health coordinator. I had no desk of my own, no computer, no printer, but I had to rely upon her break times to put information into the system. Because at the time I was a certified domestic violence counselor, in addition to my other qualifications, I was put to work conducting groups. I held a domestic violence group weekly, an anger management group, a life skills group, and a parenting group. Each day I held at least one group in addition to conducting intakes for new offenders, as well as monitoring my mental health case load.

Of course, I had paperwork from each class and information that did need to get into the computer. However, with no computer or printer of my own, I was in a dilemma. At length, I spoke with the assistant warden and asked if I could bring in my own laptop and mini-printer. He asked why I couldn't share the equipment with my colleague. I explained that she constantly needed it for her tasks, that it was basically unavailable for my use. After some hesitation, he agreed—something that probably would never happen today. So, I brought in my own equipment during my first year at Bent County.

While I could not access the internet or the Department of Corrections' programs, I could prepare tests, weekly progress forms, instructional materials, and other forms that required a simple Word program. I could print them off—at my own expense. Still, having my computer and printer provided me with the ability to produce the materials needed for the groups I led.

A Licensed Professional Counselor oversaw my work, including my group sessions, as well as my counseling and monitoring duties. This counselor came to the facility once or twice a week to supervise both my colleague and me. This supervision allowed me to gain the hours I needed toward my own licensure.

In my work with the offenders, I felt a sense of fulfillment. I could actually provide them with information and counseling in areas of managing and controlling their anger in a healthy manner; parenting from prison and afterward; how to prepare an employment application and resume; and the role of alcohol and substances in bringing people to prison. These were some of the topics discussed and emphasized in the classes, as well as in individual sessions. Yes, I actually had a chance to do some individual counseling during this time period.

But the most rewarding time came when an offender demonstrated his appreciation for the services. Dwayne popped into my office just before he left to return to his wife and two small children. "I'm going home today," he said, with tears threatening to overflow. "After six years behind bars, I'm headed out."

I wished him well.

He held out his parenting manual. "I should give this back for the next person," he said.

I shook my head. "No, that's yours to keep," I insisted. "Who knows, you may be able to refer to it now and then."

He nodded. "Thank you for the class. I plan to be a good father, to try and make up for all I've missed. It won't be easy, but I'll do it."

He smiled through his sadness at how his decisions had wrecked, maybe permanently, his relationship with his children, now eight and ten years old. Throughout the group he had demonstrated his frustrations at himself for his "stupid choices," as he called them, and had taken full responsibility for his drug crime, as well as the damage done to his family and associates.

"You can do it," I assured him.

Dwayne held out his hand. I rarely shake hands with an inmate, but I did so this time. He moved to the door then and turned and said two simple words. "Thank you."

During these years there were others like Dwayne. Not all of them said "thank you." Occasionally, someone wrote a note or card. But probably only one in ten is going to turn around and thank you—if that. As a therapist, we never know if anyone has garnered an iota of truth or that their thinking changes and that will set them on a different path. Maybe one day, five or ten years later, an offender just might go, "Oh, yes, that's what she meant!"

But in those early days at Bent County, I had more Dwayne moments, and even without the Dwaynes, I had those moments when I felt I was being fulfilled. I was able to chip away at the work I felt destined to do. I was able to share and to just listen, which is the most important thing anyway with clients—be quiet and just listen, and let them do the work they need to do to find their way back.

At that time, I recognized no problems with understaffing in the mental health department nor did I recognize problems within any within other departments of the facility. Along with the other clinician, we were able to manage our inmates efficiently. Of course, just like in any business, we might get behind for a few days, but the monitoring and services were always compliant with policies. In addition, the psychiatrist, who came in once a week, managed to handle his case load successfully.

Looking back, I had no problem providing ongoing counseling and treatment for the offenders. I was able to conduct one-on-one sessions. I even designed a couple of my own classes, such as the parenting and life skills groups. I established the objectives and goals for course completion and schedules to meet criteria. In other words, the mental health component was manageable, even allowing enough time for community services, meetings, and further training.

I am grateful for this period, for the experience, the colleagues, and the opportunity to acquire the hours I needed for licensure. That year provided me with a stepping stone to further launch my corrections career.

Those early years distinctly contrasted with what followed during the next decade as CCA continued to expand its facilities, as it grew like a Langolier from a Stephen King novel, eating and digesting every available prison—even building its own. Yet, I did not understand the "behind the scenes" activities that drove the system. I focused only on doing my job, the best I could each day. Even with some frustrations, I did not probe beneath the surface, to question those who put forth the policies and regulations that drove the machine. I never thought to review the politics or undercurrent of the company. I was content with having a good job, a decent pay rate, and great insurance and benefits so that I merely concentrated on doing my work.

After one year, I left Bent County. Much of this had to do with my growing frustration with a supervisor, who seemed to micro-manage every aspect of the mental health department. In addition, conflicts arose with the warden, who would not back mental health decisions. For example, as per administrative regulation, I had denied a picture of a naked child to a sex offender, a child molester. The offender complained, and the warden overrode my decision and gave the photo to the man. Ultimately, mental health contacted the Colorado Department of Corrections' Private Prison Monitor, who overrode the warden. After that, there seemed to be ongoing conflict between the warden and me. As the tension and stress continued to rise within me, I went home each night frustrated and grouchy, full of complaints and criticism. Of course, this made it even more difficult to effectively function at my second job—New Lifestyles—where I conducted nightly domestic violence classes.

I might have managed my frustrations, overlooking the mostly trivial issues, but about the same time I received a promising job offer with increased pay and benefits—always an incentive. With the constant daily irritants at Bent County, the change of scenery seemed like a good idea and possibly a step up the career ladder.

Thus, I left for another position in the mental health field, but soon it appeared that I should have been more patient, perhaps more communicative with my supervisors, more specific about my concerns while at Bent County. My new job classified me as an on-call clinician. This meant that I constantly traveled between six counties, day and night, putting out fires. Mostly these calls were for people having suicidal thoughts or who had suffered a psychotic break. Some had gone off their medication and were having severe withdrawals and, as a result, increased symptoms. Some had overdosed on the street on prescription drugs or alcohol.

After overseeing the six counties, more often driving through the black of night, I felt exhausted. My body and my brain were at a breaking point. What in the name of everything holy was I thinking in leaving Bent County? I muddled along for six months, trudging through icy roads and blowing snow, sometimes with two calls at the same time, searching to find the backup clinician to assist me. Dead tired, my body and my brain reached a breaking point. My health broke down. Unable to maintain normal sleep patterns, I struggled through the days and popped antacids continually. This was not a promotion. Instead, it felt like demotion.

But the IRS saved my sanity. I had not yet received the notification for my last year's CCA earnings. So, I phoned the prison. Almost immediately, the voice on the other end asked if I were interested in coming back. Apparently, the mental health clinician had resigned, taking a similar position with the state. And, while the human resources coordinator, Sarah, explained that my tax document was on its way, she urged me to reconsider Bent County once more with a pay raise. Holding the telephone in my hand, I initially held visions of those past heated moments with the warden. I hesitated, even when Sarah suggested an interview. I finally agreed to a meeting, but later cancelled it, still obstructed by those memories. As frustrated as I was with this new job, I was not sure if I was ready to return to the stress and negativity I had experienced only six months earlier.

Sarah was patient. She phoned me back, stating that the warden wanted to talk to me. She actually put him on the line! The voice I heard on the other end had a decidedly Oklahoma drawl. A new warden now headed the Bent County reins.

So, I returned for another twelve years. Even when I returned, the next period of perhaps five years, was relatively "doable." The oncoming changes were insidious, creeping in like a python, wrapping its body into every element and then squeezing the breath out of the workers and the offenders. But, when I first returned, how could I realize what changes would be wrought over the next five years? I could not imagine how understaffing would affect the mental health department, leaving us with no time to conduct classes or to provide one-on-one counseling to those offenders with mental health issues. Basically, the understaffing ultimately affected the ability of clinicians to provide offenders with tools so they might be successful, not reoffend in the community or on parole. Perhaps the mission statements and idealism, which pervaded the bulletin boards and publications, had it all wrong. After a few years, I had to wonder. Perhaps there was a need for offenders to return, that need based solely on dollars and numbers—bodies in beds. Was that, after all, the true goal?

CHAPTER 5. PROPAGANDA VERSUS REALITY

In the beginning, I believed in the CCA mottos and the mission statement. I posted the mission statement on my file cabinet. I memorized the words in case the warden should call upon me during a department meeting so I could recite it like a mantra. Much like an initiate to a new religion, I felt that the company I worked for had it right. After all, they provided me with a 401K retirement program, good insurance, medical, dental, and vision. So, I rationalized, they must care. Words like *Professionalism, Respect, Integrity, Duty* and *Excellence (PRIDE)*, and *Loyalty* cemented the message. The facility actively worked at instilling within each staff person a teamwork spirit, a sense of companionship, that we were all "family."

The mission statement went something like this: Our Vision: To be the best full-service adult corrections system; Our Mission: Advancing corrections through innovative results that benefit and protect all we serve; Our Values; having PRIDE in all we do; again those magic words: Professionalism, Respect, Integrity, Duty, Excellence, and Loyalty.

Sounds good. For anyone seeking a position with CCA, the website provided the most positive information including pictures of happy worker bees, smiling as they went about their daily duties, and a litany of information about programs available to offenders, including re-entry classes. The site boasted a detailed history of the company, how it grew from three men with a dream in 1983, and accelerated up to today's sixty facilities with a capacity of 80,000 beds, according to the last site entries. Any company growing at such a rate over a period of only thirty plus years must be doing something right.

But, let us not stop there. CCA was named in 2008 as one of the 100 best corporate citizens by *Corporate Responsibility Officer Magazine*.[1] In addition, the national military magazine *GI Jobs* has highlighted CCA as a solid employer for veterans and also named CCA as one of its "Top 50 Military Friendly Jobs" on four separate occasions.[2]

In fact, in 2011, *Forbes Magazine* named CCA's President and Chief Executive Officer Damon Hininger as one of the "Twenty Most Powerful CEOs Age Forty or Under."[3] In addition, CCA was publicly traded in the United States, NYSE: CXW.[4]

Based on this information, there was little reason not to trust the company. On the surface and the endorsements, CCA appeared to be a worker's utopia. And, today, I still believe that most of my co-workers were diligent professionals, who did the best job they knew how to do. They had my back throughout the years while I remained at Bent County. I have no problem with them. Realistically, of course, there are those with whom I may have had a personality or philosophical conflict or a different perception of a situation or interpretation of a policy. But, that does not mean that I don't respect and empathize with them as they, too, struggled to conduct their roles in a constantly changing and stressful environment.

No, it was the philosophy and values of the company itself with which I had problems. It was the difference between the propaganda that is expounded on the mission statements, the brochures, the CCA reports, and the website versus the reality of the workplace. Words are powerful, and words paint an image of a company devoted to its employees. Those words indicate that CCA focuses on providing programs and services to offenders so that they will not be as likely to reoffend, that they will be safe and successful if sent back into their communities. That appears to be the underlying message.

For example, in the September-October 2014 issues of *Inside CCA*,[5] the theme of "Tackling Recidivism" is printed on the outside cover of the magazine. A quote on page three states, "Reentry must and will be a day-one priority at all of our facilities." This message from The President's Desk and signed by Hininger emphasizes the need for reentry programs so that offenders do not return to prison. He states, "We have to interrupt this cycle of recidivism." He continues to cite the various programs that CCA provides to do exactly that, mentioning GED, life skills and vocational courses, as well as faith-based programs, adding that these efforts have long been staples of CCA's reentry programming. This sounds good. It sounds like a company devoted to instilling educational and moral concepts—even building character in the offenders.

Indeed, a review of the magazine itself featured staff from a variety of facilities engaged in worthy activities, both in the classroom and the community, demonstrating positive attitudes and actions. Those featured are performing worthy activities. The issue included a list of staff receiving service awards. However, aside from the president's message, no other articles on recidivism are located inside the magazine. The words are there. The truth was that during my years at Bent County, I found the activities, the programs, and the focus on impacting recidivism barely visible. Lip-service was apparent in every endeavor. Yes, appropriate paperwork indicated that such activities were being conducted. Yet, the resources and the staff to adequately impact recidivism were meager, at best.

While Bent County could boast GED and faith-based programs, the reality was that other programs and activities, which might have had an impact on recidivism, were cut. A life skills class was eliminated when the instructor was terminated, but never replaced during my tenure there. However, a former colleague reported that a re-entry program has since been initiated, which provides the same goals and objectives as the Lifestyles program.

A cut in July 2012, which is detailed in a later chapter, resulted in the loss of two computer classes, which were not re-established prior to my departure. The only vocational program at that time was janitorial, which was also eliminated when the instructor resigned. Toward the end of my career there, a Certified Driver's Class was added, in which offenders could train and test on the computer, but, of course, they could not drive.

When I viewed the 2011 CNBC special *Billions Behind Bars: Inside American's Prison Industry*,[6] I was reminded of the variety of actual jobs that are offered at some of the state-operated prisons in Colorado. I noted a garment enterprise, a fish industry, a program for the construction of saddles, the animal care programs, a greenhouse, and other opportunities for offenders to actually learn a skill, which they could take to the street. At the same time, inmates were earning money.

Granted there is controversy with correctional industries. As noted in the film, one primary concern focuses on the fact that inmates work for cheaper wages than community workers. In Colorado, the correctional industry offenders now earn a spectacular $1 an hour and out of that, of course, they must pay any restitution related to their crime, child support, and purchase any personal hygiene or commodities.

There is a concern that prison industry can take over and even close down similar enterprises within a community. For example, Whole Foods recently decided to no longer sell goat's milk cheese and fresh fish produced by Colorado Correctional Industries. This decision came as a result of a protest by a Texas group who claimed that the retailer was exploiting low-cost inmate jobs.[7]

In response, Adrienne Jacobs, a spokesperson for Colorado Department of Corrections said that more than 80 percent of former Correctional Industry workers with at least six months of work experience stay out of trouble after release.[8] This track record speaks strongly for the importance of offenders having access to employment while locked up. Even so, since a large percentage of CCA facilities are located in low-population, rural towns, it is understandable that the employment of prison labor could concern those locals who might feel that any prison industry might destroy their businesses. Perhaps the concern for community good will is a significant factor in the lack of bona fide industry in the Colorado CCA facilities.

Yet idle prisoners with no jobs, no programs, and no classes definitely present a problem within the prison system. Boredom can lead directly to security issues. Idle minds sitting around in their dayrooms, playing cards, staring mindlessly at television, at some point may produce plans designed to keep officers on their feet—plans such as smuggling in contraband, instigating a riot, or attacking a weaker inmate. Of course, just because there are activities does not mean that safety is insured. Yet offering programs to keep their minds busy, as well as assisting them in preparing for a healthy lifestyle when they are released, is essential.

At Bent County, the offenders could attend GED and drug and alcohol classes, but they were waitlisted. This meant that they might not actually get into the classes for several months. Sometimes, an inmate would be moved to another facility or leave for a halfway house before he could get into the classes. Thus, he could no longer learn to operate a software program, which just might lead him into a bona fide job when he was released. Having been a tenth grade dropout, he might never see a GED classroom prior to his move. A few select inmates could become para-pros. Due to their education, often a college degree, as well as teaching or vocational experience, they could assist instructors with the GED tutoring. A few could work in the library. Most of the available jobs were related to porter activities, cleaning offices and hallways or the cell houses, perhaps just the showers. Many of those jobs took only thirty minutes. Some, such as those in the medical or administration department, might take half a day. But, such choice jobs were few. The bulk of the jobs centered around the kitchen. Almost all inmates were initially assigned to the kitchen to begin their "work experience." As evident, most of the offenders had little to do and an excess of idle time.

How would these offenders spend their day? Some men learned to crochet and made beautiful afghans, bronco blankets, and other handcrafts. Some learned to construct tiny pool tables from bars of soap and sell them to family and friends outside the facility. Others learned to make chess sets and miniature covered wagons and antique-looking automobiles, all constructed of materials they had on hand, such as paper products, shoe strings, or Styrofoam. Some offender artists drew and painted scenery or portraits to sell to staff. Other more ambitious men would read and study on their own. But, many did not have good reading skills or habits. Again, those inmates spent their days playing cards, staring at the TV, or planning mischief such as drug deals or engaging in gang-retaliation.

So, it was not as if there was nothing to do at Bent County for the inmates. An industrious person can always find something to pass the time. But the goal should not be to just pass the time. Rather, during the locked-up years, an offender should be either in school or learning a trade or skill that will benefit him when he gets out of prison. He should be in treatment for his drug addiction and his mental health issues. Unfortunately, that is not what I nor the inmates experienced at Bent County.

Instead, I heard inmates frequently complain about the lack of things to do. Those offenders who had worked steady jobs before coming to prison (and, believe it or not, there were some of those behind bars) especially found it difficult to manage their boredom and frustrations. Of course, many inmates simply liked to complain about everything. Some tended to take little responsibility for their own actions and demonstrated little patience. Many of them had a toddler mentality, in which they "want it (whatever it happens to be) RIGHT NOW."

However, that does not negate the importance of providing the inmate with education and tools so that he will have a much better chance of success when he is released back into the community. The facility is not off the hook when it does not provide services that might help the inmate avoid recidivism, whether that be formal education, trade skills, or simple tools to impact his criminal thinking.

One conversation that took place shortly before I left Bent County is indicative of the problem caused by inadequate staffing and programming. The offender had requested a meeting with me due to his frustrations and increasing depression.

"All I want is an appointment with my case manager," he stated immediately. "I just want to find out how I can progress in the system. How can I move from here to my program?" He gestured with a wave of his hand, indicating the facility.

This particular inmate, classified as a sex offender, was required to attend classes, but they were not offered at Bent County. However, as mental health professionals, we did provide offenders with the forms necessary so that they could qualify to be placed on the wait list at a Department of Corrections' facility. Once approved, when their name came up the Department of Corrections would move them to the facility that provided the sex-offender treatment program.

"Have you talked with your case manager?" I asked. He had already completed his paperwork and was simply trying to learn his status.

"Yes, it's been over three weeks. I sent two separate kites. He hasn't even sent back a note that I would be scheduled." He sighed deeply, shaking his head. I knew that the term "kite" referred to a form that requested some type of service. [9]

"You may have to send another," I replied. Then, I added, "I'll send him an e-mail. I can't promise anything, but I will do that." I wanted to give the inmate a glimmer of hope.

"Okay," he said, rising from the chair. "I appreciate it. I just need to know if there's anything else I need to do. It's time for me to be reclassified, and I know he's the only one who can do that." I thought, what if I were stuck here and just needed a bit of reassurance to get through another day? How would I manage? Granted, he was a sex offender, but he was still a human being with a legitimate request, which appeared to be ignored.

As a mental health professional, I could only do so much. But, I also knew that due to the shortage of staff, the case managers and other personnel were filling in as correctional officers. That is the most likely reason that inmate Smith's kites were not being answered. For this same reason my mental health kites grew, and I had to continue moving my appointments up. When other departments were not able to handle the requests, typically the inmates solicited help from mental health. And, too often, our hands would be tied, because the solution they were seeking simply was outside our area of practice or expertise.

Once more I felt that I was hindered by the numbers game. As Bent County doubled its inmate population, I could only reflect on the how CCA had continued to experience an enormous benefit even with a declining prison population overall. The reality was that the decline had been relatively modest in most states and eleven states actually had continuing rises in imprisonment. [10] The United States has a total of 2.2 million people incarcerated; that is, 1 in 100 of its citizens, a 500 percent increase in the thirty years since CCA opened its first facility. [11] Interestingly, state prisons hold 1,315,000 inmates, but only 54 percent of those are in for violent offenses. [12]

Yet, as we continue to house more and more people over the last four decades, keeping them for longer stays, research indicates that crime has dropped to historic lows.[13]

Many organizations and politicians have been actively pursuing alternatives to corrections and suggesting ways to lower the number of people in prison. For example, organizations such as the American Civil Liberties Union (ACLU), Rebuild the Dream, and Just Leadership USA united with the goal of reducing the prison population by 50 percent within the next ten to fifteen years. This movement, known as *Cut50*, would entail enormous changes in the sentencing system, as well as parole and diversion. Examining alternatives to imprisonment, such as probation or community services, mental illness or addiction programs, and even redefining what offenses are considered violent and suitable for prison are at the heart of their movement.[14]

Even President Obama took action indicative of pushing for a criminal justice system that is more equitable as well as saving the government money. He urged a change in the sentencing of nonviolent offenders and, as a result, he cut sentences of forty-six nonviolent offenders, the most cuts in a single day since President Johnson.[15]

Addressing the NAACP, Obama stated that the cost to incarcerate people who "have only been engaged in nonviolent offenses" is $80 billion a year. He promised to lay out more ideas on criminal justice changes. During his Presidency, Obama issued eighty-nine commutations, mostly to those sentenced for nonviolent crimes under outdated sentencing guidelines.[16]

However, those who advocate for sentencing reforms, which might reduce the number of people behind bars, face an uphill battle from the private prison industry, which stand to lose ground. CCA, along with other private prisons, took a beating in the late 1990s in a controversial reorganization. The company almost went bankrupt, but survived largely due to a leveraged buyout.[17] Small wonder that CCA remains alert to laws and regulations, which might adversely affect their profits in the decades to come.

For example, in a 2010 Annual Report filed with the Securities and Exchange Commission, CCA, the largest private prison company, stated: "The demand for our facilities and services could be adversely affected by . . . leniency in conviction or parole standards and sentencing practices . . ."[18] Even earlier in 2005, the annual report had stated:

> The demand for our facilities and services could be adversely affected by the relaxation of enforcement efforts, leniency in conviction and sentencing practices or through the decriminalization of certain

activities that are currently proscribed by our criminal laws. For instance, any changes with respect to drugs and controlled substances or illegal immigration could affect the number of persons arrested, convicted, and sentenced, thereby potentially reducing demand for correctional facilities to house them.[19]

The company's language indicates their overriding philosophy. The term "aggressive business strategy" as it applies to "building prison beds or buying them off the government and contracting them to government entities" further exemplifies CCA's quest for profit at the expense of offender treatment and successful reintegration.[20]

The private prisons have benefitted immensely by the increased criminalization of activities and the advent of three-strike laws, which have been adopted by twenty-eight states. These laws impose greater penalties and lengthier sentences on those who have been convicted of two or more felonies.[21] As noted above, CCA has been outspoken about the impact on their profit if we stop imprisoning so many people. In the 2010 annual report, they issued a strong warning related to the adverse effect on the company, citing several problems areas, such as proposed legislation that "could lower minimum sentences for some non-violent crimes and make more inmates eligible for early release based on good behaviors." The report continues:

> [S]entencing alternatives under consideration could put some offenders on probation with electronic monitoring who would otherwise be incarcerated. Similarly, reductions in crime rates or resources dedicated to prevent and enforce crime could lead to reductions in arrests, convictions, and sentences requiring incarceration at correctional facilities.[22]

In addition to profiting off those who initially are sentenced to prison, CCA also manages to add to their coffers by those individuals who circle back into the system. Keep in mind that a "felon" can include someone who reoffends by committing a new crime or who fails any of the "rules" of parole, something as simple as missing a bus and not making check-in. Those with drug charges may get a "hot" urine test or fail to show up for the test on time. Such errors in judgment can land an offender right back in prison. No excuses, no "get out of jail free" cards. Sometimes no explanation is permitted. The rule is the rule. And if an offender cannot afford, on his new minimum wage job (if he has been fortunate enough to find one), to pay for his recommended classes, to pay for his random urine tests, to pay his rent and food, well, that's his problem. So back to prison he goes.

This is a complex issue. Of course, many offenders are adverse to following instructions in general. They reject authority. They may even prefer prison life to having to take responsibility for all the various factors involved in living in the "real world." Some become institutionalized, used to the prison rules, the food, and the routines. They are in their comfort zone and have no desire to leave and, if released, may actually commit a crime in order to return to prison.[23]

However, many offenders fail simply because they do not get the tools and support they need to be successful. This lack of tools for success is good news to the private prison system. The more bodies, which are placed in beds, the more reimbursement the facility gets. And, of course, as discussed previously, the increased numbers pay necessary wages for the staff and provide jobs in rural areas and offer some economic revitalization to the community. So, having a prison in a small community is great news. In some cases, it may even mean survival of that community.[24]

That is one reason that the private prison administrators, including the warden, meet with the local Chamber of Commerce, local government, and take part in town functions, such as parades and fairs. They host toy drives at Christmas. While such participation is commendable, assisting and supporting a variety of good causes, the truth is that there is a different motive behind it. It portrays the private prison as a "friend," as an entity which gives back to the community and is providing needed services by containing the "bad guys" and keeping the community safe, while feeding money back into the region.

With this type of propaganda, it's easy to overlook the wage disparities. Based on data, the CCA prisons pay lower wages than state-operated facilities. For example, the average wage for a CCA corrections office is $34,414 per year.[25.] The Colorado Department of Corrections, however, pays an average of $3,364 per month or $40,368 per year.[26] This represents a difference of almost $6,000 per year, in that one position alone. This is only one indication of the differences that can exist between state and private wages. Of course, this will vary from state to state.

Yet, CCA, especially at Bent County, foists greater responsibilities onto fewer staff, a practice, which, in many instances, leads to overwork and safety issues. Staff who work directly with offenders often find that they are required to do duplicate paperwork, some that meets state standards and the other documentation for CCA's benefit. Overworked and burned out, the turnover rates increase. According to my calculations, at one point, the turnover in the medical department within a six month period between 2013 and 2014 was 38 percent—fairly substantial in a department that carries approximately eighteen to twenty employees at any given time.

According to the Private Corrections Institute, self-reported statistics from 2000 indicated that the private prison turnover rate was 53 percent while the public prison turnover rate was 16 percent. In 2008 at seven state-contracted private prisons in Texas that rate was 90 percent compared with a 24 percent turnover rate at public prisons.[27]

Again, a review of the CCA magazine often features different facilities, which appear to be conducting some innovative and productive programming for offenders. Some of these programs probably are functioning well and hopefully providing needed tools for offenders. Realistically, the magazine will feature those successful and positive programs and articles, but avoid negative or controversial articles. Many staff working in CCA facilities begin to recognize that suggestions for implementing programs and change seem to fall on deaf ears. Usually, this is the "budget" ears. Promises are made, but any particular requested item or program is like a mirage, looming somewhere out there in the prairie dust, but unreal and rarely reachable.

I continued to review the propaganda that circulated throughout the company. For example, CCA has insisted that it does not engage in "lobbying or advocacy efforts that would influence enforcement efforts, parole standards, criminal laws, and sentencing policies;" yet, it does exactly that, pouring money into both lobbying and campaign contributions.[28] For example, Idaho Governor C. L. "Butch" Otter is tied with Texas Governor Rick Perry for having received the most campaign contributions from CCA, totaling $20,000 since 2003.[29] From 2002 to 2012, CCA devoted more than $19 million to lobbying Congress. During the same time period, its political action committee (PAC) shelled out more than $1.4 million to candidates for federal office.[30] In 2012 alone, CCA spent "$1,790,000 lobbying Congress and federal bureaucracies on issues related to homeland security.[31]

The investment in lobbying must be working, as CCA announced in its own *Investor Relations* annual report that as of December 31, 2014, they owned or controlled 52 correctional and detention facilities and managed an additional 12 facilities owned by our government partners, with a total design capacity of approximately 84,500 beds in 19 states and the District of Columbia.[32] The report notes that CCA provides "a variety of rehabilitation and educational programs, including basic education, religious services, life skills, employment training, and substance-abuse treatment," with the concluding statement that the services are to reduce recidivism and to prepare offenders for their successful re-entry into society.[33] While all of these words are impressive, indicating through numbers and management and services, that CCA is doing a great job and making significant headway in assisting offenders to become reliable and contributing citizens, this simply doesn't jive with the facts.

Take Idaho, for example, where CCA employees falsified nearly 4,800 staffing records.[34] While Governor Otter had been supportive of the company since 1997, when it first opened, with the investigation of the records related to understaffing, the company lost its state contract. In fact, Otter had even floated legislation to allow private companies to build and operate in Idaho and import out-of-state inmates. In 2008, he suggested privatizing the 500-bed state-run facility in Orofino. Following the investigation, CCA acknowledged that falsified staffing reports were given to the state showing thousands of hours staffed by CCA workers, when the positions were actually vacant.[35]

Prior to that, Otter had ordered the State Police Colonel Ralph Powell to investigate the situation. However, when AP filed a public records request, it was learned that the investigation never occurred. In early August 2014, AP learned that 26,000 hours of mandatory guard posts were understaffed or problematic.[36]

In March 2010, the American Civil Liberties Union (ACLU) had filed suit against the Idaho facility alleging that guards were not protecting inmates from other violent inmates.[37] In February 2014, the federal judge hearing the case awarded $349,000 to the American Civil Liberties Union for its costs in bringing the action.[38] In November 2012, eight inmates filed a federal lawsuit alleging that CCA prison officials partially ceded control of the facility over to gang leaders.[39] In September 2013, a federal judge held CCA in contempt of court for persistently understaffing the Idaho Correctional Center in direct violation of a legal settlement.[40]

The state reassumed control of Idaho Center on July 1, 2014.[41]

The Huffington Post reported that in the fall of 2012, state auditors of the Lake Erie Correctional Institution in Ohio, which had been acquired by CCA earlier that year, deducted $500,000 for contract violations and inadequate staffing.[42] Closer to home, Colorado private prisons in 2015 were assessed with a total of $668,705 for staff vacancies. Of this total, the three CCA facilities were fined $403, 401, while Bent County alone was assessed $70,320.[43]

Many examples abound regarding CCA understaffing and other problems. The riot at the Crowley County Correctional Facility July 2004 is indicative of what occurs when CCA fails to adequately staff a prison. This facility lies just down the Arkansas Valley at Olney Springs about fifty miles northwest of the Bent County Correctional Facility.

The riot, which broke out in the yard, quickly accelerated, resulting in more than a dozen people injured and thirteen inmates taken to hospitals. According to media reports, four of the living units were declared uninhabitable because of broken windows, fire, smoke, and water damage. A vocational greenhouse was burned to the ground, according to Alison Morgan, a spokeswoman for the Colorado Department of Corrections.[44]

Crowley County, which opened in 1998, was originally owned by Dominion Correctional Services, but turned over to CCA in 2003. During this transition period, both Dominion and CCA were involved in a sexual-harassment lawsuit with claims by twenty-one women according to U.S. Equal Employment Opportunity Commission (EEOC). They reached a settlement of $1.3 million.[45] Most of these problems occurred while the facility was under the Dominion flag but they are indicative of the types of problems that CCA has faced across the country.

At the time of the riot, Crowley held 1,125 offenders, with 807 from Colorado, 120 from Wyoming, and 198 from Washington State.[46] As already noted, much of the hostility stemmed from the fact that inmates from different states had different rules and regulations under Colorado standards than those in their home facilities. Following the riot, according to the Colorado Department of Corrections' website, Crowley was no longer allowed to have out-of-state inmates.

The Associated Press stated that more than one hundred correctional officers and response teams from five states responded to the riot, along with a special operations team. Bent County Correctional Facility also sent a special response team, known as SORT, as well as other trained officers and staff. Displaced inmates were moved to other facilities, including all three CCA-operated Colorado prisons.[47]

The fallout from the riot continued with the filing of a class action lawsuit, which included 230 inmates who suffered emotional or physical damage during the riot. As a result the plaintiffs reached an out-of-court settlement with CCA, in which the company agreed to pay $600,000, as reported by KRDO's Scott Harrison and Joe Dominguez.[48]

Bill Trine, the plaintiff's lead counsel, stated that without the settlement a trial would have possibly lasted twenty-five weeks and could have resulted in more damages. He blamed CCA for having inadequate staffing and training to handle the disturbance and for failing to act on warnings and recommendations for improving security at the prison. He stated that CCA had ignored rising tensions between the Colorado inmates and the Washington inmates. Washington inmates had been involved in another disturbance at the same prison in 1999, he said.[49]

CCA responded that all employees had acted appropriately at the time of the riot, but stated it was cheaper to settle than to fight more than 200 claims.[50]

According to a report in *Westword*, on the night of the incident, the prison had only forty-seven employees on duty, including eight trainees to supervise the 1,122 inmates. Alan Pendergast reported that part of the documents filed in the lawsuit indicated that prison officials had "ample warning of impending trouble but failed to take action in time." He noted that CCA had been blasted over inadequate training and emergency response procedures and not only that; the Department of Corrections' "own monitoring of the prison up to the night of the riot has been cursory at best."[51]

He continued that, even after several warnings of the possibility of an incident, Crowley failed to lock down or stagger recreation time. The article noted that "the warden left at five and a skeleton crew remained when all 1,100 inmates were released for recreation."[52]

The riot apparently kicked off when a confrontation occurred between a group of officers and Washington inmates, which led to staff evacuation. Some inmates then poured into housing units and began helping themselves to free weights. They used these weights to break windows and doors, smashing the electronic control centers, busting fixtures and flooding tiers, setting fires, and rifling case manager records. Many records were destroyed as a result.

Many inmates were attempting to remain in their cells, but were driven out by smoke or tear gas after help arrived. Some reported that they were treated more harshly by staff in the aftermath of the riot than at the time of the incident.[53]

Following the Crowley riot, I met with several of the inmates who had been moved to Bent County. The inmates confirmed much of what the media had reported. Two inmates stated that they had been chased by other inmates, felt they were denied medical treatment for an extensive period of time, and neither of them had participated in the riot. Both offenders told me that they knew the riot was coming, that it had been whispered among inmates for days, and they knew that some staff members knew. One of the inmates told me, "We all knew that there was not enough staff to handle anything serious. But some inmates were just waiting for a situation for an excuse."

The good news that came out of the Crowley incident was that the Colorado Department of Corrections began a much more intensive monitoring program of all the private prisons in the state. Since that time, a full-time private prison monitor has been hired. This person travels to the private systems and makes certain that regulations are being followed. As for mental health, there had always been a mental health private prison monitor. This person would come on site perhaps once a month; sometimes this was stretched out to two or even three months.

On occasion, the monitor would touch base by phone and e-mail with the Brent facility and mental health staff, as needed. Even when I personally complained about problems related to staffing and workloads, the monitor apparently had no control over CCA decisions. The monitor would meet with the warden after the review with our department, and I'm reasonably sure that concerns were discussed. However, as long as no direct safety or security problems existed, apparently no change was warranted.

After the Crowley riot, the state tightened up many of the private prison contacts. A specific monitor would provide bimonthly onsite visits. The state became very strident about keeping a monitor in place constantly who not only made visits, but was frequently in contact through telephone and e-mails. Those serving as monitors at Brent County Correctional Facility also conducted reviews of files, of processes, answered specific questions about policies, and provided information about upcoming changes at the state level. I have nothing but praise for those who served in this position while I was at Bent County.

This up-scaling and tightening of the role of the monitor was extremely valuable, but also was a direct reflection of the problems that arose from the Crowley County riot. However, with no direct violations of the CCA contract or security concerns, little change occurred. Undoubtedly, the warden listened to the concerns, but as a cog in the CCA wheel, his ability to have an impact on the staffing was limited.

Did monitoring and other changes resulting from the riot solve the problems of understaffing? Not really. As long as CCA or Brent County Correctional Facility can justify why positions are empty, and are willing to pay any accompanying fines, then, the situation remains problematic.

At one point, I went out on medical leave. Only one licensed mental health clinician remained at the facility—for 385 inmates with mental health diagnoses. Ideally, there should have been four clinicians or a case load of about 96 inmates per worker. Another person was basically providing clerical and odd duties, until he received his certification. The ratio of inmates to staff was unacceptable. Once more, CCA demonstrated a total lack of concern for the mentally ill within the prison system. This again demonstrated the direct tie-in between understaffing and the focus on profit at any cost. While I was on medical leave, I was still considered part of the staff, and I am relatively sure no fine was imposed for the lack of a mental health clinician. Yet, the facility was left with one person struggling to monitor the offenders and somehow remain compliant with all policies and regulations.

When there is an identified deficiency, CCA issues a Plan of Action (POA), which outlines the problem and what actions will be taken to remedy the issue by a specific date. I was told that the Health Services Administrator (H.S.A) stated that she already had to do two Plans of Actions (POA) to correct deficiencies in the mental health department. She insisted there could not be a third POA.

Yet, another reality check here: just one clinician or even two clinicians could not begin to keep up with the various duties and demands of the department. Even with some assistance, such as a clerk to do scheduling or getting someone else to sit with the doctor in tele-psych clinics, the amount of paperwork and the number of inmates far exceeded the ability of even a superwoman or superman clinician. Yet, until a serious incident happened or until the financial and contractual penalties become excessive, no change occurred—not during my stay.

# CHAPTER 6. UNDERSTAFFING AND SAFETY

Offender James Batson slept contentedly in a small 8' x 8' safety cell in the medical unit. Concrete floor and cinderblock walls, windowless, the cell contained a stainless steel sink and toilet stool. Both were securely attached, the stool on the floor and the sink was attached to the wall. Batson himself lay across the metal bed frame, also securely attached to the wall and floor. This was no frills: a barren, empty, gray room, depressing in tone and style.

Just down the hallway from my office, Batson was close at hand for monitoring and easy access. He was on suicide watch. Stripped out, he had no personal clothing and was dressed only in a quilted, padded blue suicide garment, complete with Velcro strips to hold it in place. He had a suicide blanket of the same material. No mattress, no book, no hygiene articles. Nothing sharp, nothing that might provide him with an implement or fabric to harm himself.

As a mental health coordinator, my first concern was always offender safety. Batson had commented to another offender that he was "done" and had climbed upon the railing of the second level in his cell house. An officer observed him and managed to restrain him before he leaped over the rail. As a result of his statement and action, Offender Batson had been taken to the medical department, and the on-call mental health clinician had been notified. It happened on my on-call rotation.

Thus, Batson slept in a safety cell, free of any objects that he could use to harm himself. And I sat in my office, my eyes glancing now and then at the clock on the wall. It was 2 p.m.. I sighed as my fingers raced to complete the seven documents required during a potential suicide attempt. The documents illustrate a combined series of policies and administrative regulations per the Colorado Department of Corrections and CCA. These policies, regulations, and facility processes have continued to grow like a python strangling the mental health department. Some of the documentation overlaps. CCA wants the piece of paper because it is required under their policy. The Department of Corrections wants their own form, which may be similar, but sometimes significantly different. On occasion, one agency will allow for a waiver, which can save staff a bit of time. Policies are CCA rules, while administrative regulations belong to the Colorado Department of Corrections.

My fingers were stiff from the day's work over the keyboard. I was physically tired after having worked till six the previous night on new admissions. I reflected how my day had begun. I turned off my 5 a.m. alarm, grabbed a quick shower, dressed, and began the forty mile trek to the prison, gulping a cup of coffee as I drove. Clouds of blowing dirt threatened to block my vision completely. It caused me to creep unsafely down the highway, silently praying that no impatient driver would ram my Scion's bumper.

Finally, and with great relief, I made it to the safety of my office. I monitored five offenders before Mr. Batson had been escorted into my office. Yet, as frustrated as I was with the additional work, I did not resent Offender Batson. He was simply an example of the problems incurred by the mentally ill in the prison system. I forced myself to focus on the paperwork. I recognized that I would probably not be able to leave early to compensate for the extra time I had worked because of the backup in my schedule and the offenders and paperwork I yet had to handle. I could not rush through the paperwork: accuracy was critical. One error or missed paper and I would not be able to use this incident for any future case study. Collecting the case study was critical because I would be able to use it when I prepared for audits. And we did have our share of audits. Colorado Department of Corrections audits, accreditation audits, safety audits, PREA audits, and possibly one or two I have forgotten. Besides, I always considered the possibility that I might have to testify before a judge as to an incident.

Looking over at Batson, I saw an officer sitting outside his cell at a battered wooden table with his monitoring forms and a pen before him. Unfortunately, the correctional officer had two separate forms on which he had to note his observations because the CCA and the Department of Corrections required different monitoring forms. Like two opposing gang leaders, neither will waive their document. As a result, the officer on duty has to remember not to confuse the two (which can happen easily enough) because each form has different numerical codes related to the inmate's actions. Therefore, the officer on duty might have to document the inmate's status twice.

The officer's role, as defined by CCA policy, was to provide continuous observation of the inmate. This meant "eyes on" at all times. Then, every fifteen minutes or less—never more than fifteen—he was supposed to jot down the time with a specific code defining what Batson was doing, such as 19, sleeping or 10, banging head on the wall. *Continual observation*—that is what the policy says.

Suicide or mental health watch is a thankless and tedious job. Yet, this vital job insures that the offender does not attempt to harm himself. Inmates have been known to use their nails to scratch open wounds, to use shoe strings to act as a garrote (that is why they do not get shoes or strings), to rip up boxers or sheets—all for suicide attempts. Even when a camera is present and operating, observation by the officer is required. CCA's policy is even more rigid than that of the Department of Corrections, which, I believe, is a positive safety factor. Constant observation further insures against any self-harming actions. Of course, when I reflected on it, I realized that suicides were expensive and the cost of litigation would harm CCAs bottom line. So, the threat of litigation caused CCA to do the right thing.

I recalled that on that day, by mid-afternoon, there were two problems. Officer Gerald Novak was working a double shift. Because he needed the money and his supervisor had been unable to find another officer to assist, Novak had been assigned to this post after already working one eight-hour shift. He had been working fourteen hours, and his eyes were very weary. As a result, he was sitting at the table, not standing. Therefore, he was unable to constantly view the offender. That was his first mistake.

His second mistake was linked directly with the first. I heard heavy breathing, followed with a type of mumbling or muttering. I stepped out of my office into the hallway. A glance to the south, toward Novak's post, revealed that both of his arms were down on the desk, his head flopped over them. I heard a deep snort, followed by snoring. I approached him quickly.

"Excuse me. Better wake up." I point to the policy lying on the desk under his right arm. "Continual observation," I reminded him.

Startled, he jumped up at the sound of my words. "Sorry..."

"You are required to keep constant watch," I repeated.

He nodded and mumbled something half under his breath. But, he straightened up, stood up, yawned, and stared into the cell at the inmate, sprawled out on the mattress-less Klingon bed in the cell.

I returned to my office and began pecking away at the keyboard, attempting to complete the suicide watch notes before the day's end. Fifteen minutes later, I exited the room, heading for the bathroom. I spotted the officer, once again sleeping at his post. Once more, I warned him, but then I moved down the hall to my supervisor's office. I reported the officer—not something I enjoyed doing, but necessary. Her quick phone call to the shift commander soon resulted in Officer Batson being replaced.

Only later did I learn of his sixteen-hour shift. I almost feel guilty for reporting him. Yet, for the safety of the inmate and my own licensing credentials, it was necessary. The word "*understaffing*" jumped out at me, not for the first time and certainly not the last time, while I worked for CCA.

Understaffing has been a major problem of CCA for many years. I have already pointed out my personal concerns with understaffing related to mental health and the day-to-day frustrations I had at my inability to do the work I was trained for and hired to do, which our code of ethics demands. However, a major concern with the understaffing concerns safety. Both the Idaho and Crowley County incidents are prime examples. Safety of both offenders and staff always should be the number one priority in a prison system.

One event demonstrates the lack of safety regulations related to staffing. On a specific day, when a clinician was out on medical leave, the other worker was stuck in the tele-psych clinic for the day; yet, the facility had forty-three new offenders arriving. This meant that I alone had to conduct forty-three intakes.

Due to the large number, the event was scheduled for the gym. When I entered the gym with several members of the medical staff, we were placed in an area separated from the inmates, who sat in chairs across the gym, perhaps thirty-feet away. Intake officers were in the same building taking pictures, getting fingerprints, and gathering the data they needed for their files. Case managers were in another section providing intake information to the inmates, while gathering required data for their files. About six officers were scattered throughout the open gym. But, as the intakes progressed, some departments finished their labors and left the building, taking a trained officer here and there with them. Soon, the case managers were gone, as were the intake personnel. Only medical and I remained.

In the meantime, the offenders had shuffled around in the room, no longer confined to their chairs across the room. As they were called forth by one department or another, they settled in different sections. Soon, many were sitting in small groups, chatting easily with each other. Some had drifted as close as five feet away from my area.

As the various department staff completed their portion of the intakes, they left. Soon the medical staff also had completed their documents. Thus, due to my staff shortage, I did not have time to complete my offender screens. Now, I alone was left in the gym with forty-three offenders. I had perhaps five intakes left. At this point, I looked around and noted one officer standing in the doorway. He was chatting with an inmate, both looking out the door, their backs to me, and perhaps thirty feet away.

At that moment, it occurred to me that I was basically alone with forty-three inmates. I did not panic nor at any moment did I feel threatened by any individual or the group itself. I elevated my awareness sensors, and I simply completed my intakes as a professional. Yet, as I later reported to my supervisor, it was not a safe position in which to put a staff person. Fortunately, nothing untoward happened.

These references are minor irritants only. They do not even begin to compare with some of the safety issues that have arisen in other facilities due to the lack of staff. The list of incidents attributed to staff shortage offer reasons for concern. For example, after CCA had purchased the Lake Erie Correctional Institution in 2011 (cost $72.7 million to Ohio), state audits found patterns of inadequate staffing the following year, delays in medical treatment, and "unacceptable living conditions" inside the prison, including inmates lacking access to running water and toilets. As a result, the company was docked $500,000 due to violations.[1]

Several other incidents with privatized facilities show a pattern of inadequate staffing. The American Civil Liberties Union (ACLU) noted that a twenty-three-year-old inmate, a citizen of Hawaii, was murdered in Saguaro Correctional Center in Eloy, Arizona, on June 8, 2010. The family filed a lawsuit against the State of Hawaii and CCA as a result, stating that the company's "pattern of greed-driven corner-cutting and short-staffing" contributed to his death. A man died because CCA failed to "adequately staff the prison."[2]

The Eloy Detention Center, a separate immigration facility, also located in Eloy, Arizona, has had more known fatalities than any other immigration jail under contract to the federal government, according to documents obtained in 2009 under Freedom of Information Act requests by the *New York Times* and the American Civil Liberties Union.[3] Between 2003 and 2009 Eloy has had 14 deaths, or 9 percent of all the deaths at nearly 250 detention centers, with 5 suicides. Dr. Allen Keller of New York University stated that the facility needs to "look strong and hard at its mental health care."[4]

In May 2012, a riot at Adams County Correctional Center in Natchez, Mississippi, claimed the life of one officer and left sixteen staff members and three prisoners injured. Twenty-five prisoners had been held hostage during the disturbance. The facility held about 2,500 low-security inmates, most of them held for coming back to the United States after being deported, according to Emilee Beach, a prison spokeswoman.[5] The riot was quelled by staff, Mississippi Highway Patrol, and the Federal Bureau of Prisons.[6]

The riot resulted in the death of officer Catlin Carithers at the CCA-owned facility. One year later, when Stockholder Alex Friedmann requested a moment of silence for him at the annual stockholders meeting, CCA Board

Chairman John D. Ferguson refused to honor the request. He stated that he had been honored in other ways.[7]

According to the *Clarion Ledger*, Friedmann said that "They would not give 30 seconds of respect (for Carithers). It speaks volumes how the company thinks of its employees and how it treats them."[8]

Friedmann also owns CCA stock in order to communicate issues with executive. He has previously served a six-year sentence at a CCA prison and is Managing Editor of Prison Legal News, a nonprofit watchdog organization.[9]

CCA spokesman Steve Owen responded to Friedmann's request in an e-mail, stated that he would "stop at nothing" to disparage CCA and its employees," referring to Friedmann as a "professional corrections critic" and stating he "attempted to exploit the tragic death of Catlin for his own personal agenda." Such remarks only underline the disregard the company holds for anyone who criticizes them, as well as for the value of staff.[10]

In 2013 the family of Carithers filed a lawsuit, saying CCA was negligent in his death, noting that an informant predicted the riot and suggesting Carithers was on a "hit list."[11]

Frank Smith, who is the field organizer for the Private Corrections Institute (PCI), a nonprofit arm of Private Corrections Working (PCWI) Group said:

> The big problem is CCA tries to cut corners in every possible way. They short-staff, they do not fix equipment, and things just get more and more out of control, and that is what leads to these riots. It is just about maximizing short-term profits.[12]

Inadequate staffing continues to plague CCA facilities. When investigative reported Shane Bauer spent four months undercover as a correctional officer at Winn Correctional Center in Winfield, Louisiana, he noted the 12-hour shifts, where there was almost never more than two floor officers per general population unit or one per 176 inmates. When questioned by Bauer, they stated that the staffing pattern at Winn was "appropriate."[13]

Bauer noted that in the entire prison of 1,500 inmates there was only one full-time social worker, no full-time psychiatrists. He was told that about one-third of the inmates have mental health problems and 10 percent have severe mental health issues and roughly one quarter have IQs under 70. The social worker noted that her case load was 450 inmates but she wasn't likely to see them more than once a month.[14]

This understaffing issue directly affects safety and security on every level. For example, Bauer notes that Winn reported 546 sex offenses in the 2014 fiscal year, a rate 69 percent higher than that of Avoyelles Correctional Center, a publicly operated prison of comparable size and security. He adds that Department of Corrections records indicated that during the first four months of 2015, CCA reported that 200 weapons were found at Winn, making it the state's most heavily armed prison.[15]

In a previous section, I discussed the riot at Crowley County Correctional Facility. Located only about fifty miles from Las Animas, the implication to Bent County strongly indicates the potential for serious fallout associated with understaffing. As mentioned earlier, in a subsequent lawsuit, a key factor cited was the staff shortage at Crowley.[16]

With the realization that correctional facilities are working with offenders, a portion of whom have violent histories, staff must prepare for disturbances. The potential for assaults or even riots continually exists. Therefore, it is critical that all facilities have adequate, trained staff who remain alert to rumor and possibilities. Paranoia is not called for, but an awareness of one's environment and surroundings is essential. When corners are cut and staff are required to work extra shifts, and when staff does not have the resources to maintain quality care, safety becomes a greater risk.

Bent County houses only those inmates classified as minimum and medium level and those who require only medium mental health monitoring. Those offenders with high mental health needs cannot remain at the facility, and once their needs rise, they are shipped to a Department of Corrections' facility. Therefore, Bent does not have the crises and the suicides or attempted suicides present at other, usually, state facilities. Nevertheless, Bent receives offenders who are mentally unstable and who require more intensive monitoring. There is no guarantee of safety whatever level of placement or needs the inmates have.

Complacency is one of the key issues surrounding safety issues. Because Brent County Correctional Facility does not house "higher risks" inmates and because there have been no serious incidents on their watch, staff can become lackadaisical. For example, an officer on post at the cafeteria easily chats with another officer or inmate; his attention is on the conversation, and not on the situations going on in the dining hall. He does not see an inmate passing drugs to another or gang information being exchanged or sugar packets being stuffed in pockets. And, of course, some staff are working only for their paychecks. Their attention is not truly focused on the offender or the moment.

One of the more frustrating actions I have seen in medical is the inappropriate pat-down. Staff members are trained before they ever take to the floor on how to do correct pat-downs. Yet, so often I see the medical officer simply running his hands briefly over the inmates' sides and back, barely acknowledging the legs, using only a short pull at the pants. The inmate would then come into my office, leaving me at risk, since he could have a shank or other weapon in the edge of his shoe or even tucked into his underwear. On one such occasion I specifically asked an officer to completely pat-down an inmate.

His reply to me was, "I already did."

I shook my head. "Please, do it again, correctly."

He did so, but was obviously not happy with me.

Safety and security are but a few of my concerns related to understaffing and the critical importance of spending the time and, yes, money, to correctly staff and train staff in facilities. Yet, mental health workers at Bent County did not have the staff, the time, nor the tools to perform their jobs safely or adequately.

# Chapter 7. July 2012

The visitation room was packed with waiting staff, gathered at the behest of the warden. Very Important People, from the Corporate Office were visiting. The big company was no longer to be addressed as "Corporate." The language adopted more recently was *Facility Support Center* or *FSC*. About 100 of us sat there on brown metal folding chairs, facing a table where seats had been positioned for the arriving big wigs.

I glanced about the room. The off-white walls contained postings of visitation hours and rules. A series of windows marked the far right wall. This area was a throwback to an earlier era when the inmates visited through the glass partition on the opposite side. Today, almost all visitation occurs in this open room, mixing adults and children, wives and girlfriends, friends and acquaintances all in one large room with a couple of officers. In front of the glass panels stood stacks of glistening, oval-shaped tables, which would be pulled out and set-up on visitation day. A large box of toys graced the floor in an area known as the children's section, along with a container holding DVDs and a wide variety of toys for the youngsters who visited their dads on weekends. Above the movies and toys, suspended from the ceiling hung a TV.

Toward the far left, facing east was an exit door. On the opposite side of the room a storage area housed board games and miscellaneous equipment. A unisex bathroom graced this area. Behind me, as I was now facing the front of the room, was the check-in station, where staff signed in upon arrival. Stationed next to that were four metal vending machines for soft drinks, candy bars, sandwiches, and various snacks. I glanced over my shoulder and noted the two entry doors near the check-in area, one for those coming directly from the bowels of the facility, the other closer to the administrative areas.

As I viewed the area surrounding me, I heard the murmurs of the staff. Speculation had begun. Rumors were already in the process of morphing into facts. A voice on my left suggested that a sister Colorado facility was about to be closed and this might be a positive thing, since it would result in more inmates for Bent County. At that time, we were already up to about 1,200 offenders, which varied weekly.

On the other hand, another staff person stated, with declining prisoner projections in Colorado, this announcement might mean that we were to be closed. Another person chimed in; our warden had already assured us time and again that this would not happen, that we appeared to have really good folks on our side at both the state level and with the top level of the company, that our audits, and our resources were so positive, a closure was not likely. The chatter around me continued, full of nervousness; everyone was concerned for his or her job. At a recent warden's meeting, department heads, including myself, had learned that the facility's contract with the Colorado Department of Corrections was assured for at least the next year. But, that was the limit of my knowledge as far as the agenda for this meeting.

So, we waited. At length, the warden led two official-looking men wearing funeral suits into the room. They were joined by the assistant warden and an administrative assistant. Bearing emotionless countenances, they slid into designated seats behind a table at the front of the room.

The warden announced their names and titles, none of which I remember. Later, I would lament the fact that I had not taken paper and pen with me to the meeting, that I had no specific notations or names, only the memory of the actions and decisions of the fallout. After the meeting was completed, the speeches delivered, and the excuses made, I came to think of them as the henchmen, those sent out to do the dirty deed that those reigning above them deemed too murky and muddy for their hands.

I remember certain specifics and outcomes without all the explanations and excuses that were presented that day. The bottom line: positions were to be cut; some staff and programs were to be eliminated. The excuse: declining inmate population. Reading between the lines, that meant declining profits for the mother company, CCA. I did not realize it at the time, but what was happening at Bent County was typical of what occurred at other privatized facilities—cutting staff means more profit.

Seventeen positions were to be eliminated at Bent County. This meant that several programs, such as the computer classes (two were running at the time) were axed outright. CCA officials piously said they did not want any member of their "family" to suffer hardship. As a result, anyone whose position was terminated could relocate to another CCA facility—maybe in Georgia or Utah or...well, the company would find a spot for these people somewhere, if at all possible. I thought: please tell that to the officer who has a mortgage on his home in Las Animas, Colorado, two children in the local school system, and a wife who teaches at the high school.

There was another wrinkle to the process. If a department head was designated to be axed, and he had employees working under him, there was a way he could salvage his job. He was allowed to bump someone under him and save his position. A couple of people decided to do exactly that and managed to keep their jobs and their paychecks.

One man did not go along with this strategy, Dominick. He served as a department head. His values said, *I can't cut someone under me because I choose to keep my job.* Already frustrated and overly stressed about the working conditions, his ethics said, *I can't do that.* He left his position. I later learned that, after several weeks, he had gotten another job, with decent pay. And, to this day, his wife reports much, much less stress. I ran into him about a month ago, and he assured me that he was doing very well in another position and that getting "fired" was probably the best thing that ever happened to him. He was a hero, in my book.

That D-Day was the turning point, the pivot of my "love affair" with CCA. While I had had moments all along, and had even quit for a brief six-month period, that day determined my future allegiance. In the course of one hour, those two henchmen had managed to dissolve any loyalty I'd had for the company. They had painted a masterpiece of CCA's true colors for me and for many of my co-workers. My own values and my sense of fairness had been violated. It truly was a reality check for me. I clenched my teeth, basically kept my tongue under control, as I marched back to my office. Inside, I was seething. I needed to retreat to my "happy place" and try to place some perspective on what I had just witnessed and heard.

The Company had made that difficult, if not impossible. Months later I still grappled with the incident and the fallout. For example, I recall Robert Jamison, an officer who had been considering a move across the state to be with his elderly parents. Because he was contemplating the move already, Robert decided that he would go ahead and leave his current job and the community. He told me his story, how he approached the administration with his proposition. He concluded that by leaving, he would be able to save another person's job. That is exactly what he proposed.

Before he left Bent County Correctional Facility, he told me, "I thought I would be doing a good thing. I was told that I could go ahead and leave, but that would not save one position." He went on to tell me that the list was already in place, and his suggestion, while worthy, could not be considered.

Robert was not the only one. Another person essentially told a similar story. Both stories were incredible, but credible at the same time. Were the two employees angry and exaggerating their experience? No one could confirm or deny either way. However, in the light of the manner in which the cuts had been presented, I was inclined to believe them.

Had anyone been asked to consider pay cuts to keep their fellow workers? Had anyone been asked to take an early retirement? To my knowledge, this did not happen. While I don't know everything that goes on behind closed doors nor do I pretend to, I do know that staff received no options.

The blanket announcement struck fear within the staff. No one knew if they would have a job at the end of the month, myself included. Rumors circulated. When one person after another was called into the supervisor's office, tensions mounted. When Robert told his story, frustrations rose that affected staff morale. And when Dominick refused to fire his subordinate and took the hit himself, anger mounted on a scale that I had never felt at Bent County. Suddenly, staff started questioning the values of those who sat on the Nashville thrones and made strong-armed decisions that literally altered the plans and lives of seventeen people. In fact, the decisions produced a chain-reaction, infecting the staff motivation and production. Weeks, even months later, the sting remained apparent within the facility. And it certainly affected our department, the mental health clinicians.

Yet, even with this earth-shaking announcement and the fallout that occurred, we were assured that Bent County was safe, that our doors would not be closed. CCA was in business for the long-haul and cuts were necessary so that most of us would keep our jobs. Of course, what we were not told was that the company would continue to make a hefty profit and that future negotiations would insure CCAs continuation in Colorado.

When working at Winn Correctional Facility, reporter Shane Bauer affirmed the cuts to programs, noted that many vocational programs were axed, with hobby shops becoming storage units, access to the library was limited and the big recreation yard empty much of the time since there weren't enough guards to watch over it. Offenders complained about programs beings cancelled, along with canteen and law library hours. Of course, CCA insisted that the resources and programs were "largely available to inmates." He reported that the work program was cut during contract negotiations with the Department of Corrections, but acknowledged some gaps in programming due to "brief periods of staffing vacancies."[1]

I reflected back on this July 2012 meeting many times as I questioned the authenticity of my work at Bent County Correctional Facility. On too many days, I felt that I had taken on the philosophy of many workers— that I labored only for my paycheck and the insurance, for my 401-K, and my dental and vision benefits. When I caught myself feeling that my actual accomplishments were useless and that I had taken on a piss-poor attitude,

I am reminded that now and then I may have provided some benefit to an offender.

Some reinforcement came when I retrieved a letter from an offender, Michael. He wrote asking for a verification of his classes for use in his transfer to a therapeutic community. Michael wrote, "I so much appreciate your doing the individual work with me when I most needed it. I believe I would still be waiting for my classes, if you hadn't helped." I keep this letter at home in my bureau, and I pull it out and reread it now and then. It is the one thing that helped when I felt as if I had morphed into a "working for the paycheck" type of employee.

I think of Michael from time to time and wonder how he is doing. He is an example of how the system can fail an individual. He had been convicted of vehicular homicide after he had stopped for a couple of beers with friends after work. He was a construction worker but in charge of high-profile multi-million dollar projects. He had already had a couple DUIs. On the third one, he killed someone. As a result, he was not only convicted of criminal charges but was hit with a civil lawsuit as well. He ended up losing his home and all his assets. Later, his wife divorced him.

When he came to my office, he was seeking treatment, but had been told that due to his Parole Eligibility Date (PED), he was not eligible for several years. He said, "I know I have a problem. I need help now."

I believed him. I personally believe that treatment should be given when the client is ready. That is something I learned in my early training. Yet, due to both the Colorado Department of Corrections and CCA policies and regulations, he was ineligible.

I looked at him, and though I knew I had no time for individual treatment, I decided I would find the time. I explained to Michael that I was licensed in drug and alcohol work and would see him weekly, but I could not provide him with a certificate that indicated he had completed a specific type of class. However, I could provide him with a letter noting what work he had done and his current progress. He agreed.

And so we met for several weeks. I was not called on the carpet to justify my reasoning and behavior, but I was certainly willing to face any consequences. I felt that Michael's current needs demanded current treatment, not some far-off program that might or might not ever materialize.

This story provides an example of how, when treatment is needed, it often becomes impossible. Wait lists are far too long and are encumbered by items such as parole eligibility dates along with too much paperwork and duties to deal with the offender in a moral and caring manner. Basically, it simply goes back to understaffing, as related to the number of offenders housed in a specific facility.

Treatment, programs, tools—all are needed if an offender is to successfully reintegrate back into his community. But when CCA walks in and arbitrarily cuts seventeen positions, it becomes impossible for the facility, as well as the individual workers to meet the needs of the offenders. I firmly believe that Bent County has never completely recovered from July of 2012. The repercussions were still evident in the lack of programs and staff when I finally left my position three years later.

This incident was just an example of CCA's continual thirst for profit. It was even more evident in 2013 when CCA negotiated a provision between the governor's office and its Colorado lobbyist, Mike Feeley, that guaranteed at least 3,300 prisoners would be housed in CCA's three Colorado facilities at an annual rate of $20,000 per inmate.[2] Regarding these guarantees of revenue, In The Public Interest (ITPI) has written that "Colorado originally intended its private prisons to be used for overflow purposes, but the bed guarantee provisions allowed it to become the first priority for placement."[3] ITPI noted that more than half of the state and local level contracts they analyzed contained bed guarantee provisions; the occupancy requirements were between 80 and 100 percent, with many around 90 percent.[4]

Interestingly, in 2013 CCA had sent a letter to forty-eight states offering to purchase their public prisons for a twenty-year contact, including a 90 percent occupancy rate. Fortunately, no state accepted.[5] Not to be deterred, CCA proceeded with its state contacts, which "guarantee a consistent and regular revenue stream, insulating them from ordinary business risks.[6] In other words, the taxpayers bear the risk, while CCA is guaranteed the profits.

While one might infer that these guarantees are reflected in the original contracts with the state, that, in fact, is often not the case. Instead, the guarantees are written in under an amendment, which CCA has stated as "enhancing the terms of our existing contacts."[7] In other words, by the action in 2013, CCA in its Colorado negotiations "completely circumvented the contract amendment process."[8]

With government, at least, we are supposed to have open door discussions on events that have an impact on tax dollars. What discussion and input do tax payers have when the organization is run by a corporation? Oh, sure, I might be a shareholder, but really, what say do I have about the policies and procedures or the effect of lobbying on the public and on the prison population?

The funds continue to flow into the private prisons coffers. For example, the Colorado Department of Corrections 2015 annual reports indicates that the private prisons are reimbursed at a rate of $56.02 per day and the last yearly appropriation for private prisons in Colorado is $89,040,134 with

$74,709,244 going to CCA facilities to house about 4,300 inmates throughout the year.[9]

As for the inmates, they remain warehoused, stuck within the walls of private prison promises while they function as nothing more commodities, their value determined by how many days they remain confined. They are nothing more than Bodies in Beds.

# CHAPTER 8. WAREHOUSING

Warehousing—there is no other word to describe what CCA does for prisoners. I used to hear offenders say things such as "All you do (not speaking of me personally, I hope) is to warehouse us." "No," I would retort. "We provide programs, classes, jobs, and, in here, you can come to vent, to get counseling. We can do some One-on-Ones, if you need them." That was okay, ten years ago. It seemed to me to be true then.

In those early days, Bent County had fewer than 700 offenders, often only 600, so with two mental health providers, one psychiatrist per week, and fewer sex offenders, and far less paperwork, our workload was doable. I held groups continually: anger management, domestic violence, life skills, parenting—one group per day. At the same time, we were performing intakes (much briefer, of course) and seeing our offender clients. Sure, we got behind sometimes, but I did not feel overwhelmed or that the task was impossible.

Of course, not all inmates can be salvaged; but I am also a realist and recognize that far too many have become institutionalized and do not want to be released. And then there are those who, I believe, should never get out because they are too dangerous to society, to your families and mine. Yet, with this knowledge I still felt that I was contributing in some fashion—that here and there an offender was able to benefit from the tools I offered, that he was able to quietly shed a few tears in the sanctuary of my office.

Gradually, I saw the degeneration closing in on us, slowly at first and then like a brief windstorm that suddenly picks up speed and whirls into a destructive tornado. CCA appeared to unwind rapidly over a period of three years. Just like that destructive tornado, it plucked up the soil, the vegetation, and the structures in its path, and it consumed those of us with our fatal flaws, called CARE. We were gradually sucked up, one piece of paper at a time. Then, another additional form. Then, another. Another policy change. One more duty, piled on until at long last, understaffed and exhausted, we found ourselves defeated. And, in that process, it was not just the clinicians, who got sucked up. It was the offenders, who no longer received the tools they needed to be successful when released.

When did my opinion change? When did I start defending the inmates' positions? When did I begin to realize that they were right—at least about the warehousing? My mind jolts back. I spoke about this moment of transition in my e-book *I'll Never Make Parole*.[1] That book was an intent to poke fun at the system and the silly and often unnecessary rules and processes that we, as staff, endured. The book, if nothing else, provided me with my own therapy. I could endure the muck of the private prison system a bit longer if I laughed about it. That included one chapter specifically devoted to that July day, three years ago, when everything changed. As described in the previous chapter, it was a time when I found that the values I held did not correspond to that of my company.

I not only thought about the staff, which had been ruthlessly cut with no warning or options, but also of the programs that had been eliminated, including computer training. Since everyone today needs the skills to use computers both for their personal needs, as well as their jobs, cutting this program meant many offenders were deprived of an opportunity for learning and the possibility of success when released to society.

While I have grave concerns over the lack of programs and jobs, my primary concern was and remains for the mental health treatment of offenders. Prior to my leaving Bent County, the staff had not been able to hold Post Traumatic Stress (PTSD) or stress management classes for about five months. It was not for a lack of initiative or desire. It simply had become impossible with one clinician out on medical leave for ten weeks and then two major audits back-to-back since her return—audits, for which we had to provide documentation and person power.

While I was at Bent County, inmates frequently came into my office and complained about being "bored," having "nothing to do here." Others complained: "I'm waitlisted for two programs, but I'm told the lists are long. I probably won't get into anything before I leave." More than one inmate lamented: "I'd like a job, but the kitchen is full right now. So, I sleep and play cards, get out to the yard, and play some horseshoes."

Yes, there are things to do, softball, basketball. But there is also not much to keep those idle hands busy. A few offenders are able to find work, even working as para-professionals in education, for example. Those offenders usually have a college degree and tutor other inmates who are working on their GEDs. Some inmates keep long hours in the kitchen to pass the time. But others, far too many, idle their time away by sleeping, staring at the TV in the dayroom or, if they have family or a support system and are able to afford such a thing, they stare at their own TV; or they play cards. This means that the incarcerated individuals leave Bent County with few new skills that will allow them to obtain jobs and support their families and keep from returning to prison.

Warehousing is one way to describe their stay. But, my key concern is that we, as mental health clinicians, are not even providing minimal tools to assist them in reintegrating back into their communities. And so we see, week after week, returnees, offenders returning from community corrections (halfway houses) and parole. They did not make it because.... and they all have their stories, usually focused on blaming the system, the rules, the bad parole officer who just would not listen, drugs, companions. Many, many excuses. And that is all they are—excuses.

Sure, an inmate can get a "bad" parole officer. I am sure they exist. But it's hard to leave prison homeless, with $100 bucks in your pocket, and be expected to find a job, pay for drug testing or urine analysis (UAs), and go to and pay for classes. Still, some make it. In past years I worked with some parolees on the street in the drug and alcohol addiction treatment, as well as in domestic violence situations. I know some can make it.

Why do not all of them make it? Maybe, the rules are too harsh. Maybe there is no leeway for late buses or bosses who keep them too late or allowance for them to attend a funeral when their mom dies. Maybe rules could be re-examined, but the inmates are locked up for a reason, and one reason is to protect society against the bad guys, people who have screwed up. So, those who are released receive monitoring and may need even more monitoring because of others who mess up and do not follow-up on their requirements.

But can all those who are appropriate for release make it? I don't think this is possible based on the prison system today that does not offer sufficient courses nor mental health treatment to allow individuals to learn how to handle their issues in a more positive way. Despite our job titles and the work we do, because of the way the system is set up, and the lack of sufficient staff, I don't believe that neither I nor my fellow mental health workers can honestly state we have contributed in a meaningful fashion to assist offenders to rejoin society with a better chance of success. We are basically paper-pushers.

The word "corrections" should be a clue of what our job entails. We no longer use old terms such as "prison." Instead, our goal is supposed to focus on assisting offenders to become "better," to get out and contribute to society whenever they are appropriate to be released. Ironically, CCA continually uses the term "reintegration" in their motto, and they place those important words on posters and placards throughout the facility, and these words would jump out every time I turned on my computer. Their big motto and icon took up valuable space on my desktop. One part of the logo was a big, red ugly image resembling a sheriff's badge. It proclaimed words embodied in the motto, words of Pride, Professionalism, Respect, Integrity, Duty and Excellence.

In fact, I tried to reset my desktop to show peaceful mountain scenes or a gorgeous guy to provide inspiration for my day. The computer refuses. A nasty message pops up that I have violated some security policy. I am thinking that I must have been spotted for investigation by Homeland Security simply because I preferred to see a picture of Sean Connery instead of a giant, ugly badge labeled with propaganda.

Yes, the goal is supposed to be reintegration. And the goal is a fine one. Yet, as I look about me and I see the returnees, I cannot help but feel that as a mental health clinician, I and others are failing these offenders—and more so day by day, as the paperwork and the lack of staffing makes our job untenable until we are left with the fact that we truly are simply warehousing offenders. We are making money for CCA but not helping offenders.

A fellow worker recently asked what I felt was the best way to recognize employees for a job well done. The current warden, on the surface a pleasant and amiable man, has integrated several reward systems into the facility: plaques for outstanding work in an audit, gas cards for those who have excelled in any area of service, raffle and lottery tickets for other services, plus the Employee of the Month, Quarter, and Year Awards as well as a Safety Employee of Month, Quarter, and Year.

Recognition is very important. Yet, my response was simple. "Give me the tools and the personnel to do my job." That is all I need. Unfortunately, this simple request is not so simple when you work in an environment controlled by others who do not see the day-by-day activities that pull you from your role as a mental health provider—your training and the essence of who you are.

The reward that I and other caring individuals seek and inspires us to do our job is to see that we are allowed to work to make a difference here. We do not need the intrinsic rewards of plaques, gas cards, and other external items. We need a system that works for offenders so that we can do our job and help these men regain the promise of the American dream.

I felt that I was failing because I was not providing the offenders with sufficient tools to help them make that giant step back into the "real world." If an offender has been locked up for five, ten, or twenty years, he probably needs some assistance to get out there and be successful. Has he learned to control his emotions, his anger, or the frustrations, which are all around him every day, and ever present in the society to which he is returning? He will be viewed differently than others simply because he has done time. Will he be able to handle the rejection, the prejudice? Does he have any idea of what to write on an employment application when it asks if he has ever committed a felony? And except for what he may have viewed on television, does he have any idea how to use a smart phone?

But most importantly, has he learned about himself and what drove him to do the crime in the first place, and does he understand how to live a positive life and avoid getting caught up in the prison world again? My question often is, have I and your case manager and other worker bees given you, Mr. Offender, the insight and tools to assist you in your reintegration?

Even though we might have scored 99 percent on our latest American Correctional Association (ACA) audit that, in itself, does not necessarily translate into providing the best treatment for our inmates. Adherence to a system of standards does not necessarily provide any caring interaction with offenders. In fact, the time involved in preparing for the audit may actually detract from the actual counseling and services needed by the offenders.

Perhaps it is time to further discuss the audit process in more detail—to review the one component that further detracts from the time to interact with the offenders—the ACA factor. This is discussed in Chapter 9.

# Chapter 9. The American Correctional Association (ACA) Connection

Accreditation should ensure that a facility meets specific standards and, as a result, conforms to policies and administrative regulations. These components should ensure a high level of safety for both staff and offenders. In addition, it should provide for services that assist with the offender's successful reintegration back into the community. Finally, it should offer humane and moral treatment of all inmates under a facility's care. It should also ensure that the policies and procedures of the agency offer fair and professional treatment for all staff.

Accreditation is a voluntary process by which a "qualifying" facility simply receives a plaque that attests that it has followed good practices. Many agencies do seek accreditation, which is a costly venture but at least achievement of accreditation is, in some measure, a way to attest to good practices and a bulwark against costly litigation. Many private facilities are required to be accredited, so the accreditation becomes vital.

Yet currently accreditation, which is conducted by the American Correctional Association (ACA), ensures none of these components. These standards for accreditation are set by a private organization, a professional association, often composed of members of the facilities that are being accredited. Does this sound like the fox guarding the hen house? It is not a government body that sets these standards. In fact, the Association has fought off government regulation of facilities stating that the facilities themselves and their members are better able to set standards of best practices than outside regulators.

However these standards are set, they may lead to better practices than what might exist without them. Yet, in efforts to meet those requirements laid out in standards manuals, staff is burdened with extra duties and hours, as well as having to "fudge" or "correct" information in some cases (although I am certain that ACA would loudly deny this). That is the perception that I maintain from my experience in working with the ACA files and with staff in an effort to insure the facility's compliance with the standards.

To begin with, the mental health department had a total of thirty-three working ACA files at one time. Each file contained a summary sheet at the front, which listed a standard that had to be met, along with the components required to meet that specific standard. For example, one standard might require that the department (and facility) be able to demonstrate that it is appropriately providing services and emergency procedures for a potential suicidal offender.

In addition, the standard and the file would ask for examples to provide evidence of compliance. Thus, the file would require a mental health official to insert the correct and current policy and/or administrative regulation (state policy) that was being followed. Then, in another section, the file would ask for a case study to actually demonstrate that the standard had been met in a specific and precise manner.

Each mental health file was designated to cover every area of responsibility. For example, areas of required compliance included standards related to topics of sex offenders or perpetrators, sexual victims, mental health intakes, social services provided, and substance-abuse services. Some files or standards were almost redundant, overlapping in certain areas, but with minute changes depending upon the focus. However, each file had to be completed for each quarter, so that at the end of the year Bent County's quality coordinator could review them and determine the best studies. Along with the department supervisor, she would select the files that would best meet the criteria for the year. Although the actual audit occurred every third year, we processed and saved these working files over the months and years in preparation. Because our mental health department was overseen by the medical supervisor or Health Services Administrator (H.S.A.) that person would review and make certain the files were correct before they moved on to the quality coordinator.

This required a lot of work, especially on top of all the other duties that mental health staff had to perform daily. One, two, or three staff members were required to devote their attention to this at various times throughout the quarter to be absolutely certain that the files achieved a high level of perfection. Thus, attention was paid to what was written and not necessarily what was practiced.

Certain standards were mandatory. A facility had to comply with these or risk immediate failure in the audit. Other standards were listed as non-mandatory but a facility had to require proof that they could pass a high number of these as well. As a rule, I compiled the mandatory files. These files included standards that absolutely had to be met or the agency could not pass the accreditation. But, we never failed a mandatory standard—not on my watch.

The required paperwork was both time consuming and frustrating. I recall spending extra hours, as well as several weekends, unpaid, of course, completing these files. The use of supervisory staff to do extra work without pay was one of the ways that the privatized facilities achieved their profit margins. As we will see in future chapters, this exploitation was particularly egregious when staff was called on to come out to the facility despite bad roads and inclement weather at all hours of the day or night.

On one occasion, I had a Saturday evening family event planned but was told I could not leave the facility until the files were done. When I arrived that morning, the files had already been laid out on a huge table in the administration's conference room some distance from the medical department. All three of us mental health clinicians, as well as the nurses' supervisor and the health services administrator, labored to insure the paperwork in the files reflected compliance with the standards. We worked from 8:00 a.m. onward, with a brief stop for lunch. We were determined to complete and, yes, perfect each file so that it would pass careful scrutiny. I glanced at my watch every now and then, planning to leave in time to visit with my granddaughter. I had already explained to my supervisor the previous afternoon that my granddaughter was in town only for the day. I was already missing most of the day with her in order to assist with the files, but I had arranged an evening supper together. However, my supervisor seemed to have little empathy or recollection of our conversation.

Late afternoon arrived; we were getting close to completing the project. As a file was reviewed, if a signature were missing or any particular item was found to be incorrect or lacking in evidence or the case study was inadequate or incomplete, one mental health person would be instructed to go back to the medical department to locate a better case study with all the components needed, every piece of paper, and all forms signed with the correct dates and times. Basically, the three of us were acting as runners. Insuring the paper was in proper order did not really assure that the services they described also were in proper order.

Finally, we were down to one file, with three runners and two others present. I looked at my watch again. I was out of time. I needed at least forty extra minutes for travel time. I approached my supervisor. "I have that family supper. I need to go," I reminded her.

She looked up at me, fire in her eyes. In an elevated and gruff tone, she firmly stated, "No one can leave till the last file is done."

I cringed. As I looked around the room, my head throbbed. It had already been a long and tedious day. I scanned the four staff members present, including the two "runners," as I called them. Only one file remained. Did she really need all of us? Anger boiled up inside me, threatened to unleash itself in a fury with words I would never be able to reclaim. I saw no need to be there. I saw her only as acting like a bully with her controlling and micro-managing manner.

In a moment of rebellion, not like my usual self, I glared back at her and stated, "Well, I am leaving. You do what you need to do on Monday." I stormed out of the room, found my coat, marched to the lobby, my hands shaking, bile threatening to spew from my throat.

An officer stood at a post in the lobby. I had known him even before I had taken this job. He took one look at me. I am sure my face was red, eyes blurry from tears, and I was probably shaking. "Get out of here," he instructed me in a firm, but friendly tone.

I did so, shoving through the glass exit door and stopping only at the steel gates that held me as much a prisoner as those offenders locked inside. At least I felt that way, as I trembled in anger, waiting for master control to push the buttons that would reward me with my freedom. As I sped toward my car, my blood pressure threatened to explode into a full-blown stroke. I wanted nothing more than to flee and never return. The truth was I simply did not want to spend another day working at Bent County. My mind boiled over with rage and contempt for an organization, as well as the facility that would permit people working off-the-clock for excessive hours, with no concern for family activities and no extra compensation. Yes, this "family" of CCA was not in reality so family friendly.

Even as I exited the parking lot, I fretted over the problems that existed in our ACA process. No matter how carefully a clinician might labor to produce each document required, say for a crises contact, something could go wrong. An item could be circled wrong on a monitoring report or, worse yet, the officer on a suicide watch could have entered the wrong time or failed to initial his time. A nurse could fail to document that she had done a check on the inmate who was placed on a suicide watch. Little things—sometimes. Big things—other times.

Our role was to "fix" the error for the ACA files. That is, if a signature were missing, we had to go get it. If that person no long worked there and was unavailable for the signature, the push was to "make it work" in the words of those supervising the process. Usually, I would know that the person had seen the inmate, that it was simply an oversight. That might be easily remedied with a telephone contact to affirm the information and determine if they would stop by and sign the document. Of course, cutting and pasting can work with today's excellent copy machines. But trying to forge a name is not a good idea and is fraught with legal consequences and violates my code of ethics. Again, this means that the paperwork was in order but the actual process may not have been. I do recall phoning a doctor once and getting his okay for a fax, which he politely completed. Most often, if you phoned a Department of Corrections' facility for paperwork long gone, you would never get a response.

I remember one incident that was actually amusing—in a sense. I was desperately attempting to locate a case study for someone who had been on a suicide watch for a specific quarter. In fact we were struggling to find a complete, precise and, if you will, perfect case for the past year. The process is simple. Whenever someone has been on a suicide watch, we would make copies of all the paperwork after the fact and file those in anticipation of future needs. Therefore, I began searching through potential studies. As I disposed of case after case in utter frustration, I located one that was the most complete and which belonged to a former offender, Joe Brown. Brown had been gone from Bent County for perhaps a year. Only one item was missing from his case study. As I recall, it was a monitoring report.

That particular inmate was now residing at another facility. I began the telephone contacts to the mental health department of the state facility. I left messages. I received no call backs. This specific inmate's file was an excellent example, but efforts to obtain that one piece of paper seemed fruitless. Time was running out and the file was past due. I was ready to shove the pages together and hope that it would somehow pass muster. Let's keep in mind that this was a mandatory file.

Late Tuesday afternoon I opened my computer to run the weekly "move list." The move list is simply a printing of all the offenders who are leaving the facility and those who will be arriving the next day. To my utter amazement, I found inmate Joe Brown was returning. I practically leaped from my chair with joy. There was a Movement god after all!! The very first thing I did when Brown's file arrived the next day was grasp that one piece of paper, copy it, and add it to his ACA packet.

If his monitoring report were left missing, my only recourse would have been to construct a brand new monitoring report, which would have been impossible with no information. However, if I had his initial report where the only problem was that times had been entered incorrectly, I may have been able to change the report to indicate the correct times. Keep in mind that the entry of wrong times did not mean that the officers who sat on watch did not do their job; it usually just meant that they did not understand the "fifteen minutes rule." Those monitoring were to enter fifteen minutes between watches or less—never more than fifteen. Any time more than fifteen minutes entered would negate the form and, in some cases, the entire case study.

This would not present a problem as long as the officers still worked at the facility. A new form could be constructed, but all the signatures of those on duty would be required—a tedious process to be sure and sometimes an impossible one. In addition, the times would have to be changed to meet the ACA requirement. If the people no longer worked there (and the turnover rate was quite high), it was almost impossible to track down a former employee. That meant, locating another case study. In other words, it would require starting the process all over again. Once more, additional work for the mental health clinicians and hours taken away from counseling sessions, and, as described above, frequently time with no pay.

Other problems with auditing included fixing simple errors such as obtaining signatures on an intake form or getting a clinician to correct a box she had incorrectly checked indicating that the offender should be directly referred to mental health. The easy fixes were just doing the whole thing over again with original dates and information and substituting that paper for the original one, which contained the errors. The reality, of course, is that the form was now correct, just a simple oversight.

But "fixing" a case study when critical information or signatures were missing and could not be reclaimed—that was a challenge. In that case, it would mean we had to locate a different case study, which was exactly what I was trying do when I could not find all the paperwork from Mr. Brown's case study. During a quarter, there might be only two or three appropriate case studies that met the criteria needed for that particular standard. As a result, if an error or errors existed in all two or three studies, that might mean that there existed no study to demonstrate compliance with that standard.

One good study per year was all the quality control department really needed. ACA auditors came every third year. However, to locate the most perfect study, which would indicate a standard was being met, our quality coordinator required that we complete the quarterly paperwork so that the best study could be reviewed and entered into the finalized files at the end of the year. (I have been told that not all facilities require quarterly files.) Thus, at the end of the third year, the audit year, all standards would have been met to the very best of the various departments' abilities.

As part of the accreditation process, the ACA appoints outside auditors to come to the facility to verify that the facility has met the standards both on paper and in reality. They are supposed to talk with staff, inmates, and administrators. The ACA auditors often made preliminary audits ahead of time, so files could be guaranteed to meet the standards. Secondly, and most interestingly, if a file had minor problems it could be cleaned up during the actual audit. In a bank audit, if the accountants have screwed up, it's too bad, but ACA doesn't work that way. During the two to three days that the auditors were on board, if an item was found to be in error, it could be corrected before the end of their visit. In fact, in some cases, the auditors were nice enough to provide a later deadline for compliance.

All of this maneuvering was for the sake of reaching a 97 percent or above figure. This would allow Bent County Correctional Facility to show excellent accreditation scores and be listed in the CCA magazine and other publications as such, as well as receive a frame-able accreditation certificate.

As a private non-governmental organization, ACA provides self-created standards. According to its statement of accreditation, the program's goal "is to help ensure the overall level of professionalism within a correctional facility and to safeguard the life, health, and safety of both the staff and inmates." Nearly all of the CCA facilities are accredited by ACA.[1]

The ACA standards were initially modeled on the Hospital Corporation of America's (HCA) model of standards.[5] The Hospital Corporation of America was also formed by a group of three, two of whom were physicians, in 1968, also located in Nashville, Tennessee.[6]

ACA was originally founded in Cincinnati as the National Prison Association in 1870 by a group of reform-oriented individuals.[2] In 1954, the name of the association was officially changed to reflect "the expanding philosophy of corrections and its increasingly important role within the community and society as a whole."[3] Approximately 80 percent of all state departments of corrections and youth services are active participants. Also included are programs and facilities operated by Federal Bureau of Prisons and the private sector. ACA accredits more than 900 prisons, jails, community residential centers, and various other correctional facilities in the United States, using their independently published standards manuals.[4]

Much of the concern with ACA falls on the heads of those who have been associated with and held leadership positions in the organization. For example, in 1995 the ACA's President was T. Don Hutto, one of the three founders of CCA. Hutto pushed strongly for privatization, an act that many considered a conflict of interest as he had been director of the prison system in Arkansas in the 1970s. During that time, the U.S. Supreme Court found that the entire Arkansas prison system engaged in cruel and unusual punishment.[7]

In addition, James A. Gondles, Jr., the American Correctional Association's (ACA's) executive director since 1990, had long history of mistreating staff. As Sheriff of Arlington County, he was accused of sexual harassment—"acts of abuse of power," including fraternizing and having sex with female deputies. In 1988 following a number of lawsuits on both himself and the county alleging acts of abuse and power, such as bullying top aides and bragging about having sex with female deputies, he settled out of court for $25,000 and publicly apologized.[8]

Christopher Epps who was ACA President from 2013–2014 was indicted on dozens of charges for taking kickbacks for nearly $1 billion worth of private prison contracts. He also resigned from his full time job as Corrections Commissioner for the State of Mississippi on the same day.[9]

Aside from controversy about leaders, ACA asserts that it provides a number of positive services, with the major function being accreditation of prisons, jails, and juvenile facilities. This accreditation is solely based upon their own published standards. Yet, the actual performance of this function "does not assure that minimum professional standards are observed," according to Elizabeth Alexander, Director of the American Civil Liberties Union's (ACLU's) National Prison Project. In fact, she writes that the ACA process actually substitutes the standards and accreditation process for any form of more meaningful corrections oversight.[10]

Concern exists that ACA uses their standards and accreditation process to prevent outside scrutiny. For example, they proclaim a list of accreditation benefits to prisons. They state that the cost of insurance will decrease to those who receive accreditation because their process makes it more difficult for a prison to be successfully sued. Thus, it ensures a stronger defense against litigation.[11]

The premise appears to be that prisons are safer from being sued because the ACA process ensures that the conditions in accredited facilities are better. Alexander documents several cases in which the evidence simply has not borne this out.[12] She cites one case in which she represented a prisoner from the maximum security facility in Lorton, Virginia. The inmate had alleged a denial of medical care for his glaucoma and skin cancer under the conditions of confinement. Interestingly, this facility had been accredited by ACA just before the litigation began. However, an internal report had acknowledged that the facility failed to meet the ACA standards.[13]

Upon review, the plaintiff learned that the ACA inspection team simply waived the failure to meet the standards and accredited the prison anyway. The jury was not impressed and awarded the victim about $175,000.[14]

In another case in June 2001, a Detention Center in Suffolk County in Massachusetts received a 98.96 score by ACA. Shortly afterwards, seven guards were charged with federal crimes for assaulting and abusing prisoners. In addition, several women prisoners came forward to report rapes and other forms of sexual abuse by male correctional officers at the jail.[15]

In 1996, another case in an accredited Louisiana juvenile facility featured a horrifying situation in which twenty-eight children were treated for broken bones and other injuries within a single week. On one day alone, eight children suffered broken eardrums as result of beatings by the staff. However, ACA never revoked the accreditation.[16]

In April 2015, CCA notified Winn Correctional Facility that it planned to void its contract, which had been set to expire in 2020. Shaun Bauer, who spent four months undercover as a correctional officer in the facility, reported that the Department of Corrections later sent him documents noting that in 2014 they had reviewed CCA's compliance with its contact and had asked for immediate changes. They identified several security issues, including broken doors and camera, unusual metal detectors and asked for increased recreation activities, improved training, additional staff, more medical and mental health employees.[15]. In September 2015, Winn was taken over by LaSalle Corrections and CCA's message to shareholders merely stated the facility wasn't making enough money.[17]

Interestingly, in 2012 Winn passed its ACA audit, with a near-perfect score of 90 percent, the same score it received in the last audit three years earlier. In fact, CCA's average score across all its accredited prisons is also 99 percent.[18]

One of the realities of the ACA process is that auditors can waive compliance with standards. Small wonder, when one  reviews another individual associated with the organization. In this case, the head of the ACA Standards Committee, Ronald Angelone, was the former (controversial) director of the Department of Corrections in Virginia. Angelone had refused to allow the Office of Protection and Advocacy for Persons with Disabilities to inspect the Wallens Ridge Supermax Prison in Virginia. This occurred after the National Prison Project sued the prison over the treatment of mentally ill prisoners, due to a suicide and another death after an inmate was being shocked with a stun gun and then placed in restraints.[19]

Prior to his current position, Angelone served as director of corrections in Nevada until 1994. The National Prison Project sued Nevada because of its unconstitutional use-of-force policies. In both of his positions, he had advocated dangerous and reactionary practices and indifference to public accountability. Yet, ACA chose to put him in charge of the Standards Committee. Alexander states that, "Absent complete restructuring, the ACA is as much a barrier to meaningful reform of prison conditions as it is an ally."[20]

Criticism surrounding ACA includes the same concerns directed at CCA and the privatization of prisons. The concept of making a profit at the expense of inmates, as well as that of the staff, does not sit well with prison watchdogs. Concern exists that taxpayers are shelling out for fancy conferences and the substandard or overpriced services to prisoners.[21] Such funds, of course, are funneled indirectly to ACA. State funds are directed to the Department of Corrections who pass them along to the various prisons, including CCA facilities, which then pay their fees to ACA.

By 2000, the number of prisoners had surpassed 1.3 million in this country. With more than 1,000 prisons in operation, that means with each new one comes "a bevy of contracts for construction and services."[22] Therefore, within the ACA bi-annual conferences, opportunities are evident for vendors to cash in on enormous profits to be made by providing services and goods to prisons. These conferences have come under fire due to the numerous concerns that presenters and promoters largely benefit the private prisons. For example, attendees and exhibits include numerous companies that supply goods to the prisons, such as transportation, phone service, and food products—all of whom make a profit on the backs of prisoners and at sometimes excessive cost to taxpayers.[23]

The ACA conference is where many of these transactions are completed. In reviewing the 2005 conference in Phoenix, which she attended without disclosing her purpose, award-winning journalist Silja Talvi reported that the program had a definite militaristic theme. Even the three keynote speakers were prominent conservatives or military officers: retired general Anthony Zinni, Michael Durant (the pilot of Black Hawk Down fame), and disgraced Homeland Security nominee Bernard Kerik.[24]

This conference (and most other ACA conferences) was financially supported by CCA, the GEO Group, Correctional Services Corporation, and Correctional Medical Services. One workshop focused on how to handle prisoners who self-medicate and featured footage of a non-violent paranoid schizophrenia in Utah being forcibly extracted and tied to a restraint chair. After sixteen hours, he died. Facilitated by Todd Wilcox, medical director of the Salt Lake County Metro Jail, this imagery was supposed to be an example of how to avoid costly litigation. He is quoted as stating, "Don't get personal with this. It is just business." He went on to refer to some mentally ill patients with Axis II disorders "as people we affectionately call the assholes."[25]

Talvi reports that the real draw of the conference were exhibitors, where the discussions were all about increasing profit margins, lessening risks and liabilities, winning court cases, and new, improved techniques and technologies for managing the most troublesome prisoners.[26] Dozens of companies hawked merchandise such as restraining chairs, drug-detection tools, suicide-prevention smocks, and prison insurance. Many competed to sell private health care systems, commissary services, and surveillance systems, including Internet and phone services. Prison phone services are not necessarily bid to the lowest, but rather to those who can generate a substantial profit to the prison. Typically their contracts overcharge prisoners and their families generating an estimated $1 billion per year.[27]

Private food service businesses, such as Aramark and Canteen, also attend the conferences and feature large ads in the ACA conference magazines. Both have had their share of problems. Aramark's low bids have succeeded in getting contracts in many jails and prisons. At the 2005 conference the company could boast that it provided more than a million meals per day to prisons nationwide.[28]

The company proclaims that it adheres to ACA standards. However, in Dauphon County, Pennsylvania, a grand jury investigated charges of over-billing and poor food quality. In July 2004, New Mexico prisoners at Los Lunas, fed up with their low food quality and "inedible" meat-type products, organized a hunger strike. Similar problems have been reported in at least a dozen states.[29] Again, privatization is the source of the problems.

As the prison industry has grown, so have all the supporting systems surrounding it. The ACA organization is a prime example of this, with its hawking of wares, its growing membership—along with dues; classes, and certificates (costly); and, of course, charges to the prisons for procuring their accreditation.

The cost for accreditation can vary widely from state to state and prison to prison. ACA insists that the critics are wrong because accreditation results in insurance savings. Of course, being a part of the American Correctional Association provides opportunities for networking with other members, for promoting careers, for locating those who can best supply products and commodities to the prison system, and for those who stand to profit on the heads of the offenders and support policies and programs that keep more people incarcerated for longer periods of time.

Author Clif LeBlanc reported that when budget deficits threatened the prison budgets in South Carolina in 2003, they decided to drop ACA accreditation in four facilities to save about $250,000. They replaced the audit with their own in-house evaluations. Allegedly, the cost to accredit each prison was about $140,000, with the additional cost ranging from $90,000 to $100,000. ACA officials contested these figures, stating that the cost for South Carolina was about $7,000 per prison.[30]

However, when factoring in the staff time, South Carolina officials stated that it ran about $35,000 to $40,000.[31] When I first read this, I felt that that cost was extremely elevated. However, I sat down and began figuring the cost in man- or woman-power for the three-year period of preparing for the ACA audit.

As you may recall earlier in this chapter, I gave an extensive breakdown of our process at Bent County Correctional Facility. Omitting one or two members of the mental health staff, I figured my own wages. At the time I was earning about $23 per hour. During each quarter, I would spend approximately two solid weeks on the ACA files myself, not including the numerous collecting, copying, filing and saving of potential case studies and multiple other documents. Multiplying this by the three years, I came up with a whopping $22,080. Granted that this was money I would have been paid for my services anyway. I cannot even begin to put an exact dollar figure on the number of staff members and the time spent in preparing for the audit. Even if only thirty people worked on it for the three years, this figure could range from $450,000 to $660,000, using a range of $15 per hour up to my $23. Some employees, supervisors, and nurses earned more than I did, and some, clerks and some officers made less. Also you must factor in that some people spent less time and others spent more. Therefore, accurately gauging the total cost is difficult; even if the cost were $200,000, that is a lot to pull from the budget. The time spent on this accreditation exercise could have been better spent in working with the offenders and providing safety and security to the prison.

However, my greatest frustration with this entire process remains the failure of the mental health staff (including myself) to counsel, monitor, and facilitate programs for those offenders with mental health problems because we are too busy gathering ACA information, processing it, preparing files, and often working (because we are salaried) with no pay. And then we received a Plan of Action requirement because we were unable to complete our offender monitoring in a timely manner. Small wonder that I began to recognize the futility of trying to make any inroads or changes within the mental health component at Bent County, as well as the inaccuracy of the entire ACA process.

Toward the end of my time at Bent County, when the inmate counts rose to 444, just the monitoring alone was an impossible task. Yet, somehow the three, and then two of us, were required to compile all of the information for ACA. The eight hours per quarter may not seem like much. But, when you compound that by the three of us in the department, it amounts to a lack of twenty-four hours a quarter—not to mention the salary factor.

Again, I am not even considering all of the "lost time" to the entire facility. That includes every department, security, investigations, medical, case management, education, and maintenance. ACA has about 500 standards per facility.[32] Every department has to complete these working files. Every department must give up time for the task. It amounts to a loss of time and staff that actually interrupts and detracts from the job of rehabilitating offenders.

And in the end, the question that remains is the following: Who audits the auditors? The ACA was to be the watchdog and standards were to focus on rehabilitation and redemption of the human spirit. Today, human beings behind bars are "little more than commodities to be traded on the open market."[33]

# Chapter 10. The New Minority Industry

My forefathers and foremothers were immigrants. I don't know if they were legal or not. Probably the only claim I have to being a real American is the Cherokee blood that I have been told flows through my veins. Like my dogs, I am a mutt and proud to be. Does that mean that I believe everyone should be admitted to this country without question? Of course not. We must have rules and screenings for folks who request admission to our country. However, to punish those who want to enter for a season to work or to punish children and families because the father or mother is illegal, seems not only unreasonable, but inhumane.

Yet, that appears to be exactly what is happening today. Immigrants, who often consist of minorities, are, in some cases, being swooped up and detained in a brand new form of punishment for simply crossing a border without paperwork. Illegal entry has become more than just deportation. In fact, it has become another enormous profit-maker for the private prison systems.

Interestingly, this all comes when fewer offenders are entering the system due to a reduction in crime. Some of this reduction may be due to the legalization of marijuana in several states. Most people would think that if fewer offenders are entering the system—there would be fewer offenders entering the gates of CCA facilities.

Don't be ridiculous. From the very beginning of the private prison concept, CCA has made provisions for such a phenomenon. Oh, those in power might not have conceived from the outset that they needed to provide for hard times, but instinctively they may have anticipated that hard times would befall the corporation, times when inmate numbers would decline. In fact, they made several statements to that effect, as recorded earlier in this book. Namely, they noted that if laws changed and the courts began assigning lawbreakers to programs instead of directly to prison, they might be in trouble. This was never a secret.

Immigrant detention presented them with an opportunity from the outset; it could prevent significant loss of profits and stabilize CCA's future. Whether they planned it or not, the very first facility they opened paved the way for their future profits. By incorporating the U.S. Government into their packaging, they have been able to avoid serious financial problems, in spite of the declining crime rate. Thus, immigrant detention coupled with the restructuring under the aforementioned Real Estate Investment Trust (REIT) enabled CCA to further acquire enormous profits. All of this was taking place right under the noses of taxpayers.

The history of this immigrant detention began with the establishment of the very first CCA private prison in the United States, in 1984, through the Reagan Administrations' Immigration and Naturalization Service (INS). The INS was later made part of the Department of Homeland Security, and its enforcement operations and was renamed the Immigration and Customs Enforcement (ICE) agency. The contract was to house detained immigrants at the Houston Processing Center in Texas.[1] This opened up a very lucrative source of capital and gave CCA a promise of a bright future through the detention of immigrants, who are largely minorities.

After its initial start up, CCA went through a period in which it almost went bankrupt. However, after the company was bailed out by Lehman Brothers, the expansion of immigration detention led to the pursuit of even more federal contracts to incarcerate immigrants.[2]

Since that time, the number of immigration detention centers has exploded, with the U.S. government managing the largest immigration system in the world, encompassing more than 200 immigration jails. In 2004, under the Intelligence Reform and Terrorism Prevention Act, ICE was required to increase the number of immigration beds available by 8,000 above the preceding fiscal year's number, each fiscal year from 2006 to 2012.[3] ICE was also under pressure to use these beds. In fact, the Chairman of the House Subcommittee on Homeland Security, Harold Rogers (R-Kentucky), stated that one of the key issues was he wanted no empty beds.[4] In 2009 Congress began a requirement to fund a minimum number of beds (currently 34,000) dedicated to detention in its annual appropriations bill. With this bed quota, the number of people detained rose each year (from 383,524 in 2009 to 477,000 in 2012).[5] There is some indication, however, that bed numbers are declining, as ICE has reported a reduction in an overall apprehension of 406,595 in 2015 while 462,463 were removed and returned.[6]

How do these numbers affect CCA? Fewer illegal immigrants are entering the United States, but 62 percent of immigration detention beds are operated by private companies, such as CCA and the GEO Group. This had led to local "lockup" quotas in many regions.[7] After CCA regained its footing, it garnered strength. In 2003, the Houston Processing Center was one of the first to include a guaranteed minimum of 375 persons. Over the years, this contract has proven to be lucrative, with the August 2015 National Immigration Center reporting that the per diem rate for offenders was $102.97.[8] Guaranteed minimums increased from this 375 to 750 between 2003 and 2008.[9] Now these guarantees appear to have spread to every type of immigration detention facilities.

CCA's minimum guarantees as of 2012 stand at 1,935 immigrants. In addition to Houston, they have guarantees at Elizabeth Detention Center in Newark, New Jersey, 385; and San Diego Contract Detention Facility, 900.[10]

The impact of the quotas goes beyond the bed numbers. For example, when ICE contracts with local or state facilities, it may also contract for other services, such as security, transportation, and food. In addition, some local governments under ICE agreement may then subcontract with private companies to operate the detention center or provide detention-related services. That means that minimum guarantees then can apply to all three ICE categories: contract Detention Facilities, Service Processing Centers, and Intergovernmental Service Agreements.[11]

Further impact occurs when, whether contracted or subcontracted, the facility receives the per-bed payment as if the guaranteed population were detained. For example, CCA may be paid for a food service contract with a guaranteed minimum as if they provided food for the guaranteed population, even if the number of people detained was actually lower.[12]

Furthermore, a practice known as "tiered pricing" means that ICE receives a discount on each person detained above the guaranteed minimum. This provides an incentive to not only meet the minimum guarantee, but to fill correctional facilities to capacity to take advantage of discounts for additional immigrants.[13]

Once more, it boils down to Bodies in Beds, and for the private prisons, it is a gold mine, a means of keeping profits at a maximum level. As the Detention Watch Network, an advocacy group which seeks the end of inhumane detention and deportation, notes, these lockup quotas are particularly troubling when "combined with easily manipulated enforcement, detention, and release practices," adding that private profit can "affect government decisions to deprive immigrants of liberty at a concrete, local level."[14]

Note that ICE controls the release of immigrants through the manipulation of bond and parole decisions. A recent example of this power was their virtual "no bond" or "high bond" policy relating to asylum-seeking Central American families. Mothers and children had passed an initial eligibility screening of the asylum process and previously would have been released. However, instead they were detained for long periods of time.[15] This demonstrates that bond and parole decisions can be adjusted to ensure that quotas are met.

However possible changes in family detention practices were recently announced by Homeland Security Secretary Joh Johnson as a result of the July 2016 Circuit Court of Appeals rejecting a key part of the Obama Administrations' interpretation of a settlement surrounding immigration detention for minors. The initial deal required quick release of children only for those traveling across the border alone and did not impact those traveling with families of their mothers. However, the appeals court found the 1997 *Flores* v. *Reno* settlement does apply to accompanied minors.[16]

Johnson stated, "We are looking at whether to change the practice in any way in the light of the 9th Circuit ruling."[17]

With the ruling, the judges clarified that the agreement does not apply to the detention of parents or other adult family members. However, one immigrant rights advocate said he doesn't expect much change because many of the immigrant families are passing the initial test of claiming asylum and are promptly released at that point.[18]

Keep in mind that ICE is not just about the Hispanic or Latino population, although the bulk of the population stems from Mexico, Guatemala, San Salvador, Honduras, as well as other Central and South American countries. However, ICE oversees all immigrant population, which means that their "clients" include those from the Philippines, China, Canada, Russia, Ukraine, India, even the United Kingdom.[19]

Just how do CCA and other private prisons such as the GEO Group manage to continue garnering business for these lucrative immigration contracts? In 2011, for example, the federal government paid $1.4 billion to the two corporations, nearly a third of their total profits. CCA managed to garner 43 percent of their revenue that year from the federal government.[20] A 2011 report found that nearly half of all ICE detention beds were operated by private prison corporations.[21] Thus, the criminalization of immigration greatly benefits the private prison organizations, such as CCA.

In a 2011 statement, CCA stated that immigration reform would be detrimental to their business, noting that it "could affect the number of persons arrested, convicted, and sentenced, thereby potentially reducing demand for correctional facilities to house them."[22]

How do CCA and other private prison corporations manage to influence ICE, and the House and Senate, the U.S. Marshalls Service, and the Department of Justice? That is quite an agenda. But, it is no secret. And it is no different from what CCA has managed on the state level, expending big dollars for lobbyists.

For example, CCA's in-house lobbyists were paid $1,070,000 in 2011 and $980,000 in 2012. Bart Velhuist, Jeremy Wiley, and Kelli Cheever lobbied on the Department of Homeland Security's appropriations bill, particularly on provisions related to ICE detention, as well as the House of Representatives and the Senate on homeland security issues related to the private prison industry.[23]

Joining them in the effort were the firms of Akin Gump Strauss Hauer & Feld; McBee Strategic Consulting, LLC; Mehlman Vogel Castagnetti Inc; and Sisco Consulting. CCA shelled out $1,730,000 for their services in 2011 and 2012. They spent most of their time and money on the House and Senate, but they also visited the US Marshals, the Department of Justice, and the State Department. Some of their interests include "the construction and management of private prisons and detention facilities," "monitoring immigration reform" and "provisions related to ICE detention." [24]

Before I began the research for this book, the only ice I had ever heard of was the substance in my deep freezer that clinks into my glass when I pour in my iced tea. Or maybe the stuff that is left behind after the snow has melted on my driveway and left me with slippery, life-threatening sheets of, yes, you guessed it, ice.

The new ICE, in some instances, can seem to appear as dangerous and threatening as that on my driveway. ICE is now under the auspices of the Department of Homeland Security. This is the group that supposedly is in place to protect all of us Americans from dangerous terrorists and others or those people who dare to cross our borders and invade our country and bring crime with them. During his campaign, President Trump, had stated that all those folks who cross the Mexico-US border are "in many cases, criminals, drug dealers, rapists, etc." He went on to state that the United States is "a dumping ground for Mexico," warning that a "tremendous infectious disease is pouring across the border."[25]

I am not certain why Mr. Trump would even consider sending them back across the border when they represent an enormous profit to the private sector, that is, the private immigration facilities. In fact, with the January 2017 executive orders, it is anticipated that the daily number of detained immigrants will double. Obviously, the current detention centers simply can't manage that many people. A White House document in January 2017 called for ICE increasing the daily incarcerate number to 80,000 people. The previous year ICE detained more than 352,000 people, each day typically 31,000 and 34,000. Doubling this would mean adding more facilities, either by building more facilities or contracting for space, primarily through the private prison sector. [26]

Since the election, two new for-profit detention centers are opening in Georgia and another private prison company, Management & Training Corporation is reportedly seeking a contract with ICE to reopen Willacy County Correctional Institution, a troubled detention camp that held up to 2,000 ICE detainees in Kevlar tents between 2006 and 2011.[27] Concern for this scrambling for beds, could mean that standards of care and safety are overlooked. For example, a prison in Cibola County, New Mexico, owned by CoreCivic (formerly CCA), had its inmates pulled and its contact was cancelled by the Bureau of Prisons. This followed a pattern of longtime medical neglect in the 1,100 bed facility, months without a doctor. Yet in less than a month after the last federal prisoner was moved, ICE was negotiating an agreement with the county and CoreCivic to detain immigrants in the newly vacant facility. Currently four hundred immigrants are housed there.[28]

Carl Takei, staff attorney for the ACLU's National Prison Project states that ICE contracted for the same company, for the same prison: "There weren't any substantive changes." [29]

While Bent County Correctional Facility is not a designated immigration center, it has, in fact, housed many ICE detainees during the time I worked there. Most of the time, these were Hispanic/Mexican offenders, with little or no English comprehension. Often they expressed concern about Colorado laws and specifically plea bargaining. Not able to afford private attorneys, they relied heavily on the overworked, underpaid public defenders who knew little about their case or personal situation and in some instances, probably did not care, although I am told they were provided with bilingual public defenders or translators.

For example, while working for CCA as a mental health provider, I would continually perform intakes for the inmates, some of whom spoke very little English. Occasionally I would find one person illiterate in the language and would need an interpreter. These people needed to know what was in the paperwork they were signing, in their own language, in the hope that they would understand it. I would note the ICE detainee label on the first page of their files. Upon questioning the offender, if he spoke decent English or through an interpreter, I would frequently find that he was scheduled to return to Mexico when and if he completed his sentence in the States.

More than one inmate shared with me that he had family in Colorado and that he had lived in this country for many years, yes, probably illegally. He did not wish to leave his family and go back to Mexico; his family was already struggling because he was locked up and couldn't pay the bills. He just wanted to get out and do whatever paperwork he needed so he could stay. Sometimes these immigrants would tell me that they would come back anyway, if at all possible, to take care of their family. Only one inmate told me that his wife and children were planning to join him in Mexico, if he could not stay. And, yes, I had one inmate tell me that he had families in both places. Stinker!

But the profit, in itself, is not the only problem arising from this new industry. Beset with allegations of abuse, litigation, and understaffing—not unfamiliar to CCA's history in their other facilities—the treatment of immigrants who supposedly belong in prison and possibly may have mental illness has raised many concerns for those who actively monitor the issues with private prisons

The CCA immigrant connection does not stop there. Just as in their "regular" or other facilities, they have encountered their share of lawsuits. They have also encountered litigation surrounding their hesitancy, if you will, to fully disclose information. Little if any transparency is there, and CCA tends to fight when anyone or any organization threatens to expose this secrecy. Immigration is not an exception.

For example, a 2011 lawsuit filed by American Civil Liberties Union (ACLU) alleged that several immigrant detainee women were sexually assaulted while in custody of the U.S. Immigration and Customs Enforcement in Texas. They were being transported from the T. Don Hutto Family Residential Center in Taylor, Texas. Three ICE officials were named, as well as Williamson County, Texas, the manager of the Hutto facility, the former facility, a guard, and CCA.[30]

The lawsuit alleged that the officer was transporting the women to the airport or the bus station from the Hutto facility and sexually assaulted each of the women and is also known to have assaulted at least six others between October 19, 2009 and May 7, 2010. Furthermore, the lawsuit asserts that the officer had the opportunity due to CCA allowing male officers to transport female detainees without the presence of another officer, much less a female officer. CCA is accused of failing to implement and enforce the contracts, policies, and standards "clearly and obviously designed to protect" the women under the Intergovernmental Service Contract with the County.[31] In addition, ACLU reports that since 2007, there have been 56 allegations of sexual abuse of immigrant detainees in Texas along and a total of 185 complaints to the Department of Homeland Security about sexual abuse in ICE custody. [32]

While the immigrant issue is a prime source of income for CCA, the reality is that discrimination appears to be at the heart of the American justice system. One has only to examine the numbers and the race and ethnic records to realize just how prevalent this practice runs throughout the system.

It is no secret that the majority of offenders populating the prison system are minorities, largely comprised of Black and Hispanic-origin males. According to the Sentencing Project more than 60 percent of the people now in prison are racial and ethnic minorities. For Black males in their thirties, one in every ten is in prison or jail on any given day. The impact of the War on Drugs has resulted in two thirds of all people in prison for drug offenses being people of color. [33]

A move to reform the criminal justice system met with national attention, when then President Obama, in addressing the NAACP's 106th national convention in July 2015, outlined several steps being taken on the federal level to impact reform. They included the signing of the Fair Sentencing Act, which reduces mandatory minimum sentencing for the simple possession of crack cocaine and the focus on the "Smart on Crime" initiative, which refocus on worst offenders and pursues mandatory minimum sentences 20 percent less than the previous year. Finally he noted that he has commuted sentences of dozens of people sentenced under old and unfair drug laws. [34]

The disproportion becomes even more evident in private prisons, according to a study published in the *Journal of Radical Criminology* by University of California Berkeley doctoral candidate Christopher Petrella. He notes that the 60 percent figure is actually higher in some states, and reaches 89 percent in California's private prisons. Prisoners over fifty years old are predominantly white, based upon historical sentencing patterns. Those in the twenty- to forty-year-old range are more likely to be black, Hispanic, or some other minority. [35]

He states, "I came to find out that through explicitly and implicitly exemptions written into contracts between these private prison management companies and state departments of correction, many of these privates... write exemptions for certain types of prisoners into their contracts...And, as you can guess, the prisoners they like to house are low-cost prisoners...Those prisoners tend to be younger, and they tend to be much healthier." [36]

Petrella's study looked at nine different states with large private prison populations, including California, George, Oklahoma, and Texas. While the contracts do not explicitly mention race, they do reference health and age. Therefore, the prisons can avoid housing those with chronic medical conditions. According to a 2012 report from the ACLU, elderly prisoners today (over the age of forty) cost $68,270 a year to house, while non-geriatric prisoners cost $34,135 per year.[37]

Steve Owen, a senior director of public affairs at CCA discredited the report, stating it is deeply flawed. He noted that CCA's government partners determine which inmates are sent to their prisons, that the company has no role in the selection. He also stated that their contracts are mutually agreed upon and the government partners have significant leverage in the provisions. He added that contracts can be cancelled at government's decision and that CCA works within the needs and preferences of the referring agent.[38]

Owen then goes so far as to state, "Finally, under longstanding company policy, CCA does not lobby for or in any way promote legislation or policies that determine the basis or duration of an individual's incarceration."[39]

While on the surface this statement appears accurate, CCA does pay funds to lobbyists, as listed earlier. How much that affects legislation and policies could be debatable. However, CCA's high-ranking membership in the American Legislative Exchange Council (ALEC) provides a disconcerting picture.

Critics maintain that ALEC continues to feed the nets and bank accounts of the private prison industry. The organization bills itself as "the nation's largest bipartisan, individual membership association of state legislators." Its membership consists of over 2,000 state lawmakers (one-third of the nation's total legislators) and more than 200 corporations and special-interest groups.[40] In the early '90s, ALEC's Criminal Justice Task Force was co-chaired by CCA. During those years, the National Rifle Association (NRA) another task force member, initiated a campaign to introduce two pieces of ALEC-inspired legislation at the state and federal level. As mentioned earlier these laws, known as the "truth in sentencing" and "three-strikes-you're-out" have resulted in an explosion of numbers in the prison system across America.[41]

The impact of these laws, in which CCA has paid a large role, has rolled across the United States with a reckless abandon, from Washington, California, Georgia, Delaware and North Carolina, to Arizona, Mississippi, and Virginia. And today the growth has continued to encompass almost every state in the union.

ALEC members listed in 2010 include CCA, the Geo Group (second largest private prison company), Sodexho Marriott (nations' leading food services provider to private correctional institutions), the Koch Foundation, Exxon Mobil, Blue Cross and Blue Shield, Walmart, and Rupert Murdoch's News Corporation, just to name a few.[42]

Arizona State Senator Russell Pearce (R-Mesa), an executive member of ALEC's Public Safety and Elections Task Force, has been at the forefront of passage of legislation, including S.B. 1070, the Support Our Law Enforcement and Safe Neighborhoods Act, signed into law by Governor Jan Brewer. The Arizona law, as well as the ALEC model legislation (No Sanctuary Cities for illegal Immigrants Act) both include sanctions aimed at those who employ illegal immigrant and tougher penalties for human smugglers.[43]

With the Arizona law that provides for law enforcement officers to arrest anyone they consider to have probable cause to commit a crime, such as not having proper documentation, and forbidding localities from ignoring them, both Pearce's Arizona law and ALEC's model legislation effectively convert every state, county and municipal police officer into an enforcer of federal immigration law. The reality is that, under both Arizona and Sanctuary Cities Act, which carries the repeat offenses as felonies, the door has opened for greater number of arrests and lengthier sentences. Good news for CCA and the other private companies![44]

No lobbying indeed, Owen. From January 2008 to April 2010, CCA spent $4.4 million lobbying the Department of Homeland Security, Immigrations and Customs Enforcement (ICE), the Office of the Federal Detention Trustee, the Office of Budget Management, the Bureau of Prisons, and both houses of Congress. Of the forty-three lobbying disclosure reports CCA filed during this period, only five do not expressly state the intent to monitor or influence immigration reform policy or gain Homeland Security or ICE appropriations.[45]

Indeed, through the efforts of ALEC, the private prison enterprises, their high-paid lobbyists, an industry has been created that is thriving on the backs of our minority population, whether they be Black, Hispanic-origin, Asian, or another minority. And, of course, CCA and the other private prisons are now banking on immigrants through strict laws, lengthier prison terms, and greater and greater profits, with little or no oversight—and all at the expense of the American taxpayer.

All these numbers and figures only come into sharp focus when I recall a meeting that I had with one prisoner, Jesus. When he entered my office, I flipped open his file and noted the ICE acronym on the cover sheet. He dropped onto the chair, his eyes lowered, and he slowly shook his head. "Tell them to go away, por favor," he pleaded in broken English.

I knew what he was trying to express. The voices continued to ravage him. He had been on a suicide once when his demons told him to kill himself. He fought them and came to me for help. So he spent two days in the safety cell until he stated that he was not going to kill himself. Still, his demons would wake him in the night; sometimes he was screaming and his cellmate complained loudly to the shift commander.

I wanted to help him. But he did not want to take medication. He reported that he would pray harder for them to go away, as he was convinced his problem with the "demons" was because he "broke the law."

When I asked him what law he broke, he reminded me that he had "no papers" and also confessed that he got angry with his wife when she kept yelling at him, and the voices wouldn't stop, so he struck her. I knew he'd done more than strike her, he'd broken her jaw. And, of course, then authorities learned he was illegal. Off to jail with him, and the voices didn't stop.

As I met with Jesus, I could not help but ponder on his ICE label. He had three more years of prison. He was mentally ill and had a heritage that frowned upon the taking of medication. This thirty-some man with his brown skin and piercing dark eyes looked to me for help. I would do the best I could with the limitations of Bent County Correctional Facility. Yet, I recognized that Jesus was only one illegal/minority held in the private system—only one of the thousands who even now sit in detention centers across the United States. And every one of them was adding dollars to the prison coffers.

# CHAPTER 11. AUGUST 2014

In August 2014, my best helper, Ellen, quit. I had watched Ellen's frustration steadily growing, along with mine. One worker had been gone for an extensive period and when she came back, she was on restricted duty. Now, another one was resigning. Ellen and I struggled to keep our sanity and to prevent our work frustrations from spilling over into our private lives. I had suspected that she probably would resign before I made my own break. Her individual and group work excelled, and there never was a complaint from an inmate. Her skills at the computer amazed me, as I sought her help on numerous occasions, specifically on spreadsheets and templates.

So, she was leaving. No on-call weekends; standard work hours, a chance to be home with her family and enjoy her son for a few more years. Who could blame her? I envied her. Ironically, we had both applied for the same position with a local homeless coalition, but I think I had asked for too much starting pay. However, my age was also probably a factor, although it should never be. Most probably her talents in conducting therapy and interviewing skills made the choice an easy one for the board. Today I am assured that her new employer made the right decision.

Her leaving was the culmination of all the frustrations and pent up anger inside me. Why did our job have to be so consuming that we could not do our work? It remained and continues to remain an enigma to me. It is akin to those old adages, which came first the chicken or the egg? We must work to get a paycheck and have benefits such as insurance. Yet, the work is mentally and physically debilitating.

I have always been grateful for my paycheck. I worked hard to get here. I raised four wonderful, successful children, by myself those last few years. I thank CCA for that and for the learning opportunities I have had. And there are many, many good employees behind those prison walls that I commend for their dedication and keeping me safe every day. But through all of this, runs a sour chord, the melody broken by the continuous pressure and by the nagging reality that I was not able to provide counseling to those offenders as I should.

So Ellen and I both, in our frustration, had applied for a job with another organization. We both had interviews on the same day, actually running into each other as we met with the hiring committee. I recall one of the interviewers asking if everyone at Bent County Correctional Facility was "deserting a sinking ship." It seemed as if it was time to "flee" or at least to move away from the system that had no concern for our well-being and, more importantly, for the progress and treatment of offenders.

During that interview, I probably destroyed my own opportunity. At the end of the three-panel screening, as I was leaving, I remarked to the group that my colleague, whom they had already interviewed, was one of the best clinicians I had had. "I will hate to lose her, should you select her, but you will be getting a great therapist."

A couple weeks later, she gave her notice. Ugh! Back to two clinicians to handle the incredible *case loads*. Surely, now someone would act. Surely, between the Health Service Administrator, the warden, the private prison monitor, the CCA district director—surely all of these folks in their positions would recognize the needs of staff and offenders, would move at a reasonable pace and get us some help. Truthfully, even at this junction, I had no hope. My experience over the years had jaded me as to the prospect of any positive responses from the powers that be.

As a result, I also had almost left for a position in Pueblo, Colorado, but it would have required me to move from my community—a move that would have meant selling my home and relocating. At the time, this did not seem like a valid option. I struggled for several days over this decision, knowing I would have a lesser *case load* and not be on-call. In the end, I realized that I could not make the transition.

Maybe there was an element of hope in my remaining at Bent County. So, I decided to stay. I realized that as long as I was staying, I had better shut up and quit complaining about my case load, my lack of time, and the wrongs done to the offenders. Still, it nagged at me—somehow I should be doing more. Somehow I should be able to make a difference in this line of work.

A week later the warden arrived in my office. No doubt his concerns revolved around Ellen's resignation. For the past year, our team had been vocal about the need for another counselor. As our mental health offender numbers grew, so did the treatment level needs. Yet, our requests fell on deafened ears. Oh, people apparently listened. My supervisor heard my ongoing chatter about the overwhelming paperwork and lack of time to do any significant work. She received my monthly reports. She appeared to be concerned; she appeared to be passing the discontent up the line.

The Assistant Warden listened, expressing concern. The Department of Corrections monitors listened, but, they were not employed by CCA and did not have final say in the day-to-day operations. Of course, if the company is violating or not-conforming to the terms of the state contract, pressure can be applied. But otherwise...Still, they listened like any good therapist, allowing us to vent, nodding and shaking their heads appropriately.

So, the warden arrived in my office. I had spoken to the previous warden regarding these same issues. However, at that time, the workload had not yet become so overwhelming. N We had reached a critical mass or 444 offenders with mental health diagnoses and the need for treatment. In previous years, my experience and sense was that the inmates' needs had been less intense. Now, we were getting more and more arrivals with chronic and severe diagnoses, as well as heavier medication needs. In the past, the paperwork had been manageable to a certain degree. Yet, the last year had seen an increase in the paperwork, with additional forms to be completed. For example, PREA screening forms, segregation sign-off sheets, and additional suicide watch paperwork, as well as follow-up paperwork on all crises added to the work load.

The warden carried himself with self-assurance, a perpetual smile adding to his friendly and open demeanor. I sometimes have difficulty describing him, as it seems like he comes off to me like "everyman," or maybe it is more like a company man, a man immersed in the politics and workings of the institution.

That day I listened to his remarks. He was aware, as I had been vocal about the fact, that, I, too, had applied for the same position as Ellen. The warden was a calm man of reason and, like me, a pawn in the private system structure. He could empathize. He could listen. He could nod his head. He could also pass along statistics and requests. But like myself, he was caught in the bureaucracy of a quasi-military system that equates profit with progress.

He expressed his concern that we, the mental health staff, had not waited until September, when the Powers that Be would be deciding if our needs merited a fourth mental health coordinator. The implication being, of course, that our staff should put on-hold any opportunities for advancement and their own personal needs, all with no guarantee of relief. I understand that he could make no promises. He was clear about that, and I respected that. But neither my staff nor I could bypass a chance to improve our mental, physical, and spiritual dimensions all on the slim chance that we might someday have additional staff, especially since the historic failures of our requests were evident.

Of course, now, the problem had intensified. With the loss of Ellen, we actually needed to hire two counselors based upon current case loads, which were not decreasing. Finding two counselors who resided in a rural area or were willing to relocate might be compared to a Criss Angel illusion. Complicate that by adding in another equation—locating "quality" therapists, and, indeed, the quest appeared impossible.

I explained one critical reality to the warden. As mental health staff, we are not just dealing with our Offender with Mental Illness (OMI) population of 444. Actually, we were dealing with all 1,385 offenders. Once more, I explained that we, as mental health staff, saw every single inmate upon arrival when we conducted an intake review. After that, we followed up with all those who had OMI status or those who were sex offenders and needed code evaluations for programming or placement. I reminded him that roughly half of our population at any given time were sex offenders, who required screening for codes and placement. We were also dealing continually with crises—those contemplating suicide or simply wanting us to advocate a move for them. All of these factors played into the workload of mental health.

The warden nodded. He did seem to "get it," but he candidly and honestly stated as he had several times before, "They do not consider that." They, of course, being CCA and, I suppose, the Department of Corrections. Of course not. My old adage, which I referred to as the CCA new motto, came to mind: "Do More with Less."

Keep in mind that we also had numerous conversations with the Department of Corrections Private Prison Monitors. Over the years that I worked at Bent County, we had five different monitors. Some of them were more serious, some more prodding, some more fun. Some dressed inappropriately for the prison (in my estimate). We had a grandma, a cowboy, a pregnant lady. Some went to lunch with us; others were strictly business, preferring to pop in, take up two hours of our day, and pop back out in the early afternoon. Still others preferred to review files and comment on our handiwork. Some met with our supervisor to share concerns. All met with the warden during their visits.

So, we had monitors to discuss our concerns about understaffing. We had monitors so that we could complain about the amount of documentation and lack of time to complete required tasks. Yes, we did. But how did that actually impact us? It didn't. The only thing it served to do was provide some free counseling for us counselors. We were able to let off steam. But, as far as impacting our concerns, it did not have any impact. I am not saying that our monitors did not do a good job. I feel that they did an okay job with the ability and resources that they had to work with. They consulted with the warden. From that consultation the monitors could express their concerns and unless the prison was violating some policy or safety measure, in reality, they had very little power.

If a major problem arose, of course, change could be affected at the Department of Corrections' level. A prime example of this was the Crowley County Correctional Facility riot mentioned in an earlier chapter. In that case, because of the damages and injuries that occurred, the Department of Corrections began much closer monitoring. The result of this event impacted both the state and CCA. In fact, it resulted in litigation and CCA shelling out some of its precious profits to those injured.[1]

Even with all the repercussions, Colorado has maintained its close alliance with CCA, still building into their contracts and addendums the fees to support the for-profit enterprise. Yet, litigation and negative significant events did not benefit our mental health department. Well, it did have an effect, in that we received several inmates from the riot at Bent County.

So, the message was clear. The Mental Health Department had no clout and had no way to effect change within the facility. Instead, in spite of staff turnover and resignations, the expectations remained the same. And the larger part of the message rang clear—the offenders and their treatment did not count.

# Chapter 12. Salaries and Profits

When I began working at the Bent County Correctional Facility, one of seventy facilities at this writing owned by CCA, I was employed by the hour. As long as I worked my forty hours per week, I got paid for each hour, minus taxes and other deductions. If I were ever required to work overtime, I would then get paid for those extra hours. That rarely happened, unless there was a crises requiring that I be on-call after hours.

Maybe that is why our status changed. Somewhere along the way, perhaps about the third year, we mental health workers became "salaried," also known as "exempt." At the time this occurred, the then Health Services Administrator assured me that this would be for my benefit. She stated that if my child had a ballgame, I could take off early and "flex," make it up another day. Since I had no children in school or playing ball, this was irrelevant. However, doctor and dental appointments or banking, business needs could be accommodated much more easily.

I did not balk at this. Actually, I had no choice. It was the company's decision. At about the same time, they changed our titles. Previously, the mental health job duties were divided into two categories: mental health specialist and mental health coordinator. The mental health specialist did not require licensure, but that person could perform under the supervision of the coordinator. They could perform less intensive duties, scheduling, assisting in monitoring offenders, and conducting certain classes. On the other hand, the mental health coordinator was a licensed position requiring a master's degree. That person oversaw the specialist and could perform any duty within the department.

With the change, all mental health workers were titled as "mental health coordinators." This meant that only those with master's degrees and licenses could hold that position. Thus, it limited applicants. It also did one other thing. It added to confusion for applicants. Those seeking jobs in the field often made an assumption that the position was one of a supervisory nature. Even the job description implied this. The summary section of the job description stated that the person "Coordinates and directs activities of personnel engaged in providing mental health services to inmates/residents." It implied that the person would be overseeing a mental health department and other clinicians. That was not the case.

As a result, those coming for an interview had, at least on three occasions, held the misconception that they would be supervising the mental health department. This had to be explained to those applying for the job, twice during the actual interviews when I was present, and on one other occasion when I was not present, but which was revealed to me after the fact.

Earlier, I had listed the number of activities the position required. Just in case anyone might assume that this was an exaggeration, one has only to review the five-page job description last revised in May 2008. Essential functions include: daily mental health activities, six items; regular/weekly mental health activities, six items, and this list was followed by thirty-four bulleted items. Then, the qualifications were listed.

The qualifications are found on the CCA website under positions available and were a detrimental factor in locating mental health staff throughout my stay at Bent County. The area that has created a challenge reads, "Five years clinical experience, which includes two years in a comparable job position required." Bent County was located in a rural area, and it paid lower mental health wages than the state or other companies; this became an issue when our department critically needed help. People simply could not meet both the five years and two years in comparable position criteria. Undoubtedly, some clinicians did not bother to apply. We later learned, according to the supervisor, that five applications had been thrown out at the corporate level because they could not meet this standard.

And, the description very clearly stated that the position was "Exempt." This is another way of saying that the coordinator's position was salaried— forget overtime. On the surface, "salaried" sounds good, right? This was a misconception, based upon stereotyping of those in power, who leave for their golf game in the afternoon. I had no experience in the real world of salaried workers. I should have because I once worked as a newspaper reporter/editor; basically, that was the same—attending night meetings, getting up early to check the wire service, and covering county fairs on weekends. Yep, it should have raised a question.

Salaried or exempt means you get paid a straight salary. You do not get overtime. You do not get paid for extra trips when an offender goes "crazy" and requires a Saturday 10:00 p.m. forty-mile trip down the Arkansas Valley with no mileage compensation. It actually means, in realistic terms, that CCA gets free worker bees. In the case of mental health counselors, this can mean anywhere from two-to-twenty extra hours per week. If a particular evening crisis should fall in the early part of the week, unless another activity bars that, you can flex and take off early at the end of the week. However, with Friday and Saturday crises, forget it. You will have to eat those hours.

In the Bent facility, we had two days of intakes up until the last six months prior to my leaving. That generally meant late days, so one might try to flex that off the clock, but if hit with an evening crisis, again, you might have to go down in flames. And, if you were a conscientious worker who despairs at getting too far behind, and you have twenty files that need documentation sitting in your desk, you might decide "What the hell." You come in on a Saturday, unpaid, of course, just so you can catch up. Speaking from a personal point of view, I have done exactly that in the past, just so I could relax a bit and start the next week with less stress.

At a certain point, I decided that I could no longer work all those uncompensated hours. I did not encourage my fellow mental health worker bees to do it. Please do not work "off the clock." CCA does not seem to mind. They do not fault us for it. Only the assistant warden here has recommended: do not do this. "If you get everything done, then they [CCA] do not see that you need help." Words of wisdom. Yet, even that did not seem to work—at least for my department.

Salaried with no compensation for off-hours crises contacts? Really. Even our SORT (SWAT) team received compensation for being on call. I used to complain about it, but over the years, sounding like the so-called broken record, I quit complaining. Oh, I mentioned it to new wardens, but the response was anything but encouraging. During the last year of my sojourn at Bent, I had mentioned it several times as our workload and the number of crises contacts had increased substantially.

About two weeks prior to the writing this section, the warden came into my office, and I brought it up again. I reminded him that Ellen was leaving because she would have no more on-call days, she would have regular hours. I reminded him that the SORT team was paid for their on-call status. I also reminded him that we received no overtime for this and no mileage. I pointed out the large number of crises contacts we now had, the numbers of which continued to grow. I pointed out that the nature of our offender population had changed. We no longer housed so many "minimal" offenders. We had always had "moderate" offenders, of course, but they were much less "needy" regarding their mental health problems. We also had considerably more sex offenders than in the past. All of these variables had led to more volatile and difficult-to-manage offenders. The warden did listen, but...

Several weeks later, after I was off work for about twelve weeks due to medical issues, the warden and I had another talk, in which the "on call" issues arose once more. He reminded me that this on-call provision was in the job description when a mental health coordinator was hired. I agreed, but I reminded him that people were usually not aware of all the variables that were entailed in the "on-call" status, such as the extra mileage on one's vehicle, the extra time on weekends, all of those extras with no bonus or overtime. I remind him that the SORT team (like a SWAT team) gets extra pay for this duty.

I even explained that the nature of inmates arriving at Bent County had changed over the years. We in mental health were only too aware that we had more "mouthy" offenders, more little "gang bangers," more offenders who are victimized, and who victimize others. We now had more racially biased inmates who are vocal and active about their beliefs. That did not mean that we had not always had some of those. It is a part of the prison culture. But, the intensity of the behavioral and emotional levels had risen along with twice the number of inmates than were previously housed at the facility. Thus, the problem had increased exponentially.

All of this goes back to understaffing. Understaffing, of course, relates directly to safety and security. And it directly relates to all three of the mental health staff who were seeking employment elsewhere at that time. Other departments also had heavy turnovers for a variety of reasons. Of course, some people discovered, after accepting the job and completing training, that corrections was not what they deemed it to be. A week or two spent in a classroom does not provide a clear picture to trainees as to the reality of the prison world. A day or two of learning martial art techniques for dealing with passive-resistant inmates does not present a clear picture either. CCA officers do have additional training beyond that given to the clerical and other staff, as mandated by the American Correctional Association standards.

Once people "hit the floor" so to speak and were actually dealing with offenders, they might find that the workload was not what they expected. For the first time, they now came face to face with the criminal element, people who are doing time for assault, rape, and murder. They find themselves surrounded by rival gang members who most probably will try to intimidate and scare them. Their expectations of prison life may be based upon the variety of stereotypes they have viewed on TV or in the movies. This in itself does lead to staff bailing out after only a few weeks. But the ongoing pressures of the environment, over a period of time, can also drive away even the most resilient of employees.

In my case, somehow I managed to remain calm in the storm. Perhaps this was my mental health training. I was able to sit in a tiny room with a 300-pound gruff "shot-caller" and not lose my cool. (For those of you not familiar with the term, a "shot-caller" is like the boss, the guy inside who barks the orders to his gang members.) At times, and after a developing a level of trust with the offender, I pulled out the box of Kleenex and watched as this big mountain of man with a loud booming voice and an aggressive manner bawled like a baby. That was my reality; that was where I saw that the lack of resources and staff affected my clients, the mentally ill inmates. And, we were sinfully failing them.

As I reviewed my own experiences as an exempt employee, I found that CCA has been successfully sued several times for this very issue. In 2009 CCA also settled a claim in federal court and paid $7 million over allegations of unpaid overtime. The guards and other staff claimed they were regularly required to work off the clock. The agreement was reached in February 2009 and approved, but it was promptly sealed. However, it was unsealed on September 1, 2009, in Kansas by U.S. District Judge John Lungstrum. As is typically the case, CCA did not acknowledge fault in the case.[1] Also, typical of many of these CCA lawsuits, is the sealing of litigation cases. However, *Prison Legal News* argued that this settlement was a public document, because CCA contracts for prison space involve tax dollars. Of course, CCA lawyers argued against the unsealing.[2]

A federal court in Kentucky unsealed a CCA settlement on August 13, 2014. The case had settled in November 2013 with the company agreeing to pay $260,000 to supervisors who claimed they were denied overtime and required to work extra hours without compensation. Again, CCA objected to the unsealing of the case, but *Prison Legal News* had once more intervened to make the settlement public.[3]

In August 2014, CCA was required to pay $8 million in back wages and benefits to current and former employees at a prison in California City. An investigation revealed that 360 employees were underpaid because their positions were classified wrongly as exempt. The lawsuit stated that the positions included former managers, supervisors, investigators, and accountants, who regularly worked more than forty hours per week without overtime pay. The complaint accused CCA of violating the Fair Labor Standards Act.[4]

One would think that with even a few lawsuits around the "exempt" status that CCA would be more cautious about the labeling of exempt status. Yet, an examination of the overall profits of the company only indicates that there is no incentive to alter the process. After all, laying out a few million here and there in comparison to the millions saved through allocating exempt status appeared to be worth the risk.

I recently learned that Bent County is now conducting "power shifts," mandating staff to work extra hours due to the shortage of staff. According to one staff member, at one point they were thirty officers short and were using case managers who had been previously trained as officers to perform correctional officer duties. My understanding is that they were getting paid for these hours. Another staff person recently reported that he had just completed a sixteen-hour day. Though they were getting paid, this exhausting work schedule could lead to unsafe conditions and endanger both staff and inmates.

I made the choice to continue working under the exempt status, after I realized that I did not have any positive alternatives. That is the dilemma of workers who need jobs, who reside in areas where decent-paying jobs are at a minimum, and who truly care about their profession. Nevertheless, it does not redeem those who take advantage of workers for their own benefit.

Alex Friedmann, *Prison Legal News* editor and Human Rights Defense Center Associate director, said it best: "The public has a right to know how its tax dollars are being spent when government agencies contract with for-profit companies like CCA to operate prisons and jails, especially when such companies are accused of violating the law to increase their profit margins."[5]

## Chapter 13. Do More With Less

On a certain day I had an unusual duty assigned by my supervisor. I was to complete a spreadsheet. It contained a line for a date and name at the top, with columns for a start and stop timeframe, plus a long column to write in an activity. The purpose of this paperwork was to document every single activity of my work day. Staring at the empty paper, my frustration rose. Now, I would have to spend additional time completing this paperwork instead of working with inmates.

The first entry I posted was for ten minutes that I had spent screening offender requests. The requests, known within the system as "kites," consist of paper forms submitted by inmates who may ask for a variety of services, often associated with appointments. I had to review each one separately, research any needed response, and document the response on the kite. Each morning I had a pile of anywhere from six to twenty kites.

On most days during the last two years I was with Bent Corrections, I felt like Indiana Jones as he was rushing down the tunnel with a gigantic rock just behind him, the rock ready to crash into him at any moment—or worse to run right over him, crushing him with its weight. The longer I had worked at CCA, the more I felt like that rock was going to crush me. There was no catching up. There was no way to leap to one side and avoid the collision. Sometimes that rock followed me home, into my dreams and woke me at night with the enormity of my task.

As a mental health worker, I should have had control over my emotions and the ability to multitask and handle the mountain of work. Yet, the workload continued to grow like some type of a virus, spreading into every moment of my day, even interrupting my lunch hour. I was trained as a therapist. I entered this field to help others. And for the first five, even eight years of the work, it seemed productive, rewarding at times—as rewarding as work can be with correctional offenders. Still, my hope has always been to make a difference in at least one life.

But, during the last few years of my work with this CCA facility, I no longer felt that I was making a difference in anyone's life because I was not given the tools and the time to do so. The paperwork stream grew to an uncontrollable size. The staff demands and duties grew so enormously that it was impossible to do meaningful work with clients. Numbers and case loads continued to increase, but no additional help arrived.

Instead of being given some help when I, in my naivety, had asked for assistance, be it clerical or counseling, I was asked to prepare a report documenting my activities for every single minute of the day.

My colleague, a true organizer, provided the spreadsheet. We included the number of inmates we dealt with for each activity. On the mental health case load alone, we had more than 400 individuals—more than 200 each. Before this, a colleague shared our burden, which meant that we each had more than 133 mental health cases. But she was no longer with us. The case load did not include the 48 percent of the 1,385 inmates in our prison who were sex offenders and required screening.

Supposedly, this categorization of how our time is spent would prove that we needed help. At least that was the reason (political term) that we received over our protests. I pointed out to my supervisor that since I could write any activity and time frame on the lines, the process of detail notation was basically meaningless. Despite my protests, I was required to continue this time-consuming documentation for a solid month.

At some point, it dawned on me that there was another explanation for this documentation. It could be used to show that we were not working efficiently. Someone suggested, "Perhaps you may be able to find ways to better use your time." I wondered what else I could have sacrificed to get more time to work with inmates. I had already almost totally given up my daily lunch hour. As the paperwork load increased, and as a mental health professional, I was unable to maintain the quality and production that once existed. I rushed through my appointments with offenders, touching briefly on the key issues or needs of each session. As my colleague stated, "I used to do hour sessions. Now I am fortunate to get thirty minutes. I used to schedule four or five each day. I am now averaging two." Her dilemma resonated with me.

This lack of time and concern for each inmate made me wonder: Was it intentional? If the inmates did not get the help they needed, they might not be able to make parole; or if they did leave, they might return because they had not achieved the skills they needed to successfully cope with life on the outside. Again, the issue of bodies in beds was clear to me.

While it may seem that I am whining a bit—just a bit, of course, I think it is important to understand that mental health professionals, at least in our facility, a CCA prison, had an enormous list of responsibilities to perform, some might be only annually or monthly. Others might be weekly and some daily. But they are all there, fraught with frustrations. Note that the duties can be reassigned or alternated at the whim or discretion of supervisors and, of course, with the mother company. The following laundry list is not to elicit sympathy but only to offer explanation for our frustrations in attempting to find methods to be more efficient.

Duties of Mental Health Staffer

• Intakes of all new offenders arriving at facility. The turnovers or those offenders entering and leaving were incredible, an average of thirty per week over the past year I was at Bent County.

• Initial follow-up of offenders designated as having mental health diagnoses within thirty days.

• Ongoing monitoring of all offenders diagnosed with a mental health condition. At the end of 2014, it was 444 inmates (Note that a contact with supervisor indicated this number had dropped to 385 as of March 2015).

• Screening for sex offenders who need referrals for programs. The classes were not offered at the Bent facility, but the mental health staff had to see the offender to fill out paperwork and to answer follow-up questions. At the end of 2014, about 700 offenders at Bent had sex-offender codes.

• Answering all requests from offenders. Offenders completed a form, as noted earlier, known as a "kite." Offenders may be inquiring about medications, reporting side effects, asking for increases in medication, or asking to go the clinic for medication. Or, they may be seeking programs. They may want to be moved from their current cell house or to another facility. Regardless of the request, each piece of paper had to be handled, and the answer researched, if needed. In fact, these kites often required an appointment with mental health.

• Must conduct extensive evaluations of those offenders placed on mental health or suicide watch. This process requires a minimum of seven documents, along with phone calls or contacts to the Department of Corrections and psychiatrist.

• Mental health staff rotate sitting in tele-psych to assist the doctor once or twice per week.

• Those on watch must be followed up daily with directives and a clinical note written. If taken off watch, the inmate must be followed up daily for a week with notes on his status, then once a week for two weeks. Finally, if he remains stable after one month, he can be discharged from monitoring.

• Staff also teach classes to new staff and conduct the annual training for old staff. As of this writing, mental health staff was teaching suicide prevention and the Prison Rape Elimination Act (PREA) classes weekly. That duty was later removed, as mental health simply did not have the time, and it was felt that the PREA class was best conducted by the PREA coordinator.

• Mental health staff must also attend forty hours of re-training each year, as well as computer-based training, and additional training that may be required by CCA and the state department of corrections. In addition, clinicians must complete requirements for training based on renewal of their licenses due every other year.

Gather and maintain case studies and dates for the ACA and PREA files. Complete the ACA working files. (See Chapter 9 on my perception of ACA and its accountability process, particularly as conducted at Bent County.

• Attend meetings: monthly meetings with medical; weekly with warden; weekly mental health department meeting, monthly telephone or in person mandatory meeting with Department of Corrections' supervisors; meetings related to the Prison Rape Elimination Act (PREA) to offenders charged.

• Filing. Until the last three months of my stay, mental health clinicians were doing all their own filing. This is comprised basically of paperwork that arrives from Colorado.

• Screen and enter information regarding the disability status per mental health on inmates.

• Schedule inmate appointments. No clerical services were available at this writing. That duty was reassigned to a clerk following my resignation.

• Schedule inmates for the psychiatric clinic. Shortly before my resignation, this chore was mine alone due to the lack of clerical help. That duty was transferred. However, it still requires ongoing consultation and monitoring.

• Filing. Until the last three months of my stay clinicians were required to do all their own filing. This is comprised basically of paperwork that arrives from the Colorado Department of Corrections related to past testing, court documents, prior screens, and other information of offenders now residing at Bent County. Rarely is there paperwork from our staff, who file as we see the inmate.

Whew! I'm stopping right there. I'm certain I have missed a significant number of duties. Those are listed under "other duties" in my job description. This list provides just a brief glimpse into the ongoing job duties I had while I was at Bent County. It provides a clue as to why I became discouraged and frustrated with the entire process and felt overwhelmed and pulled from one activity to another with no means to do the real work I was educated and trained to do.

We documented these daily activities for a month. What was the outcome? There was no follow-up at the time.

I asked, but my supervisor stated that the documents had been forwarded to the district director. The hope was that CCA would see the need for additional staff, but, not surprisingly, no new mental health clinician arrived. Promises were made. Last year the promise was that we would either get our own clerk or another clinician. In the six months prior to my leaving Bent County, no new funds had been appropriated for another clinician this year, "maybe next." Every potential clerk hired had been sent to other departments.

My suspicions remained—the goal must have been to find ways for the mental health staff to be more efficient and cut costs and/or staff even further. However, funds could be found in other departments. For example, it seemed there were never enough case managers. Before I left, Bent County had fourteen case managers with case loads of approximately 100 inmates each. Yes, this number brought additional frustration to the mental health department because we realized that we were actually managing and seeing the same number of inmates.

Because we in mental health would literally see each inmate at least once after his arrival to the facility, that meant that the two of us had a case load of 700. When there were three clinicians, our case load was at 467. However, for CCA and the Department of Corrections' purposes, not everyone counts toward a mental health case loads. The warden told me that CCA and Department of Corrections only count the Offenders with Mental Illness (OMI) numbers, or about 400, so that still meant that the two of us had 200 inmates each to monitor, and when we had three mental health staff that meant a case load of 133, still difficult to appropriately manage even under the best of circumstances.

Even if some offenders "did not count," they still had to be seen and their problems had to be considered, handled, and documented. I appealed on several occasions and with two different wardens for more help, based upon the numbers and the amount of duties.

Several times I was told that we were supposed to be using the medical clerks. Yet, all three medical clerks had their own assignments and did not have any time to devote to the needs of the mental health department. One part-time clerk was assigned to the file room only, as well as following up on mail. Another basically did consults with outside medical providers, as well as caring for intake files, processing those outgoing and incoming documents, and arranging transportation for outside medical appointments with the transport team and providers. She was known as the "go to gal" because she would make time to help with projects and emergencies, but her days were packed. The third clerk did scheduling for all the medical providers, x-rays, the eye doctor, specialty doctors and providers, the nurses, and the nurse practitioners. Her schedule was packed also, but about the time I went out on medical leave, she took over the psychiatric and mental health appointments.

On one occasion, the warden asked if we could we use a clerk from another department—part-time, temporarily. "Yes, of course," I replied with a sense of joy and sudden achievement emulating from my spirit. We would appreciate even a few hours of a clerk's time. A clerk could help with filing, scheduling, running errands, pulling files, and preparing intake packets. I emphasized that I did not need a full-time clerk, but someone who could come for a couple of half-days a week. Even that amount of time would provide a respite for mental health and allow us to focus on monitoring those offenders classified as mental health clients.

Yet, each time I met with the warden, I felt that getting additional clerical help was fruitless. The answer always was that such a decision and request was in the hands of the mother company. The need had to be processed through a district director who then moved the request further up the line and on and on, seemingly infinitely. And, of course, as always, everything depended upon the budget.

One warden actually agreed that we might have a clerk. He said that this clerk would be designated for "mental health only." He let me know that Sharon was in training and would be assigned to me when her classes were complete. He would inform me when she arrived.

A man of his word, he did so. About 7:30 one morning, he phoned, informing me that the new clerk would be coming down to shadow me and receive instructions. However, the morning passed, and she had not yet arrived. My thought was to call the warden back and find out what the snarl was. However, in search of a file, I walked to the records room and saw a strange woman with our regular clerk, and both were engaged in filing a stack of medical documents. Confused, I inquired as to her name. "Sharon, I'm the new clerk," she responded.

Still confused, I stated, "I am sorry. I thought the warden was sending you down to work with me."

Now it was her turn to look confused. She said, "The supervisor told me to help file these records." She shrugged her shoulders. "She told me I was to do this." I nodded and left the room, walking straight down the hall to my supervisor's office.

My boss, known as a Health Service Administrator (H.S.A.) was in charge of both medical and mental health. My inquiry was simple. "I'm confused," I told her. "The warden said he was sending Sharon down to work with me, and I was to be her direct supervisor..."

Almost before I could voice my concerns, she jumped in. "Right now, I need her to get those files all put away and the paperwork filed, as well. That is a priority. When that is done, then she can help you."

But that never happened. Once when Sharon seemed to have a break from the medical duties she was being assigned to, I managed to catch up with her. Great! I thought. I sat down with her and began to explain how to fill in the preliminaries on an intake packet, thinking that this would take a huge load off my back and allow me a whole extra half hour or hour a week.

Unfortunately, my supervisor popped in right at that time. She immediately put a stop to that plan. "I don't want her doing that," she snapped at me, her eyes flashing. "She is not a trained mental health person and should not be doing that." She turned on her heels, practically yanking Sharon out of her chair as she fled the room.

I sighed, feeling the old blood pressure threatening to smack into the ceiling. *Really?* I thought. Sharon was simply going to write names of the new incoming inmates on the packets, along with their Department of Corrections' numbers. Clerical work. This was nothing that required special training or a license. Still, the boss had spoken.

When I complained to the warden, he was very much aware of the phone call only a week before that had promised me the new clerk. His quick reply was simple. "Right now, medical has more pressing needs." In other words, an H.S.A. trumps the warden in the decision game. I left his office, my frustration mounting. I recalled the mental health department motto I had cited numerous times: "We are the poor step-children." That simply, meant that some other department or person seemed to almost always take precedence over mental health.

I believed that until the mental health department was hit with a poor score by the accreditation board or had a bad audit, there would be no help forthcoming. In fact, any effort would be thwarted. And, as I describe in another chapter, even with the next warden, who offered encouragement and appeared to understand our dilemma, there were no changes. Usually, the lack of assistance was attributed to budget problems. My question: who was in charge of the budgets of the various CCA facilities? Just how do funds get appropriated?

Of course, I am not a numbers cruncher, but I am realistic. I do know that there are many areas that require funding, some areas are much more of a priority than others. Yet, somehow, in spite of all the blame placed on mental health for offenders who murder others and do horrific acts in the community, which leads them to prison, there still appears to be little need to make mental health a bona fide priority.

This is true even though U.S. courts have clearly established that prisoners have a constitutional right to receive medical and mental health care that meets minimum standards.[1] Apparently, the "minimum standard" is all that is required. Therefore, prisons can get away with providing unethical and poor quality care and still meet that standard. CCA has been sued many times over healthcare and mental health care. Yet, they are still not priorities. Perhaps, it is cheaper to pay the fines for not meeting these minimum standards than fulfilling them and offering treatment that would help inmates.

For example, the American Civil Liberties Union filed a lawsuit against CCA and the U.S. Immigration and Customs Enforcement (ICE) agency on behalf of three female detainees who were being transported from the T. Don Hutto Residential Center in Austin, Texas, when they allegedly suffered sexual abuse while in custody of ICE. One CCA employee and three ICE officials were named in the suit. This is not the first time that that allegations have focused on this CCA Austin facility. In 2010 a guard was charged with numerous counts of sexually abusing female inmates.[2]

Again, the same philosophy seems to persist with the understaffing issue. It seems that understaffing apparently is okay as long as the mental health department managed to pass the audits. Understaffing is okay as long as the facility managed to demonstrate that positions are covered in some manner so that it does not fake records, as the Utah facility did. It is okay as long as it could be justified by salaried staff putting in extra hours that are not compensated.

At some point, I realized that it did not really matter if staff had to work extra hours (thanks to exempt employees) or experience burn out. Clinicians who leave in frustration are replaceable, and others with appropriate credentials, can be hired instead. But, until the failings of the department and the inability to maintain case loads and duties become a critical problem, no additional help will be forthcoming. The bottom line: money saved = profit ensured.

In 2014, a mental health clinician was out for about ten weeks on medical leave. I felt that Loki, the Trickster, had somehow conspired to create havoc in our midst during this month of Hell. Twelve individuals were screened for possible suicide potential. Both of us, the two remaining mental health clinicians, were wearing out the asphalt driving back and forth to the facility. A few incidents occurred during regular hours, but even so, monitoring and follow-ups meant excessive hours—also uncompensated. In addition, four other non-suicidal crises occurred that month. For each crisis or potential suicide we had to go to the facility, but we were not compensated for our travel time nor for the hours we spent resolving each crises.

Each crisis contact requires extensive evaluation, a minimum of seven pieces of paper, initially, plus the daily notes and dispositions. At the end of the watch, all case studies must be compiled along with an audit cover sheet that goes to the Colorado Department of Corrections. The time involved in completing each evaluation is appropriately three to- four hours, resulting in the clinician cancelling any other appointments scheduled that day.

For myself, who at the time taught classes to new staff, as well as conducted annual in-service classes, prepared monthly reports, ongoing auditing reports—all outside of keeping my case load current, it added a sense of overwhelming helplessness. I felt caught up in a system that continued to demand more of me as a mental health clinician, but which subtracted significantly from my ability to provide counseling and therapy to offenders. I struggled to maintain a positive attitude and teamwork mentality that CCA professes as necessary components to successfully meet the goals, personal and professional, within the organization. That is when I formulated a new motto for CCA. "Do more with less." I often stated this in a joking manner, but in reality there was more truth than jest in the remark.

With a mental health case load of more than 200 each at this time, both Ellen and I felt the impact. We spoke with our Health Service Administrator (H.S.A.), the warden, and our Department of Corrections' liaison, better known as the private prison monitor. Both as a team and individually, we expressed our concerns and frustrations about not being able to adequately and safely handle the numbers. We had already asked for a fourth clinician several months previously, a request that had apparently been submitted to CCA, with no response or at least no action. It was as if our requests and concerns had been swallowed up in some black hole. Our warden had been clear that all he could do was submit the request within the budget, but could not make any guarantees.

With the third mental health clinician's return, we struggled to catch up. Yet, even with her back, catching up seemed to be an impossible task. During that interim, the workload had only increased. Due to her temporary disability, she was put in charge of working on the American Correctional Association (ACA) files for the first three weeks. We had no clerical help and certainly no evidence of obtaining a mental health clinician, even part-time. As a result, our ability to meet the required timelines, according to administrative regulations and policies, lagged far behind.

We were getting more flak from the Department of Corrections, and more pressure to complete approximately thirty working files for the American Correctional Association (ACA) accountability process. We seemed to be doomed. Sandy labored over these files, so I give her total credit for taking on the bulk of that work. As outlined in a previous chapter, this is a tedious and time-consuming task, one I have personally toiled over for many years

During this month, with the addition of the suicidal and other crises, we struggled onward. Like faithful workers, we triaged our days. I recall leaving about an hour open each morning when possible, to simply review the inmate requests, follow up on them, and complete any outstanding reports or other emergent duties. We generally had a call from a case manager needing information about some offender's sex-offender status or the need for something called a "transition report." Those reports were required when an inmate was leaving on parole or for a community corrections program outlining any programs the offender had completed for mental health, any diagnoses, medications, and mental health recommendations for his future needs.

Just those items and communication with staff, supervisors, and clerks would require at least an hour. But, I never knew when another crisis would hit. Already backlogged with an inmate on suicide watch, I realized I had to do an update on his status, at least two pieces of paper, possibly four, if he and I decided he was safe to return to the general population. In the meantime, as I checked my schedule, it was time to begin the daily appointments.

I double-checked the status of my outstanding monitoring through the computer. I was already sixty offenders behind. I sighed. Each one required at least a thirty-minute appointment, and depending on their status, possibly longer. I generally liked to allow forty-to-fifty minutes, but as our time crunch had begun, I was allowing thirty minutes, trying desperately to obtain the information I needed in that timeframe and hoping to get the clinical notes typed right after the meeting. The truth was that this just did not happen. As their needs increased, and their issues became more complex because of the lag in their mental health appointments, they required MORE time, not LESS.

In an effort to "catch up," I would schedule extra appointments—possibly eight or nine inmates on days that appeared more open. However, then I found that I could not enter the notes after each session, and the files would pile up in my desk, along with the files of new inmates who I had seen. I struggled to catch up. Sometimes I found myself rushing, my hands even shaking with the stress and pressure. My biggest fear was that I would miss something, that I would not probe deeply enough or ask the right question, and an offender would take his life.

Of course, I complained and asked for help from my supervisor, and to my warden. In the mental health department, two of us were trying to manage those 400 mental health patients. Then, there were all the other inmates who required our services, as well—all 1,385 of them. I grew angrier as I realized I had been working in a system that cared so little for its employees, that was content with understaffing, that made its profit on the back of workers and offenders.

And, as I described earlier, the profits did not stop with CCA contracts and addendum agreements with the states. No, the big profits to be made were more far-reaching and insidious, encompassing the minority and immigrant population.

# Chapter 14. February 2015

February 2015. I sit at my computer, attempting to compile readable and logical sentences related to my experiences with CCA and its Bent County facility. I retraced the events that led me on this journey of more than a decade, and I wonder why I remained in my position. Only when I was laid up with a blown-out knee, which required surgery, did I begin to question whether the stress surrounding my job had contributed to my current medical condition.

Of course, I cannot blame CCA for that. I am seventy-two years old. Age certainly played a huge role. Yet I consider the source of some of my distress from the constant walking on concrete floors and trudging up and down a steep flight of stairs to conduct weekly segregation rounds. I even recall the Friday before I went down, cringing as I mounted a flight of twenty-four stairs, hanging onto the rail, and cringing even more as I retraced my path down—one step at a time. Was that a factor? Who knows?

More probably the primary contribution was stress, plain and simple. I have related many of my frustrations and my anger surrounding the lack of adequate staffing and my inability to provide services and tools for offenders. When the stress mounts, the body and the brain react. My reaction had been an upsurge in my bitchiness, as increasingly I felt inadequate in making a difference in my role as a mental health coordinator. I felt depressed and, at times, helpless in the cogs of the system that paid my salary.

While I wrote this section, I reflected on those feelings that seemed to permeate every work day. I would sometimes go into my office and shut the door, to isolate myself because I realized that I was behaving badly, that I was openly vocalizing my anger. And I do appreciate some of my co-workers who were patient with my outbursts. I felt that I was on an accelerated conveyer belt. The workload continued to increase with no help in sight.

Not typically a praying person, I nevertheless felt myself leaning toward some type of intervention. Since we were not getting a company intervention, I thought it more likely to seek a divine one. Surely, after struggling all these weeks and months and all but begging for help, surely the administration and those higher up the corporate chain would recognize the resulting problem—the morally reprehensible attitude and failure toward our clients—the offenders.

Each time I read the statistics about reoffending, each time I viewed a newscast where a former inmate had shot or assaulted someone after being released, I cringed. While these cases were not mine personally, I had to wonder if we, as a prison system, were not failing those offenders who might be appropriate for rehabilitation. But the truth was, we were not providing any tools for them to learn new techniques, find new resources, or discover a sense of motivation within themselves so that they might be able to succeed when released back to their communities.

On January 31, 2015, I had made my weekly Walmart trip. Along with the usual household supplies and groceries, I purchased twenty composition books. I had put off this purchase for several weeks, a part of me insistent that the facility should provide these books for the offenders to journal their emotions and behaviors. Because I was not able to meet with my case load clients in a timely manner, I had decided that having them journal in between visits might be very beneficial. However, it was often difficult to source the journals through the usual channels. On occasion, I would get a dozen or so, but then, whenever the budget was tight, weeks or even months would go by, and often the response was that they were *back-ordered*.

Thus, I would sometimes purchase them myself. On this day, I already had a list of about 20 clients for whom I wished to assign journaling or replace their already filled journal. Little did I know that these journals would not get to the offenders for several months.

On February 1, 2015, I woke in a positive mood, did some laundry and household chores. Shortly before noon, sudden sharp pains struck on the inner side of my left knee. Great! These pains were so excruciating that I was unable to walk. I stumbled to my recliner, and spent most of my day there, struggling with the intense pain. The following day, I went to the medical clinic and began the process of discovering the problem. An MRI and several visits later, I learned I had a torn meniscus. New to my vocabulary, I learned that the meniscus is a piece of cartilage that acts as a cushion in the knee joint

Of course, I knew that the knee had more than its share of arthritis present. As a result of this, I was unable to take the journals to the facility. There would be no driving or working for several weeks. I was confined to my recliner, awaiting possible surgery.

When the doctors questioned me about any injuries, I told him "no," I hadn't fallen. No football injuries, no dogs knocking me over. However, I did admit that when I mounted those stairs to gain access to the second level of segregation, I felt the intense pull on my knee, both going up and coming down. I would take the stairs slowly, one at a time. Often, I joked that should I win the lottery I would install an elevator. At such a revelation, one of the officers on duty simply retorted: "Ms. Binder, you know better than that. We would never see you again!"

In reviewing my activities with the doctors, I did a flashback to the Friday prior to my Sunday "attack." It had been very evident that I should have been avoiding those stairs. The only blame I could level at the facility would be for the lack of better accommodations for the elderly and the handicapped. I wondered whether the Americans with Disabilities Act (ADA) rules would be applicable here. Otherwise, the onus was on my own medical condition.

Instead, my thoughts and empathy then resided with my colleague who then struggled to maintain her equilibrium. I had spoken with her at least weekly while I was on medical leave, and I heard her frustrations, as she was the sole mental health worker to monitor, supervise, and accommodate the total case load. While the numbers were beginning to decrease just prior to my exit, still, they remained impossible to handle adequately. They had decreased from the all-time high of 444 to 385 at the last monthly report. This was largely due to cooperation with the Department of Corrections, which was actively attempting to send fewer offenders with mental health problems.

Prior to my medical leave, the procedure to locate another clinician began, finally. The word went out through word-of-mouth and apparently the mother corporation's website stated that we were actively seeking a clinician. My hopes had risen. However, being a realist, I knew that our chances of locating anyone in our region, the Arkansas Valley, were limited. The few licensed clinicians who lived in the area had positions or were self-employed. Still, progress was being made.

As the weeks passed and no applicants appeared, my frustration grew. My supervisor had mentioned that we might need to use temporary placement clinicians. I was fine with this. The same process had been used for the medical team when they had been short-staffed. Yet, that had never occurred while I was there. Using temporary agencies for mental health can be problematic, as they may not be familiar with policies and requirements and processes in corrections and those of a specific facility. Therefore, they may require lengthy training. The other problem, of course, is that they are much more costly. That presents a major consideration for a company, whose key focus is on profit.

In my own search, I went online and located the advertisement for the Mental Health Coordinator's position at Bent County Correctional Facility. Reading the description, my anger erupted. No wonder we had no applicants. I clicked on several job sites and discovered that the ad was the same on all sites.

The notice called for someone with experience that no candidate in our area was likely to match. Curiosity claimed me. I went to the actual CCA website and clicked on the position. Sure enough! Right there was the crux of the problem. Our own company was advertising the position with this criterion. The other job sites were simply running it word for word. I did not know whether this was an intentional calculated act to pretend they were seeking someone or an unintentional blunder.

I brought this problem to the attention of my supervisor and e-mailed the warden as well, stating that there was no need to be so selective. We did need licensing, if at all possible, or the ability to be licensed in near future. Other than that, I was not so caught up in those time lines. About two weeks later, my supervisor popped into my office again. She said she was "livid." She reported that five applications had been discarded because they did not meet the requirements of the posted position. I have no way of knowing if this was true. I only know that this two-month process advertising restricted criteria had produced no interviews. The result was that offenders continued to be shorted on treatment. It appeared to be, as it often did, that when it came to mental health needs, CCA couldn't care less. They were focused on saving money by not hiring for that position until they were placed in a compromising position where they were forced to act.

However, sometime later I reviewed the current position description and learned that, indeed, it had been revised. It now read in part: "Postgraduate clinical experience, including experience in a comparable position, is preferred." Perhaps my complaint, but more likely the threat connected with fines for positions not filled and/or the pressures from state monitors, played a role in altering the language.

Eventually, we did get someone who was interested in working for us. However, he was not licensed. My understanding, when I sat in on the interview with him, was that he needed his 500 hours of supervision, which I or another licensed person could sign off on, and, *voilà*, we would have help. He was hired. However, he had to wait about a month to give notice to his current employer and to get in the next training class. That meant we would not see his services until February.

By that time, I was out on medical leave. My colleague reported that he completed his two weeks of training, but had been unable to do any actual work; he was only shadowing her. The lack of licensure prevented him from providing the relief that she needed in my absence. At that point, I was somewhat amazed that the remaining mental health clinician continued working.

While in recovery from my knee surgery, I was not isolated from the activities at Bent County. Though the wonders of e-mail, texting, and, believe it or not, actually talking into a cell phone, I was able to maintain some connection to the medical and mental health departments. Unfortunately, much of what was reported served only to remind me of the understaffing issues and the subsequent lack of services for the offenders.

A key factor in my frustration, as I sat nursing my knee back to some semblance of normalcy, was what I have termed *The Dismantling*. This dismantling, as I noted elsewhere, refers to a tracking system that had been created to indicate how many offenders were seen on a specific date, week, or month and what services were rendered by which clinician. Over a period of two or three years, I had made better use of this system to assist me in auditing the mental health department—my own activities, as well as those of my fellow clinicians. This system enabled me to prepare my monthly reports, much more efficiently. At a glance, I could determine exactly how many offenders had been seen by which clinician, and specifically what services were rendered.

However, I learned that our supervisor had decided (no phone call to me, no consultation) that many of the service codes that were used to indicate the type of activity had been eliminated. The primary activity information remaining in the program were the codes that specifically referred to the Offender with Mental Illness or the OMI code, which reflected the required quarterly monitoring. As previously noted, I came to believe that this alteration occurred because CCA did not want to recognize all of the duties required by mental health, which would have necessitated additional help.

Because our mental health department had lagged sufficiently behind in this area, we had been given a black mark and the word came from above, like the voice of a god, demanding that we had to get these offenders seen and "become compliant." The word went forth—and this was even before I left—that x amount of offenders had to be seen daily to "catch up." So, the supervisor had assembled a Plan of Action (POA) to provide a strategic method of doing so. A POA is an indication of a requirement or action not being correctly done or followed. It might be compared to a "black mark" on the department or person. Therefore, the supervisor completes a plan to correct the deficiency.

This initial POA came about before I went out on medical leave. At that time, we had more than 400 offenders (444 at one point) to monitor in addition to our other duties, which I outlined in an earlier chapter. To monitor these offenders with mental illness (OMIs) quarterly, to address any crises, to keep up with the daily inmate requests, as well as who-knew-what was thrown at us daily, simply was an impossible task. Now filter in the loss of one of my staff member the previous year for ten weeks due to medical problems. Even when three of us were healthy, we had requested help two years before with growing numbers.

However, the mental health department was not to blame for this POA. We did nothing wrong. Being salaried, we worked overtime with no pay when such actions were required or needed. We often cut short or eliminated lunch breaks altogether. Along the way, possibly about two years before, I had quit *giving* Bent County and CCA extra time. I would not come in on a Saturday of my own free will to "catch up." I departed my office when it was time to go for the day. Of course, I stayed over for crises and for intakes, when necessary. But, discouraged, drained, and depressed, I began pulling back. If the department received a black mark because we were "behind," that was Bent County's—no, make that CCA's—problem.

Just prior to my medical leave, Brent County Correctional Facility did hire the other clinician I had referred. However, because he did not yet have all of his credentials, his duties were limited. He could not screen the offenders with mental illness (OMIs) unless a licensed person signed off for him. He could do clerical duties and other activities that did not require oversight. My contacts with my other licensed colleague and the medical department indicated that his duties were minor; the supervisor was dictating his activities, with no input from the remaining mental health clinician. However, I have since spoken with this clinician while he accumulates the required hours toward his certification. He now has complete duties in the facility.

Throughout my downtime, I felt that I would be able to pick up the pieces, review the current numbers, and resume my role as the lead clinician. However, in the interim we had received another black mark, and the supervisor had to put together another Plan of Action. The word passed on to me was that this "would not happen again." In other words, we, the mental health staff, had to clean up our actions and be more efficient. We had to meet our quotas with no excuses.

My colleague reported to me that the warden had confirmed the intent of the POAs, stating that if it was necessary, he would fire the whole mental health department and start over. Sitting in my recliner, nursing my bandaged knee, I sighed. It was a sigh of frustration and anger. *Really?* I thought. And secondly, *Not my problem. This is a CCA problem*, because they chose to try to run a facility with far too few staff bodies. And that included the mental health department.

I had had excellent assessments each year during my history at Bent County. This current action seemed like a threat, and a childish one at that. The true responsibility lies in CCA's decisions not to provide appropriate staffing, especially during critical times. Time was also wasted in analyzing how the clinicians could improve their work habits to better handle their duties.

A large secondary problem lies in the "speed" at which the company operated in making hiring decisions. For example, even when our inmate numbers continued to rise, reaching that all-time high of 444, and we met twice collectively with the warden and several times individually, no help arrived. No postings—online or in the facility—occurred. Some political statements were made, which seemed to hold us off for a few more months, but nothing substantial came of this.

Thus, the mental health department was, over a period of time, specifically the past two years, being dismantled. A major dismantling, referred to earlier, occurred with the scheduling system. At the insistence of the supervisor, almost all the service codes had been eliminated. In other words, they were removed from the scheduling program. The service codes had been initiated to indicate the reason an inmate was seen. For example: sex offender, kite, crises, suicide watch, Hepatitis C referral, Code of Penal Disciple review, segregation round, segregation evaluation, and intake—among others. The purpose of the detailed coding was to get a legitimate handle on why we saw inmates, who was seeing them, when, and to do adjustments in the department based on this information. When completing monthly reports, for example, it was easy to push the appropriate buttons, and access statistics. I could actually print a pie chart, which indicated the areas which needed more attention or where my clinicians needed to improve their time.

Now, this tool was gone. My big question was *why*. At the time, I decided that I would save that question for a face-to-face discussion with my supervisor. I was informed that mental health did not need to focus on that issue, that the changes were made because the time to input this data was simply taking up too much time.

Reality check. This process actually saved time. I did not have to go pull a file to find specific dates and times I had seen a certain inmate. I could track his appointments, as well as the specific reason he was seen, right on the screen. A phone call from a case manager with a question as to when and why I saw an inmate was right before my eyes. That had been changed without me being consulted, when I was only a phone call away. Now, I had to put the case manager or investigator or shift commander or whatever department was inquiring on hold. I had to tromp to the file room and locate a file before I could find an answer.

But that process, that system which allowed for better accountability, had been dismantled. I pondered the reasoning behind this sudden change. If the program indicated only that offenders with mental illness (OMI) activity was generated by mental health, then there was no need for additional help. Our complaints could just be traced to our own lack of organization and planning. After all, the computer no longer showed all those "extra" duties, which we performed. Basically, they were nonexistent.

By wiping a large portion of the service codes out, our supervisor had now taken care of the problem. No record was in the system to indicate the variety of activities that mental health clinicians performed. Any report going to the warden, district directors, or on up-the-line would indicate that we were inefficient. I recalled the month that two of us spent a large amount of time documenting every single activity we did with the timeline spreadsheet. I saw now that it had been a useless activity. It was supposedly designed to indicate that we needed help. No, we later realized that it was designed to find ways to point out our inefficiency and to emphasize that the mental health department did not need another clinician to handle the workload.

This process was continually slicing away at the mental health department's activities and running interference with systems, and questioning the integrity and organization of the staff. As a result, it had served only to further disintegrate the department and destroy the morale of the clinicians. And, I believe, this was an intentional act on the part of Bent County.

In response, I developed my own plan that I was going to implement upon my return the following month. I would further explore the changes and consult with my supervisor. Perhaps I could better explain the department's needs and concerns. Perhaps I had not been open enough in my earlier requests. Perhaps she would be able to clarify my concerns regarding the codes.

However, in the meantime I seriously began considering my options. I had a job interview scheduled and was also reviewing possible retirement. It appeared that any hope of hiring another staff person, any semblance of CCA acting on data that more staff was needed in our department, had been thrown out by those in power—the offenders be damned. The people who sat in Nashville and took home their enormous paychecks and bonuses did not care about reintegrating offenders into the community. CCA desperately needed all the Bodies in Beds they could keep.

## Chapter 15. Medication Management

I shuddered at the current numbers. Out of 1,388 offenders residing at Bent County Correctional Facility in May 2015, 444 were classified as mental health clients. Of these, 318 were currently on medication. I was printing the tally sheet just as an officer appeared at the door.

"Jacobs here," he announced in a weary monotone.

I shoved my report in the top desk drawer, totally frustrated. The next client was a sharp reminder of my lagging schedule. I had not seen Sam Jacobs for 120 days. The Department of Corrections' criteria required that we monitor inmates who are have a chronic or severe mental health diagnosis at a minimum of every ninety days. Obviously, I was not meeting their criteria.

But, more importantly, I was not meeting my own criteria—or more accurately my own moral code. I felt an obligation to remain in contact with those on my case load. Sam had been diagnosed with bipolar disorder by a psychiatrist at the state hospital five years ago. His lawyer had been working on a possible insanity plea after he had severely assaulted his wife. The original charge had been attempted murder. The mental health ploy fell flat, and Sam was now serving a ten-year sentence.

He shuffled into my office and slumped down onto the corner chair.

"Good morning. How are you, Sam?"

Sam shrugged his shoulders. "Okay." But his head was bent, his eyes downcast.

"Is something wrong?" I probed.

"Do I have to be here? I don't want to."

"No, I can't make you, but before you leave, tell me why you don't want to visit."

He shook his head, his lips tightly shut.

"Just answer a couple of questions for me, and then I'll dismiss you. Okay?" He nodded in agreement, but his eyes remained locked on his prison-issued shoes.

"I see where you haven't been coming to med line? Why is that, Sam?"

Still a pause. I noticed that his legs had been shaking steadily. Now, his hands seemed to tremble also.

"Do you think you need an adjustment on your medication?"

He shook his head rapidly from side to side. "No, no, no..." he said, his voice now taking on anger, elevated.

I gave him a moment, waiting, making certain he was not becoming too volatile for this session.

"It doesn't work. I have to stand in line for an hour and then the nurse argues with me and sometimes I get the wrong pill! They keep changing my appointment with the doctor, and I never get to talk with you. You're too busy!"

With that outburst, he stopped and dropped his eyes back toward the floor.

What could I say? He was right—at least about my lack of availability. I had no excuse. Guilt rose up inside me. I did not even try to make an excuse. Instead, I did only what I could for Sam that day. I used my ever-ready supply of "Band aids." I applied them with care, making sure I provided him with enough reassurances and excuses to hopefully encourage him to continue with whatever relief he could get from the medications. Certainly, he was not getting any help from me—not in the form of appropriate counseling or therapy. "I am so sorry, Sam," I began. "As you know we've been short-handed in mental health. I'll put you down for a follow-up appointment next week..."

He cut me off. "That sounds good. But it never happens. I come in and there's a big sign posted that all appointments have been cancelled."

"That does happen sometimes," I admitted. He was right, of course. Too often appointments got cancelled at Bent County. It seemed unavoidable. An inmate in cell house six might make remarks about killing himself. Therefore, I would have to stop everything I was doing and deal with that crisis. If there were a facility lockdown or if one clinician was out on a medical leave and another was stuck assisting the psychiatrist in tele-psych clinic—or any one of these events should occur, that means that Sam Jacobs will have to be rescheduled. And if the schedule is full for the next month or six weeks, then Sam may end up at the end of the list.

Sometimes when I had an unexpected crisis occur (and they were almost always unexpected), I would literally slam a book down on my desk (in the presence of no one) and, with my voice slightly elevated, but hopefully so no one could hear me down the hall, I would yell, "NO, NO, NO. Not today." I know that the clerks had heard me briefly explode, perhaps all of thirty seconds, and then I would take a deep breath and renew my spirit and start my day again.

Of course, it was not the fault of the client in crisis, not the clerks, not even mine. It was the same old routine of too many numbers, too many mental health offenders, and not enough staff and time to manage in a safe and healthy manner. The problem was the primary reason I wrote this book: to examine why profits trump help for clients and result in clients coming back into the system instead of getting out and living responsible lives outside of the prison. How can those offenders with behavioral health issues be successful when the mental health department is understaffed? How can staff be expected to perform in a timely and ethical manner when they are stumbling over mountains of new client and reams of paperwork?

With the numbers of inmates on psychotropic drugs, the tele-psych clinic runs into the same problem as the mental health department—trying to get offenders seen within a ninety-day window. If the psychiatrist should take a two week vacation or leave for a week at a much needed conference, the clinic will get pushed back. If there is a lockdown, the clinic will be cancelled. But here's the other issue. Medication was ordered, renewed, but any counseling or therapy rarely occurred due to our inability to follow-up in a timely manner.

Would those inmates send a request enumerating their side effects? Sometimes, but not often. Frequently they would get frustrated and just quit taking the medication and then would end up with elevated symptoms, sometimes decompensating, sometimes experiencing suicidal thoughts or plans. Sometimes they might become so frustrated with the lack of follow-up and their own emotions, that they would state they were having suicidal thoughts. Or, they might perform an act that could be construed as suicidal, such as climbing to the top of the rail on the second tier or scratching their wrists with a pen. After all, they realized that any suicidal remarks or attempts are a sure route to mental health. These desperate acts get the attention of not only the counselors, but of the entire facility as well.

The other side of the improper management of medications and symptoms is the safety issue. Offenders may become irate at not having their needs met. They may become vocal and act out. They might even attempt to steal medications from another inmate or locate illegal drugs within the facility—all in an attempt to manage their own symptoms and emotions. When they get too vocal, disobey orders, make threats to staff, then, their behavior merits a write-up. They may end up in segregation. Unfortunately, for the mental health inmate, this may be the worst possible scenario.

As I mentioned earlier, one of the first rules of therapy I learned as a new mental health provider was that it is inappropriate to provide medication to a client unless you are also providing therapy. Yet, in corrections, at least at Bent County, we did it all the time. I have never been comfortable with such a procedure.

This situation only occurs because of numbers—too many offenders who are classified as having mental health diagnoses and issues—too overwhelming for mental health staff to adequately provide therapy hand-in-hand with the needed medication. Of course, another question arises: are all of these offenders, in our case, 440 actually diagnosed correctly, and, even if so, do they actually need medication? Or, would they profit more by having classes and therapeutic sessions without medication?

These questions are difficult to answer. Offenders are excellent at faking symptoms. Many offenders have been drug users on the street. They are chemically dependent and now, faced with sentences, some very lengthy, they crave medications. Thus, they are frequently able to relate, in a very convincing manner, appropriate symptoms to the psychiatrist. I am not blaming the psychiatrist. I have worked with many excellent psychiatrists who screen, evaluate, and diagnose to the best of their abilities. But, many offenders are Oscar-contending actors, excellent at manipulating and lying.

They go to the library and read the symptoms associated with any medication they may be seeking. They speak to other inmates to get information on the side-effects and results of any specific medication. As a result, they are prepared when they meet with mental health and later the psychiatrist. Offering medications in the system is indeed a balancing act. If the doctor withholds medication because he believes the offender is faking symptoms, then he may be subject to verbal and perhaps physical abuse, as well as possible litigation, if the inmate can prove the doctor acted wrongly. On the other hand, if he prescribes the wanted medication against his better judgment and the offender gets ill, dies, or has severe side effects, then the doctor is again subject to repercussions. It is not an enviable position.

Inmates continue to lobby for medication. I recall one Spanish-speaking inmate. He knew almost no English. He had sent a request to see mental health and thus had been scheduled for an appointment. Upon walking into my office, he sat down in the offered chair. Immediately and without a word, he pulled a fragment of notebook paper out of his pocket. Clearly printed on the paper was one word: Wellbutrin. I spoke with a translator, and we explained to him that he could not just get the medication without an appointment with the doctor for an evaluation. He left, his face indicating disappointment, shaking his head. It was obvious that he had been coached by someone, someone who probably wrote the word for him, someone who may have wanted the medication for himself, but had manipulated the Spanish-speaking offender into seeking it.

Of the more than 400 offenders in the facility with mental health issues, about 300 were on medications with a variety of diagnoses. A few may have actually been schizophrenic or truly bipolar I or II or had post-traumatic stress disorder (PTSD), indicating a genuine need for medication. A large majority of them were diagnosed with attention deficit hyperactivity disorder (ADHD), anxiety, or depressive disorders, or possibly an impulse control disorder. Of course, some of these also needed medication. But all too often they were all prescribed medication, even though there was a realization that the mental health clinician would not be able to monitor them in an effective way or provide any type of counseling.

In fact, the psychiatrist may not have been able to renew their medications within ninety or 180 days in some cases. When mental health numbers rose, the nurses would renew the medications through the telephone because the order would expire and the offender could not be seen for several weeks or months down the road. Of course, the doctor had approved the renewal and would sign the orders upon his next visit to the facility.

Frequently the requests (kites) that we received would have notations, such as "I need my Wellbutrin (or fill in the blank) renewed" or "I am having side effects with my meds (breaking out, throwing up, etc., etc.). "I need my dosage increased." "I am not sleeping even with the new meds." "The nurse keeps giving me the wrong meds, green pills instead of white." The requests all would require a follow-up, checking the offender's med orders in the computer or in their files, a contact with the nursing staff or doctor to verify orders, or an extension of the medication. At one point toward the end of my career in corrections, I was spending about an hour every morning, reviewing, screening, and following up on these requests. This especially became critical as the numbers mounted and we were short a clinician and never able to procure a clerk.

One of our roles in mental health is to explain to the offender that medication, depending of course, on the diagnosis, might not always be in his best interests. Many of the inmates, as mentioned earlier, were already addicted to drugs and simply wanted to continue taking "something." The clinician has an opportunity to explain to them that their incarceration time is a good time to "get clean." And, of course, it is not the clinician who evaluates the offenders for medication and orders the drugs.

Many of these offenders would benefit by being in a long-term addiction program rather than in prison. Naturally, this depends upon the nature of the crime and the addiction. However, all the money spent on corrections, a good portion of that would be more wisely allocated to treatment. I am so reminded of the wasteful War on Drugs, which has been fought for decades now with no success. Yet, it has managed to pack the prisons full of bodies, and in the case of CCA, that means more and more profit.

In fact, all that the War on Drugs has done is add to the prison numbers. Drugs and alcohol are a factor in about 85 percent of the cases of inmates I interviewed. It is there in their file, arrest after arrest, violation of probation and parole, one time after another. Yet, their addiction remains. And the problem remains. Offenders continue to be arrested for crimes associated directly with drugs. Their abusive habits represent a windfall to CCA and other for-profit prisons.

CCA has stated that they could be adversely affected by changes in enforcement of laws, leniency, and certain decriminalization actions. They note that "any changes with respect to drugs or controlled substances or illegal immigration could affect the number of persons arrested, convicted and sentenced, thereby potentially reducing demand for correctional facilities to house them."[1] Thus, once more, it is obvious that it is not in CCA's best interest for offenders to be placed into treatment rather than locked behind bars.

I am not suggesting that those offenders who have addiction problems should get a pass. To the contrary, the crime itself, whether it be domestic violence or robbery, murder, rape, assault, or one related to drugs, of course, should and must be addressed. Consequences are extremely essential to those convicted.

We have a criminal justice system that locks people up for snorting cocaine or smoking a joint, people who, by the way, are primarily lower class or of a minority status, and they tend to fill up the prisons. Then we leave these offenders at risk to continue their behavior, and we open the gateway to their learning to become better criminals while locked up. I especially saw this in young, naïve boys who arrived in my office with no street smarts. Before long, they had contacts and experiences that could negatively influence the rest of their lives.

When I had my own office, I sometimes provided treatment and aftercare for parolees. During one session, a young man explained that he had been incarcerated for stealing cars and altering them to meet the needs of his "clients"—chop shop activities. When I spoke to him of his future goals, he related to me that he had met people in prison who were more knowledgeable than he was and now he was able to "do it right." In other words, he had spent his time "networking" with his comrades, not a particular noteworthy activity for rehabilitation. Now he would be able to get out, return to Denver, and continue in his chosen profession. Not a bright outlook for any twenty-five-year-old.

Perhaps in states such as Colorado, which has now legalized marijuana usage, we may well see fewer people incarcerations for possession and manufacturing of weed. There may be other legal problems or arrests that arise as a result with factors associated with the cannabis industry, but the legalization may bring down the prison population in the future. Over the next few years, Colorado will be able to have a better concept of the results of the new laws.

As a Licensed Addiction Counselor, I am well aware of what drugs and alcohol do to the brain and the body. However, during the thirteen years I conducted domestic violence classes, I had only ONE person court-ordered to treatment whose crime was associated directly with marijuana. He explained to me that his wife had objected to him spending money on pot. "I work for my money!" he told her. Then, he stated that he had stood up, struck her in the mouth, knocking her down. He then sat back down in his recliner and smoked another joint. She left the house and called the police.

Every other client, possibly as many as 1,000 clients over those thirteen years, was court-referred on charges related to alcohol and other drugs—primarily alcohol, the legal drug, but that was the only one related to marijuana. Am I advocating for legalized pot? Not at all. But I do believe in personal choices, and I believe that not everyone should be behind bars for choices made, even if in some opinions they were bad choices. In the case of marijuana and other drugs, it is important to evaluate the level of impairment and provide treatment for those addicted.

One would think that the historic experience associated with prohibition would provide a message that outlawing drugs does not really work. Instead, it sometimes makes drugs attractive to those who are facing severe life issues and especially those of the lower economic class, who have poor job prospects or opportunities. Sometimes, smoking a joint may be what relieves stress and gets a person through to another day. And sometimes, in the case of marijuana, there are some medical properties that may make it appropriate.

Again, I am not necessarily an advocate of marijuana or other drug use. But, I do believe in personal responsibility. I do believe in treatment, when necessary. I believe that we, as a society, are too quick to hand out prescription drugs, which, in turn, can result in addiction. I think of this when I go to the dentist to get a tooth pulled and he hands me a prescription for Vicodin or Percocet, which I use once or twice and then throw away the rest of the pills. I am reminded of it after surgery when the same thing occurs. Our society seems to want a pill for every minor ache or pain. We want a "happy" pill and a "no stress" pill. The world simply is not like that, but somehow many people have not learned to manage moderate pain or stressful feelings. Perhaps some of this could be attributed to the media and the advertising of all the positive effects contained within prescription drugs.

I am also reminded of a veteran's experience. He had returned from service in the Middle East, where he had been wounded in body and mind. He relayed to me the trauma of witnessing his fellow soldiers blown away before his eyes, of having half his leg ripped off and being covered with the blood and guts of other men. As he described his experience in therapy, he struggled to hold back tears, in vain. His hands shook, his chest heaved, as he revealed his ongoing problems with drugs. The horror that he had experienced was evident. I allowed him time to process his feelings before proceeding.

But, then, he described how he had been provided with medication to assist with his diagnosis of Post Traumatic Disorder. He stated that the medication, a cabinet full of prescription bottles, eight to be exact, seemed to help, but he actually wanted to get off some of the drugs at times, to try to manage his feelings himself. He had become so addicted to them that each time he tried to drop one, his symptoms returned with a fury. As a result, he doubted that he would ever be free of the drugs. How tragic is that!

More recently I have come face to face with the realities of the fallout from the prescribing of opioids. Now working in the substance abuse field, I repeatedly find that a large number of my clients who are addicted to heroin began their journey with opioids. Beginning with a medical issue or some type of surgery, a need to control pain, they continued their use of the drug long after they should have. When they could no longer obtain a prescription, they turned to heroin, and some of those clients will undoubtedly end up in prison.

But let's face it, the drug companies and alcohol vendors are motivated to make money, even if it results in addiction. In the end, they are no different from the for-profit prisons. By criminalizing so much of the drug world, we have served only to open the doors for the both legal and illegal drug operations to flourish.

Those who ask for and need help should be provided it along with treatment and counseling, instead of simply being handed a prescription or sent to jail or prison. Litigation is often involved over the use or non-use of legal drugs, as well as medical problems in the prison system. Lawsuits play a huge role in all facets of prison life and CCA has experienced a number of lawsuits, including many related to inadequate medical care as the following examples show.

CCA shelled out $1.65 million and another $756,000 in fees and expenses in March 1999 to settle a lawsuit initiated by inmates at Northeast Ohio

Correctional Center, who claimed they were physically abused, not adequately protected and denied "adequate medical care."[2]

Sometimes lawsuits are settled out of court and without disclosure as to the cost. In the CCA-operated prison in Burlington, Colorado, named Kit Carson Correction Facility, the mother of an inmate filed a lawsuit in response to her son's death. According to the complaint, the inmate suffered from a hereditary condition that caused his breathing passages to swell and he died because staff refused to fill his prescription shortly before he was scheduled to be released. Because the medication could only be obtained in thirty-day lots, and he would only be at the facility for ten more days, they did not order it. The cost for the drug was about $35. On the day he died, he tried to call for help from his cell, but as much as thirty to forty-five minutes passed before staff arrived. The complaint also alleges that "unit staff had the practice of turning off the intercom in an empty cell to cut off calls from inmates in occupied cells; therefore, preventing them from "bothering unit staff with calls." The lawsuit was settled out of court in 2004.[3]

The list goes on, and I will not try to enumerate all of the medically related ones. However, it is worth mentioning that the CCA-managed Dawson State Jail in Texas was closed due to "inadequate medical care." Due to several deaths at the facility, organizations such as Grassroots Leadership and The Sentencing Project successfully advocated for the closure of the facility, noting that the facility had experienced seven deaths since 2004 that might have been prevented if those inmates had received proper medical care and attention.[4]

Following an investigative report by the Dallas/Fort Worth CBS affiliate, several allegations of medical negligence were reported. One thirty-year-old woman who was serving an eighteen-month sentence for drug possession died of pneumonia just six weeks before she was scheduled to be released.[5] Another woman died from pneumonia complications while she was serving a six-month sentence for drug possession.[6] Also in 2010, a forty-five-year-old woman died while serving a one-year sentence for drug possession. The lawsuit filed by her family alleges that she was taken off her prescribed insulin injections and given cheaper oral insulin, resulting in a diabetic coma. She continued to be denied the insulin injections and died from complications from diabetes.[7]

A January 2012 audit of the CCA Dawson, Texas, facility's health service by the Texas Department of Criminal Justice found multiple systemic failures more than half the time in a variety of medical areas, even noting that they failed basic inspections, gave inappropriate diets to sick prisoners and did not keep adequate records.[8]

Of course, CCA responded stating that its "dedicated, professional corrections staff is firmly committed to the health and safety of the inmates entrusted to our care." They were quick to point out that CCA was not the health care provider, noting that the state contracts with the University of Texas Medical Branch for care. The problem was not bad treatment, but in each case of alleged mistreatment, it was an issue of access to treatment. Regardless of the contractual system, CCA was still the "gatekeeper," still responsible for what occurs under their banner.[9]

Medical lawsuits are only some of the many litigations that CCA has had to face over the years. From sexual assault to employment discrimination to Federal Labor and Wage Law violations, many of which stem from lack of staff or staff training, somehow CCA manages to dodge numerous bullets. Needless to say, CCA admits that most times, it is less costly in both time and funds to settle lawsuits than to go to trial.

When I think about the inmates making "demands" for medication, and I have actually heard some do so, I also consider what the outcome might be if the doctor does not comply. For example, if the inmate has outlined his symptoms, even the doctor may believe that he is exaggerating or lying, but what is the doctor to do? If he refuses to give the offender the requested medication, the inmate may scream and yell, stating that he is being denied medical services. Some psychiatrists and physicians may take this threat seriously, and cave in to the offender's demands. But, even if they do not, the offender may initiate a lawsuit. With this threat, most providers will probably assess the symptoms and decide to order the medication, in a safe dosage.

All the psychiatrists with whom I have worked have been very appropriate in their ordering offenders' medication. Some of them outright refuse medication to certain offenders, but there is always that risk of litigation that exists in all that we do within the prison system. And, CCA has not been blameless in issues involving drugs. CCA has been sued numerous times for failure to provide adequate medical care. This is an area where proper care costs a lot of money but not providing care or proper care means cost savings. Therefore, the professionals working with offenders must make cautious decisions when it comes to providing and monitoring medications.

Some staff at Bent County were terminated for selling or bringing in drugs to inmates while I worked there. While I have no record of the outcome, whether charges were filed, this behavior simply demonstrates what occurs when pay is minimal. There is a temptation to make some easy money by scoring drugs.

Of course, this occurs in many facilities both public and private. In addition, lax security makes it easier for staff members who make such decisions to sneak in drugs and other contraband. I accidentally brought in my cell phone one day, and discovered it only when it started ringing! I was embarrassed, but that phone should never have been allowed through security.

Once I had an officer who waved me on by without a check. He was a family friend. I refused his wave and went through the check like everyone else. And, of course, there are always those who sneak in the drugs in exchange for sexual favors or because they are "just in love."

My concern with the use of medication within Bent County was primary from the understaffing of the mental health department, where we were not able to monitor appropriately any symptoms or side-effects from the medication. Although the medical department did an excellent job of monitoring offender side effects, I felt the guilt of not being able to do my job properly due to time constraints. In the end, it all boiled down to a lack of staff needed to monitor offenders. This lack of monitoring elevates safety and security issues, and often leads directly to litigation.

## CHAPTER 16. THE SPIN CONTINUES—OR, MORE EXCUSES

I felt my days at Bent were coming to an end. I had been actively seeking another position. My last three years had demonstrated that despite requests for changes, these changes would never occur. Instead, staff would be met with roadblocks at every turn, and the bottom line was that the mental health staff would continue to be blamed for any perceived shortcomings.

I had taken a leave of absence for medical reasons. As I contemplated returning to work, I found myself dreading my return. I was haunted with frustration, frustration at not being able to do a damn thing to help the inmates.

That theme reverberated through my brain for most of my down time. The knowledge that I had to return to work filled me with a sense of dread. While I appreciated my colleague keeping me posted on events at Bent County Correctional Facility, I also dreaded her phone calls. I realized that all human beings have different perceptions of situations. I also recognized that I could not entirely accept her statements, which would be colored by her own experiences. I knew that I had to experience the changes for myself. Yet, I also recognized that the information I had received made absolute sense and fit with my past experiences at Bent County.

No panic allowed, I told myself even as I pondered my return. My return could not be put off past twelve weeks. Even then, my doctor was not totally in agreement. In fact, he was recommending that I have a knee replacement. I held off. It had only been a month since the meniscus repair. He left it at that and signed off on my paperwork. After all, I had to work.

On May 7, 2015, I returned, and the dismantling I previously referred to immediately became apparent. My colleague had not exaggerated. Once more seated in my office, I faced the computer. Tentatively, I opened my appointment schedule. Almost immediately, I detected numerous missing service codes. I would no longer be able to see how much activity had been generated in each area and by which provider. I could no longer easily grasp areas that needed improvement or renovation.

Most of the codes referring to activities and the status of inmates were missing. For example, the code that referred to the daily checks we conducted for an inmate on suicide watch was gone. The code that indicated that mental health had seen and signed off on an inmate charged with an infraction that had placed him in segregation also was gone. Codes for referrals and follow-ups from medical to mental health for those inmates with a diagnosis of Hepatitis C were gone. As I thumbed through the selections, I shook my head in disbelief. I realized that I could no longer indicate the number of audit checks and diagnosis changes after the client had been seen by the psychiatrist. I could not find a code for drafting a client's letter requesting clemency from the governor. No code now existed to follow up on the kites or inmate requests. This entire process had been thwarted. The beauty of the prior system had been that I could easily track all services that the mental health providers had performed. It was an invaluable tool for preparing accurate monthly reports and recording precisely how much time had been spent in each endeavor.

I struggled with the program, wondering what code to place on any service. My first difficulty arrived with a letter I had written for an inmate's clemency packet, a one-page document that still required a meeting and some research. Sitting in front of the monitor, I realized that I could not accurately code this activity or many others. Most things now got placed under "sick call." Many services could not be entered at all.

Speaking with my colleague, trying to sort out the various ways to document items, I explained that I now understood her problems. I told her, "I know why."

She asked, "Why?" although I am certain she knew and was just looking for confirmation.

"CCA simply wants the record to show that all we do is OMIs (Offenders with Mental Illness) and screens for the sex offenders. They do not want documentation regarding all of the other activities that we perform. That way, they can say that we should have enough staff to perform our duties." I wondered: why does every irritant, even simple frustration, seem to flow back to the understaffing issues—and beyond that to the real root of the problem—profit.

My supervisor popped in about this time and appeared very pleasant, smiling, helpful, and considerate. I did not bother to confront her with my intolerance of the "new" scheduling system. She could have consulted with me by telephone during my medical leave. She could have queried me as to the relevance of the codes. Yet, she had simply made an executive decision, which, of course, was her right regardless of how the outcome might affect our operation.

As she relaxed in the chair next to my desk, she stated that her superiors were pressuring her and, thus, changes had to be implemented. She stated, "I am micro-managing mental health now." This statement was from a nurse who had no psychiatric or mental health background.

Okay? And why? Again, my response, or should I say my reaction, reverted to the numbers and the seeking to prove no additional staff was needed. I let her comment drop. There was no use in bucking her authority. I had a sense that my days at Bent County would be quickly coming to a close.

I interviewed for two different positions in Pueblo, neither of which seemed to fit me and my experiences. I had scheduled an interview with the Veteran's Administration, but cancelled it, due to the driving distance to the job site. And, then, unexpectedly, I received an e-mail from an organization in the community which was seeking someone with my qualifications. They were willing to work with me on salary and insurance. I reviewed my current status and the direction I wanted to go. Facing retirement in the near future, perhaps a couple of years away, I did not want to spend those months torn by stress and being physically exhausted. I was tired of the on-call process and having to track offenders on watch all weekend. In general, I was burned-out.

The negotiations went speedily. I received the go-ahead for the position. I turned in my letter of resignation. My supervisor seemed to know that it was coming and was pleasant enough when I described my decision.

The warden was not so pleasant. It was a simple example of how money and profit play such a huge role in the staffing issue. Initially, I met the warden passing in the hall, and provided him with my resignation letter. After a brief glance at the contents, he turned to me, stating, "After all we've done for you, you do this to us." I assume he was referring to my being on a twelve-week disability, and returning for a few days before resigning. He then asked me to get an appointment though his clerk and see him.

As he addressed me in this very rude and commanding manner, my thoughts did an instantaneous flashback. I leaped backward into the many, many hours of overtime with no pay, of weekends that would have been better and more leisurely spent with family, of forty miles of traversing icy roads and the wind-swept prairie. Within a matter of seconds, I had been transported back to "what I had done for them," but, of course, I realized that was irrelevant to the moment.

In the sanctity of my office, I recalled one specific night. At 8 p.m. my phone rang. Someone had attempted to kill himself, having sliced his wrists. The Department of Corrections had been notified. The inmate was in the holding cell on constant observation. However, according to policy and regulation, I was required to evaluate him and do the appropriate paperwork. Did it matter that this was in the throes of winter, mid-February? Did it matter that it had been snowing off-and-on most of the day? Of course not. I considered that I had to be up again to teach a 7:00 morning class. This meant that by the time I drove in, evaluated the offender, and completed all the required paperwork, it would be somewhere around midnight before I could drive home, only to turn around and drive back in a few hours.

Even so, this was not my primary concern. I realized that the highway would be crusted with ice. Yet, what was I to do? No other clinician was closer or available to fill in for me. Rules were rules, apparently. I must do my duty and head down that highway. (I would never do that today!). Bundling up, I started the car, turned the heater on full blast, and began the trek. The weather and even the roads were worse than I had anticipated. Snow continued to blow across the road, not blindingly so, but enough to keep my eyes focused and my foot off the accelerator. Ice-coated roads dominated all forty miles, keeping me at a snail's crawl. My hands clung to the wheel, terrified that one wrong move would send me careening into the ditch, car destroyed, or more importantly, my life gone.

Somehow I made it into the parking lot, my anti-grip shoe soles not worth their warranty. I was still shaking, trembling; my shoulders were tight, my hands stiff from the death-grip on the wheel, but I still managed for the good of the company. Right! The story does not end there.

I completed my evaluation. By that time, it was about 1:00 a.m. I considered traveling back down that icy highway in the black hours of the morning, arriving home, only to rise at 5:00 a.m. to start the journey all over again. I simply could not do that. It was either to call in late in the morning and miss my class or stay all night. At first, I thought I would just sleep in my office or in one of the beds in the holding room, but I decided against those options. I assumed that I could make it to the motel at the end of town without incident. And so, once again, I set out. I arrived, only to find that the check-in section was closed. No surprise there. I searched for a place where one could ring for help. I walked through the halls. Finally, I spotted a sign informing me to go to room so-and-so. Once checked in, I located my room. By this time, I was shivering, bone-cold from my travels, and the motel was not much warmer. Once inside, I searched for the heater, but I simply could not locate one. I checked on every wall, even the bathroom. No indicator. It was bitterly cold, and I continued my shivering regime. Finally, instead of calling for help, I opted for bed, using all the blankets I could find, plus my winter coat. I huddled there and at long last I fell asleep.

Morning arrived. I got up, tried to straighten my wrinkled, slept-in clothing to be half-way presentable for my class. Then, I looked around. Behold the heater, sitting right where most heat/control sits on a wall, under a window. I could only laugh at myself. In my exhausted and stressed state, I simply had not been able to focus. And, of course, CCA did not reimburse me for my hotel stay.

That was only one example of my willingness to serve my company. Of course, it was not the company I served, it was the offenders. So, for thirteen years, I was willing to brave winter snows, at least most of the time, except for extreme conditions. I forced myself to travel those icy roads. I drove the flatlands of southeast Colorado when dirt storms blocked my vision, creating dreaded brown-outs and opportunities for chain-reaction wrecks. I drove through blinding rainstorms, when I would pull off the road into some farmer's field to avoid a wreck.

And the warden dared to try to give me a guilt trip. Really? *After all you've done for me.* I don't think so.

So, it was when I sat in his office later in the day, I was reminded of the request that had been forwarded to the warden on March 11, 2014—at his request. That paperwork contained a twenty-point request for a fourth mental health clinician. The request talked about the increased case loads and the inability to manage the offender population in "a safe and efficient manner." The points included statistics as well as the various duties, including hours needed to appropriately handle each of those duties. That submission was supposed to be forwarded to the Powers That Be to emphasize the importance of adding a clinician to our department. Interestingly, at the request of the warden, I also provided an update to this several months later. All in vain. No real surprise.

The warden addressed some of those issues that had led to my resignation. At that time he stated that individually, the mental health clinicians did excellent work. However, the problem was that all of us were never there at the same time. So, collectively we could not keep up with the monitoring and duties in a timely fashion. In other words, we were being penalized because two of us had been out or had surgery over the last year.

My response was that neither I nor the others, to my knowledge, had taken any unauthorized time, vacation, or sick time prior to my leave. He agreed, but countered with the fact that the clinicians had basically not followed suggestions made by the State of Colorado Private Prison Monitor to reduce certain inmate codes, so they would not need to be monitored so often by mental health. I disagreed with this, stating that I myself had deleted many codes. In fact, I had a list of those I had removed.

During this conversation, I pointed out to him that we had asked for help long before our third person left the past year. At that time, our numbers were well more than 400 inmates, and with all the activities we had been asked to do, including conducting classes, it was impossible. I reiterated to him some of the reasons, including the workload, the on-call, and salaries that were factors in the loss of the last three mental health clinicians—all enumerated in this book. He agreed with some of those factors.

I also reminded him of the time when I had pointed out the various required activities we were asked to perform, and he had stated that CCA and the Department of Corrections did not count those. Most of those items were not part of the state contract, but were listed in the job description under "other duties."

The warden responded that crises contacts are part of the job description and new clinicians were made aware of that coming on board. I agreed, but I stated they did not understand all the repercussions, including paying for your own gas and day upon day of monitoring those on watch. I could recount times that I had had to be in the facility for as many as fourteen days at a time with no break. My colleagues had had the same experience due to the requirements surrounding the monitoring policy.

In the end, the conversation was pleasant enough, but my sense was that it was just the same old excuses—trying to justify the lack of staff needed to appropriately and safely manage the department. More words. Words to brush away the impact of losing another staff member. Words that would perhaps take the sting out of him being unable to control the situation. After all, he was accountable to his bosses in Nashville.

And those bosses, who controlled the purse strings, have the power to hire and fire. And if a person wants to climb the corporate ladder, that can't be done if he disagrees with the bosses. I get that piece. But the reliance upon taking the politically correct posture seems to be the norm with CCA. As mentioned earlier, their sealing up lawsuits and then trying to justify their position is but another facet of the attitude and actions that prevail.

For example, in the $8 million payback at California City Correctional Center, which was mentioned earlier, CCA claimed the payment for back wages was due to a "retroactive contract modification" by federal officials and said it had "diligently" worked with the U.S. Department of Labor to ensure employees received the wages they were due. This was again just another attempt to put a positive spin on their greedy actions.[1] So, why should I expect anything more from this CCA warden?

So I was able to get out. Some do not go that quietly. By contrast, Shaun Bauer, mentioned earlier in this book, had worked undercover as a corrections officer at Winn Correctional Facility in Winfield, Louisiana, for four months while compiling his information for *Mother Earth*. He took extensive notes and recorded conversations. He also had a colleague, James West, who was to shoot video for the story. When Bauer did not return from a nighttime shoot, Bauer phoned him, only to learn he had been arrested.[2]

Bauer left town quickly, calling in sick. James was taken in leg irons for questioning and charged with trespassing. After a $10,000 bond was posted, he was released. Bauer called in and resigned.[3]

CCA issued a statement saying that his approach "raises serious questions about his journalistic standards." Five months after he left Winn, Bauer reported that "*Mother Jones* received a letter from a law firm representing CCA, dropping hints that the company had been monitoring his recent communications with inmates and was keeping an eye on my social-media presence."[4]

He noted that the company's counsel claimed he was bound by their code of conduct. CCA had insisted on receiving a "meaningful opportunity to respond" to this story prior to publication. When Bauer asked for an in-person interview, they refused. However, they did reply to more than 150 questions, but scolded him thirteen times for his "fundamental misunderstanding of the company's business and "corrections in general." The spokesperson also suggested that his reporting methods were "better suited for celebrity and entertainment reporting." [5]

Certainly my leave-taking was not nearly so dramatic. But then I was not doing an investigative report. Rather, it was only after the fact that my perceptions and research came together to develop this book.

# CHAPTER 17. THE THERAPIST'S FLAW

Those who work in the mental health trenches, whether we are titled counselors, therapists, or social workers, have a major flaw. That flaw follows us like a shadow, pervading everything we do. It creeps into our workdays and haunts us into the night long after we have gone home. Oh, we try not to mingle work and private life, but somehow the shadow inserts itself into the family picnic.

And, if we are good—or have been—very good at what we do, then the major flaw flies into the workplace with a vengeance, creating a disruption between our actual work requirements and our code of ethics.

Our flaw is simple and prevalent. *We Care.* Yes, even though we are working with offenders some of whom have committed terrible crimes, some of them unspeakable, such as child molesters, we still care about their mental health. Even though some of them should never be released from prison, we still want them to take responsibility for their past actions, to seek out and find redemption, to live out their lives with no future victims.

Maybe we ask too much. Maybe our role should be akin to some of the officers. Come in, stand guard, watch over the inmates in the chow hall, hope there are no disruptions during your shift, check out, and collect your paycheck. Of course, not all officers are that way. But my point is that I should be able to do that—come to my desk, turn on my computer, run my scheduled offenders through like so many cattle, and leave at the end of the day, and—naturally, collect my paycheck and keep my mouth shut.

I cannot. I have tried. I tried for years, even as the population doubled. I tried as our duties increased. I tried as I asked for additional help—even a part-time clerk. Yet, inside of me an odd sensation festered—a voice crying out that what I was doing, or attempting to do with such limitations was Just Plain Wrong. It went against the very purpose of why I had gone into counseling in the first place. It went against my very moral code. I was not helping anyone. Oh, I like to think that here and there someone perhaps picked up a word of encouragement or made a significant change in his life. I like to think that. It helps me sleep a little better at night. But, then, reality snuck in again. I am not doing the work I was trained to do. I am pushing paper. With each word I type, I may be keeping my facility and CCA, perhaps even myself, free from litigation. But I am not helping offenders to reintegrate. And I am angry that it has come to this. I did not feel like this earlier in my career. I did have a defining sense of gratification at helping inmates now and then.

Perhaps my current feelings stemmed from my initial training and my perception of my role as a counselor/therapist. Was I mistaken in my memories of what characteristics define a good counselor? I decided to check some resources, just to refresh my thinking, possible to revise my expectation. Reviewing several websites, I found basically the same information. Not only should a counselor have patience (maybe I could use some assistance here), but also the counselor should be a good listener (I think I pass muster here; additionally, the counselor should be compassionate, as well as empathetic.[1] Those two terms exactly describe my "flaw."

Compassion and empathy. They go hand in hand. Compassion implies that the counselor cares and it will show in the body language and the responses to the client's issues. Empathy basically means that the counselor is able to put herself in the shoes of the clients, to understand the situation from their point of view, but also maintain appropriate boundaries.[2]

As I reviewed these words—compassion and empathy—my frustrations were further fueled by the sense that that my feelings, my character, and yes, my values, were in direct contrast to my employer's goals. CCA's profit motive ran interference with what I considered my purpose, my calling. My focus was on the offenders and on their mental health problems and needs. I wanted nothing more than to listen in a nonjudgmental manner and provide them with the tools that might assist them with reintegration. However, if their sentences were such that they could never leave prison, then I wanted to be able to at least provide them with an outlet for their emotions.

Still, I felt that I was failing, so I tried to ignore these feelings of inadequacy. I sometimes did this by justifying what I could not do by blaming the system. Ultimately, it remained very difficult for me to blame anyone else or examine the many factors that prevented me from providing the type of services that I consider vital to my clients. This is one of the reasons that it has been difficult for me to write this book. Even as I researched the issues and compared my problems with others that were often much larger, I continued to examine the offenders' various types of diagnoses and problems and the services that I could provide, which might better help them in their life quests.

I reflected on the various offenders. One of the diagnoses which continued to intrigue me was Post-Traumatic Stress Disorder (PTSD). A person can develop this condition for a variety of reasons, such as being raised in a home with ongoing domestic violence (or a war zone). While I related to the wide variety of PTSD patients, the ones, who raise more concern for me are those who actually do return from war. Sometimes known as "Wounded Warriors," these are veterans who served, most recently in the Middle East, and have returned, not just with physical wounds in many instances but with mental health problems as well. Within my heart, I often asked: How does a person who has served his country honorably end up in prison? Of course, there are many journeys that lead to the loss of freedom.

However, one of the variables, which appear in almost every case, is alcohol and/or other drugs. But why? The answer sometimes is evident in the experiences that the men have encountered during their service. Many of them have watched their fellow soldiers literally blow up right before their eyes. Even when directly witnessing a bombing incident, for example, they are compelled to continue with their current assignment. As a result, they end up with PTSD, and sometimes with physical wounds as well. And, again, my lament was that I did not have the time nor the staff to provide the appropriate therapeutically beneficial PTSD program.

However, Ellen managed to facilitate a PTSD group when she was working at Bent County. I envied her being able to do so. At the time, we did have all three clinicians, which greatly helped us to provide these vital extra services. I heard nothing but compliments about this group. Certainly, much of that could be attributed to her. She was an excellent clinician, a caring person who always prepared for her group, and somehow managed to recognize the needs of the individual participants as well. However, much of the success belonged to the use of the PTSD class which provided the offenders with the insight and tools that they needed to have an impact on their thinking and behavior.

After she resigned her position, the two of us remaining clinicians had not been able to resume the program. With the large numbers of inmates and the accompanying paperwork, along with ongoing crises, meetings, and auditing, it became impossible to lead groups due to the lack of staffing. Furthermore, it did not appear to be a class that was recognized, given credit, and certified by the Colorado Department of Corrections, at least not at that time with that specific program title.

My interest in this area is substantial. I have had several family members serve in the military including an uncle who returned from World War

II "shell shocked" He and his wife lived with us for a time when I was a child, and I remember waking up to shrill screams and loud voices. My uncle would be pulling my aunt across the room by her hair. She would be flailing, trying to get away. I still remember that scene in the middle of the night. It had a strong influence on my desire to help others who had experienced the trauma of war.

I desperately wished to address this issue—the one that indicates the journey from military service (war) to the community and then to the prison gates. I even wrote a short story, "Foxholes," found in my e-book *Meltdown.*

Another area that I touched on earlier that is associated with PTSD is domestic violence. I had once operated my own agency, New Lifestyles, which provided treatment for domestic violence offenders. In that context, I also wrote a manual for male offenders, *Hands Down: A Domestic Violence Treatment Workbook.* This book, along with its teacher's manual, indicates the heart that I have for this issue. I have been amazed at the number of inmates who came to the Bent facility and had backgrounds, if not current charges in domestic violence.

Although I am no longer certified as a domestic violence provider and cannot provide the accepted classes or certificates for inmates, I do sometimes use materials from my book for clients, when it is appropriate. I have met with both offenders and other clients and have guided them through the materials, sometimes giving them the manual for their own use. My greatest regret in working in corrections was my inability to regularly meet with and counsel this group, specifically to assist them in preventing any future victimization—to others or to themselves Again, with the shortage of mental health staff, it became impossible to do this vital work. And since practically all offenders are released, who knows how many of them go on to do further domestic violence, which might have been prevented had I been given the opportunity to counsel them properly.

The current focus on bipolar disorder is important, too. This is one of the most misdiagnosed mental health conditions, especially within the prison system. I witnessed large numbers of inmates insisting they had this condition, either by their own diagnoses based upon their having "mood swings" or because they had actually had that diagnoses before coming to prison. Once they had that label, it seemed almost impossible to convince them that it might just be possible that they had been misdiagnosed. Instead, they would insist that they needed medication.

Of course, some individuals do have a correct diagnosis. For those, it is essential that they remain on medication to control the chemical imbalances that appear to dictate their mood swings and behavior.

The other diagnosis that is prevalent within the system is ADHD, or known by its longer title of Attention Deficit Hyperactivity Disorder. Often, this is associated with children. Many people carry the condition into their adulthood. Most adults who truly have this disorder have learned to cope with their lack of ability to pay attention and their manic behaviors. On frequent occasions, I have spoken with a inmate who had been diagnosed with ADHD or ADD as a child, who for years had been taking medication, which, in effect, is a stimulant. Since there are no tests for ADHD, but it is based solely on behavior, I would question if the offender had actually been correctly diagnosed. I also recognize that a large portion of the offender population have been addicted to street drugs prior to incarceration. As a result, many of them continued to demand medication of some type to fill that gap.

I was not able to meet with them routinely to determine if they actually met the criteria for the diagnosis they had or if they were appropriate for medication management, or if they would benefit more appropriately with therapy or even both therapy and drugs. Due to the lack of another mental health counselor, I could not take the time to properly assess and counsel most of them. So, they continued down the path they were on and would probably return to prison once they had been released because nobody had the time to provide proper counseling or treatment.

I sometimes met inmates who had practically memorized the symptoms from the psychiatric guidebook, *The Diagnostic and Statistical Manual of Mental Disorders* (DSM-V) published by the American Psychiatric Association. They would rattle the symptoms off, one right after the other, often using psychiatric terminology. They would also present all of these symptoms when meeting with the psychiatrist in their search for medication. They would sometimes persist even when the doctor screened them carefully, seeing no outward signs and historic evidence of true bipolar disorder. Many of the inmates were simply drug-seeking.

As a helper person, as one who cares about the mental health of others, I often found myself torn. It is one thing to place an offender on medication when he actually has a condition where his brain chemistry is messed up—that is one thing. But the problem is that when there is no staff and no time to provide the counseling hand-in-hand with the pills—that goes against my code of ethics.

From the earliest days of my career, when I was working on my master's degree in psychology and gaining experience and the hours necessary for my certification, one truth was emphasized by my supervisor. It was simple. "Never give medication without therapy." Yet, in the prison system, at least at the Bent prison, as well as in other circumstances, I have learned that giving medication without any or little counseling is commonplace. Certainly, the manner in which we pushed the inmates through the system, monitoring them once every three months (if we were lucky and there was no other emergency), and the manner in which they requested multiple drugs from the psychiatrist, and the manner in which they faithfully lined up at the medication line in the morning and evening, belies that fact.

The increased use of medications in our society is nothing new. Yet, with my work at Bent County, I felt stifled. I might not have minded so much, if I could have scheduled individual sessions—if I could have held noteworthy groups to provide inmates with coping skills designed to ward off relapse and recidivism. It simply was not going to happen.

Ultimately, it goes back to my fatal flaw. I care. That is why, in the end, I had to leave Bent County—or should I say CCA, the true source of my frustration.

CHAPTER 18. WHAT IS THE ANSWER?

The truth is that private prisons are now so entrenched in the corrections industry that they will not just "go away." Senator Bernie Sanders (I-Vermont) introduced on Capitol Hill a bill titled "Justice Is Not for Sale Act of 2015." If passed, that bill would have eliminate for-profit prisons. Senator Sanders has accused the private prison industry of creating a "perverse incentive" to keep jails filled. Co-sponsored by Representative Raul Manuel Grijalva (D-Arizona), the bill calls for federal, state, and local governments to ban privately run prisons within three years, to reduce high fees for prisoner services such as phone calls, and to reinstate a federal parole system.[1]

The bill also called for reduction in the number of immigrants held in detention centers, many of which are privately managed. This could occur by eliminating the current minimum quota of housing 34,000 people each day. Senator Sanders called the private prison industry "disgraceful" and "morally repugnant."[2] Known as S. 2054, the bill was read twice and referred to the Committee on the Judiciary as of September 1, 2015.[3] In the House of Representatives, the bill was H.R. 3643, and on October 5, 2015, it was referred to the Subcommittee on Crime, Terrorism, Homeland Security and Investigations. It was still in process.[4] on October 5, 2015. Neither bill was enacted, but rather died with the previous Congress.

Hillary Clinton, the other Democratic presidential candidate, had previously accepted $133,246 in campaign contributions from both the GEO Group and CCA through the Ready for Hillary PAC. However, in October 2015, she announced that she would refuse future funds from private prisons and would turn over the PAC money to charity. She went so far as to state that if she were elected president, she would ban the use of private prisons and private immigration centers.[5] Even during the first presidential debate Hillary Clinton called for criminal justice reform, including the elimination of privatized prisons at the federal and state level.

Is it possible that Sander's bill will pass? Probably not. Companies, such as CCA, GEO, and MTC revolve around a system of expensive and highly effective lobbyists. They pay homage primarily to the conservative Republican candidates, historically and currently, providing campaign support and funding, in many cases. Private prisons appear to be a sound investment for those organizations and individuals attempting to profit from imprisonment.

However, the Justice Department on August 18, 2016, announced that it would no longer renew private prison contracts and would "substantially reduce" the scope of those still in effect.[6] This signals what could become a complete elimination of its reliance on the private prison industry and represents a step in the direction that Senator Sanders advocates with his "Justice Is Not For Sale" Act.

This opens a new dialog as to the future of state-run facilities, as well as immigration facilities, which are operated by the private prisons. Those two areas are not affected by the Justice Department's decision. Further examination of this decision and the implications will follow in the Afterward of this book.

In the meantime it is necessary to examine areas in which improvement can be made in those remaining facilities, which remain under the private prison umbrella. What is the solution? Is there any way in which privatized prisons can be held more accountable for understaffing, lack of programs, and failure to provide safety and security nets around staff and offenders? Is there any way, short of further litigation that they can be held responsible for exempt classifications that rob workers of their well-earned wages? Is there any way that they can provide more significant and appropriate services for all offenders, including those with mental health conditions?

One solution is to increase the amount of monitoring both by the mother department of corrections and by outside auditors. This means strict adherence to staff numbers, as well as strong penalties, both in terms of dollars and pulling the number of offenders from the supervision of any facility found fudging on staff numbers. Of course, this would mean that the current focus on number requirements, which are integrated into many of the state contracts, would have to be revised—obviously, not in the best interest of CCA.

Increased staff training is essential. The Colorado the Department of Corrections requires extensive training and CCA has its own annual training for staff, along with training for new hires. Yet, CCA's training is often superficial, sometimes staff who have previously been through training, either at hiring or since, are allowed to leave after signing in. I have witnessed this often when I was conducting a training class. People would get up and leave with the excuse that they had work to do. Sometimes, training is done through out-of-date films and PowerPoint presentations, with the class staring at a screen, while the instructor signs paperwork or engages in other activities. However, there were some excellent trainers at Bent County. Then, there were those who simply read the information off of the screen and clicked to the next slide. Training should be mandatory at all times and staff should be held accountable and compelled to take make-up sessions when they leave or do not appear for the class.

While I was out on medical leave, contact with a colleague only added to my frustrations. I had commented that I would need to complete my annual training upon my return. She stated, "There is no training at this time. We are too short-staffed." She explained that the training was suspended until staff had returned from various leaves and vacations. I later learned that this was not entirely accurate. The facility had held an extensive hiring event. As a result, with the additional staff being trained, approximately twenty-four, mostly officers, the in-service training for existing staff had been placed on hold. Yet, as I listened to her, how could I but be reminded of what I consider a major problem in the private prison industry—understaffing. As stated earlier, I believe that the Brent facility has been very fortunate to have had few major safety issues. No riots yet. Only one suicide completed since the doors had been opened. As I commented to my colleague, I believed this was because, as staff, we had done an excellent job in our various roles. I cannot praise staff enough.

One corrections officer whom I admired, Donald, is an illustration. Donald had been an officer for approximately four years. He came from a military background; he demonstrated the high professionalism that a correctional officer should exhibit. His pat-downs were meticulous. He was courteous with staff and offenders. He would call inmates out of their cell house when I requested. In other words, he was one of those worker bees who managed to do a good job with a positive attitude and a smile on his face. Yet, he was firm and consistent with inmates as he need to be. But Donald was also discouraged and concerned about the staff patterns. He stated that on one particular day there had only been four officers in a certain cell house, which had more than 700 offenders. One time, the facility was about thirty officers short. He said that case managers who had been trained previously as correctional officers were called upon to serve once again as officers. In other words, they were working two different positions, as needed—"power shifts."

From a safety standpoint, someone was gambling with us. One nurse actually said, "It's like sitting on a time bomb; I just hope that we don't end up with a riot."

The next shift brought Officer Michele onboard. She had been with the facility for about eight years. She was very professional and knowledgeable about her role; she managed offenders with a "defuse" mode. In other words, she listened to what offenders had to say without over-reacting. However, she was assertive and followed through, when needed. She had a clear-cut understanding of the manipulation and minimization that was rampant in many inmate behaviors. Somehow, the conversation had carried over onto her shift. She stated that her concern, too, was for safety.

I stated that, "Well, we have fifteen new people training today, and I understand another group is set up for the next session." Michele shook her head. She went on to explain that already Bent County had a large number of "new" officers on the floor, some of them no more than six months out, and many were still unclear about their jobs. One new officer was "afraid" of the inmates and when one of them refused to turn around and get patted down, she made no effort to stop him or write him up. "I used to think the staff was there to watch my back. I no longer feel that way," she added.

That evening as I departed the facility, I arrived in the lobby to check-out. I found one other staff person waiting, also to be cleared for departure. There was no lobby officer present.

So I asked. "Where's the officer?"

"He had to go to visitation and should be back soon."

I nodded, but added, "This is a mandatory post."

"Yep," he replied, shrugging his shoulders.

Without the presence of uniformed officers who are knowledgeable, staff are placed in more and more precarious situations daily. Many of the staff members are long-term workers, with excellent skills and experience. And in-service training can occur within the time-frame required. Yet the very concept of suspending training because of "not enough staff" on board at the facility underscores the depth of the under-staffing problem that prevails in many CCA facilities, as has been documented in several lawsuits.

Decreased and controlled numbers is an essential ingredient in being able to manage offenders, particularly those with mental health needs. With the legalization of marijuana in Colorado, the result may be fewer arrests on possession and manufacturing charges. On the downside, there may be other types of crimes. However, if there are fewer offenders to deal with, perhaps the state facilities will fill their beds first and the Department of Corrections will send fewer inmates to the private systems. But, I am not counting on that basically because of the ever-present bed guarantees that CCA places in their contacts—or amendments.

More appropriate placement of offenders should also result in private prisons receiving fewer seriously ill mental health inmates. Colorado has for many years used an outdated system for classifying those with a mental health diagnosis or illness. While they have made strides in attempting to correctly identify and place them, there is still much work to be done.

The current system relies on a code known as P-codes, the P standing for psychological. Inmates are initially coded when they arrive for their first interview at the Denver Reception and Diagnostic Center. This is a 542-bed transitional facility, which evaluates offenders for medical, dental, mental health, and personal needs, as well as provides testing for academic and vocational needs. [7] Following the assessment, offenders are provided with a code in each area, which signifies their level of need. For example, the mental health codes range from P1 to P5. P1 means the offender has absolutely no history or current need of mental health treatment. P2 may mean that inmate had some previous diagnoses or history, but it was relatively benign, indicating to mental health staff that there is no need to further screen or evaluate him.

Moving along, the P3 codes indicate that the offender has a current diagnosis, needs to be monitored closely, and is most probably on medications. A P4 ranking, however, would mean that the inmate has severe mental health needs. He may have had a recent crisis, a suicide episode or a psychotic break. In fact, a P4 should never have arrived at Bent County because they are not supposed to be housed in private prisons.

Are the codes ever incorrect? Of course, since judgments are often made on the fly by human beings. It is not unique for an inmate to arrive with a lower code of P2 who is on psychotropic medications. As mental health professionals, we simply change his code to a P3 when we discover the error. Have we ever been the recipient of a P4 at intake? Several times. This may mean that he needs to be shipped back to the Department of Corrections. However, it may also mean that he was incorrectly coded. After evaluation, the mental health clinician can reduce this code.

Because offenders with P3 codes were required to be monitored a minimum of every three months, Colorado did introduce a variation on the monitoring status. If an inmate had a less intense diagnosis, such as ADHD or perhaps a form of personality disorder, but was stable, his monitoring visits could be extended to up to six months. If he was no longer taking medications and was stable, he might be an appropriate case for a code reduction.

While the code system works fairly well, it is important to note that the gathering of information at the Denver Reception and Diagnostic Center (DRDC) occurs very rapidly after the inmate arrives. If he has been in the system before, his entire history/narrative is simply transferred, with a brief update, to a new date. However, I saw few updates in these cases, except for medication changes. Much like Bent County and other prisons, even the intake center needs to have adequate staff to take time to accurately complete these interviews. A few years ago, DRDC called for staff from other facilities to assist them in the intake process due to the influx of offenders. It is hoped since Colorado's inmate population has declined, that staff will have the time to critically screen for all codes, including P codes.

Attracting professional staff is critical to the entire prison system, including the private facilities. Private prisons are well-known for lower wages compared to the public facilities. In the case of Bent County and the mental health department, it became a difficult challenge to locate trained and dedicated staff. Clinicians who have invested much time and money in their education need to be paid at a comparable rate with other professions. They are not going to relocate to a rural area with fewer amenities unless they are provided with some real incentives.

Of course, paying clinicians more digs deep into the pockets of CCA. And to even consider other incentives, such as assisting with student loans, paying for classes they must attend for license renewal, or relocating expenses—are out of the question. At least they were when I was at Bent County and with CCA.

As a result of the lower wages and, of course, other issues, I lost three excellent mental health workers in the last five years while I was at Bent. Two went to the Department of Corrections. Another took an outside job with more pay and student-loan- repayment benefits.

Crisis-intervention assistance. For those mental health professionals who are required to work a standard day of eight hours, forty hours a week—give or take, of course, a huge assist could be provided by using outside agencies, especially during the weekend and holidays. Throughout the state, agencies exist that specialize in mental health treatment. Those agencies could be contracted with to provide additional help during crises, especially when a staff shortage exists. For the "exempt" mental health workers to have to report to the facilities twelve or fourteen days in a row to check on Inmate Smith who is being held on a suicide watch is simply not necessary and represents a hardship and potential for burnout to good clinicians. Over a period of time, it also represents a loss of qualified clinicians. Of course, it does provide CCA with an even greater profit margin.

The other manner in which greater assistance could be provided requires that CCA permit its nursing staff to do the routine checks on offenders who are on suicide or mental health watches. In other words, the policy and procedures need to be changed. According to CCA policy, weekend and follow-up checks must be done by the mental health staff. The same is true with the CCA policy, which states that once an inmate has been on a mental health watch, then he must be seen daily for a week, then once a week for two weeks, then he can be closed out after a month. Again, this means at times the clinician must journey into the facility on the weekends, probably both days. Why can't that policy be revamped to allow members of the nursing staff to check on the offender? unless there is a mental health issue that needs to be addressed, this would save extra runs to the facility? Perhaps it is simply not in the best interest of CCA to use their "exempt" staff. I have been told that since my departure, this process has been modified somewhat and that a nurse can monitor an offender on watch, but is to call mental health for any significant needs outside their scope of practice.

Increased psychiatric hours are a must. Most of the psychiatrists Bent employed had other jobs or their own practice. However, with the mental health inmate numbers at elevated levels, it is critically important that those offenders have their routine visits with the psychiatrist for a review of medication, side effects, and effectiveness. That did not always happen when I was at Bent. When the number of mental health inmates rose while I was at Bent County to an all-time high of 444, with more than 300 on medication, it became impossible to shuffle the offenders into the clinic in a timely manner.

Sometimes the clinic would be disrupted by human events, such as sickness of the provider, a vacation, or a medical conference. Whatever the reason, it simply placed the offenders further down the appointment date. Increased hours, an extra day during the week, an outside backup psychiatrist—all would be very helpful in these situations, but, of course, such alterations require additional funds.

How do we change this unconscionable system? It is entrenched in this country, and it has solid political support and investors who are profiting handsomely on the backs of offenders and caring professionals alike. Senator Bernie Sanders may have the right idea, but the whole country needs to rally behind this effort and make this change a priority.

As individuals, employees have no power over CCA. Our mental health team reported our concerns and professional needs relentlessly, and the warden was never able to get the company to address the appalling abuse of staff that in turn means a lack of care for the inmates. They created situations that could only fail the inmates and that put us all in actual danger.

To keep up with bureaucracy, we scaled back more and more on services and training, for ourselves and the inmates. I no longer taught classes for staff, and my colleagues temporarily dropped their inmate classes, which was contrary to the Department of Corrections' requirements. These classes were absolutely essential in order to reduce recidivism.

Some attempt was made to assist us in fulfilling at least some of the superficial criteria with our case loads. Whereas one of my roles had been to schedule offender/clients for the psychiatrist, as well as for myself, a clerk finally took over that task.

But it was more important to get one more staff person to fulfill all the tasks and manage the offenders safely, and with a hope of assisting them prepare to reintegrate into society—and that was never done. Only lip service was paid.

# CHAPTER 19. SEVERING TIES

There I was, returned after medical leave and ensconced in my black swivel chair, my left leg stretched out before me, elevated on the shredder, an ice pack over my knee. Nothing had really changed; yet, everything had. When an officer walked by in the hall, my attention turned to the door, the door that I had entered who knows how many times. This filled me with many memories and differing emotions. This small 8' x 10' room has housed equipment, files, manuals, and a variety of records, as well as personal mementos designed to bolster my days at Bent County Correctional Facility.

I scanned the room, taking in all the various nuances and objects, the pale yellow walls, all constructed of pre-fab materials. On the one solid wall before my desk was a large poster with a scene of an autumn field, red and gold leaves ready to fall from the trees. Blazing across the photo is the encouraging word "Change." At some point I must have thought this poster would encourage the offenders.

My desk, a big brown overgrown behemoth, sat before me, taking up far too much room. I had often wished for something smaller. Atop this big desk was a big old computer box, the CPU guts, a large black box that did double-duty by holding the telephone. I also had a keyboard, monitor and scanner on the desk and a flat desk calendar with its coffee stains, notations, and many various scrawls—numbers and scribbles, which even now I don't recognize. Oh, yes, I have my own printer on a short file cabinet on my left. It holds manila envelopes, Spanish-intake paperwork, and possibly a dead mouse (computer one, of course). The printer itself merely prints black and white, no color, no scanning, no faxing.

To the left of this is a battleship gray bookcase housing a variety of manuals, mostly outdated. Black stacker trays contain papers ready for filing or discarding. A miniature covered wagon, constructed by an inmate, sits atop the bookcase. I smile at the memory of the offender sitting in my office, repairing a busted wagon wheel. The little wagon was been constructed of a variety of odds and ends found within the prison, mostly paper. The detail is amazing, a frying pan, a barrel for water, a bedroll.

Next to the wagon is a miniature pool table made from a bar of soap. The pool table has an Avalanche decal in its center. It has tiny balls and a cue stick, a sign of some inmate's intricate design sense and abundant time. The inmates built all these and more items for my office.

I reviewed the items with some nostalgia. I would miss this claustrophobic room with its packed furnishings. It had served me well. But already I was grateful to be moving into another stage of my life. Primarily, this gratitude was based upon the recent frustrations regarding my final paycheck.

Here comes another shocker. I am not the only one who's been buffaloed by the leave policy with which dedicated employees are rewarded. When I went out on medical leave, I had not yet accumulated much Paid Time Off (PTO), with only two hours to my credit. As a result, my facility immediately deducted forty hours off my collective time, leaving me about thirty-eight hours in the hole when I returned to work.

I did not realize this at the time. When I resigned and began calculating my final paycheck, I discovered that I would be docked for the days I did not work, since I had not accumulated enough "down" time. Instead of simply being cut loose and not paid for the missed days and paid only for my remaining workdays, the thirty-eight hours was deducted at the rate I would normally be paid. I spoke with the human services coordinator, who explained that this was policy. You are actually penalized for not having enough vacation or sick time accumulated; instead of it being counted as simply no pay for days not worked, you actually owe the company.

A former officer who left about two months after I did had the same experience. Because he had been out on medical leave shortly before quitting and had no leave accumulated, he too was short-checked. To me, this is just another way for CCA to retain a few dollars from people who through no fault of their own have had to take medical leave. It is one more scheme to put more dollars back into the coffers of the mother company.

Because CCA has an employee assistance program, I thought that perhaps I could apply and receive some help with my medical bills. After all, I had been paying in $5 per paycheck since the program started. I gathered all my medical bills and filed the application, hoping I might get a few hundred dollars.

Instead, I received a letter about two weeks after I left Bent County stating that I did not meet the criteria. Well, probably not, since I no longer worked there. Still, I could not help but reflect upon the negative outcome associated with my final days at Bent County. While I understood the logic behind this refusal, it only served to fuel my belief that CCA was primarily concerned with dollars, not with people. In the end, all of the policies, the rules, the exempt status, the failure to hire needed staff, and the docking of time—all add up to the same primary purpose. Every decision and every activity, no matter how minute, was focused on profit. Ultimately, it is and only was all about Bodies in Beds.

# Afterword

The issues discussed in *Bodies in Beds* came under closer scrutiny on August 18, 2016, when the Justice Department announced that it plansplanned to end contracts with the private prison industry. Deputy Attorney General Sally Yates made the announcement, stating that a number of factors were involved, including the higher incidence of safety and security problems in the private prisons, as well as a general decline in the number of federal inmates.[2] Yates cited a recent audit that found that the privates "simply do not provide the same level of correctional services, programs, and resources" as publicly run facilities.[3] The audit report had collected and analyzed data from fourteen different privately owned prisons and indicated a higher problems with safety and security incidents than comparable Bureau of Prisons (BOP) institutions, including higher levels of assaults.[4]

In response to the decision, both CCA and MTC issued statements saying they were disappointed with the decision. They also said that they disagreed with the conclusions of the audit that preceded the Justice Department's decision.[5]

The decision callscalled for a phasing out process in which contracts willwould not be renewed or the Bureau should at least "substantially reduce their scope, Yates wrote in a memo. The reduction began with a non-renewal three weeks before the announcement when it did not renew a contract for 1,200 beds. The policy change also includesincluded a change in current solicitation for a private prison contact, cutting the maximum number of beds required by 60 percent.[6]

The decision doeswould not impacthave impacted state prison systems or the federal immigration authorities for prison housing or the U.S. Marshals Services, which uses private facilities to temporarily jail suspects and convicts.[7] However, the impact on states could occur if they absorb some of the inmates being housed by the Justice Department facilities.

A CCA spokesman said the contracts affected by the announcement amount to only about 7 percent of their business and that the company has been expanding into other services, such as re-entry for prisoners who are ready for release.[8]

GEO reported that it has a "longstanding relationship" with the Bureau of Prisons and highlighted its rehabilitations programs. "The impact of this decision on GEO is not imminent," the company said.[9]

Privately held Management & Training Corporation said it was disappointed in the announcement and that it will result in "a very heavy cost to taxpayers."[10]

The announcement was met with a flurry on the stock market, with CCA shares sliding 40 percent and GEOs down by 35 percent that day. Nevertheless, the process of ending private prisons held under the Justice Department system by reducing as many as 10,800 prison beds down to 3,600 beds will, in all likelihood, take years.[11]

For some, this decision by the Justice Department was long overdue. In fact, some feel it did not go far enough. Senator Patrick Leahy stated that is it "an important first step, but it is not enough."[12] Not covering ICE detainees or those in state and local prisons is a mistake, according to many liberals. Democrats have criticized Homeland Security Department's use of privately run facilities, particularly the detention centers that have housed thousands of immigrant families seeking refuge from violence in Central America.[13]

ICE did issue a statement, following the Justice Department announcement. Spokeswoman Jennifer Elzea noted that the agency provides several levels of oversight in order to ensure that detainees in ICE custody have safe, secure, and humane environments. "ICE remains committed to providing a safe and humane environment for those in its custody."[14]

The efforts made to thwart the private prison industry have fallen with the advent of the Donald Trump administration. The Obama administration's decision to stop using federal private prisons came to a halt on February 23, 2017, when the Justice Department rescinded the order. This reversal was announced by Attorney General Jeff Sessions who wrote that Obama's order had "impaired the bureau's ability to meet the future needs of the federal correctional system."[15]

Stock prices in private prisons have jumped since Trump won the election and with Sessions' order, they rose even further.[16]

Even so, criticism of the tactics used by the private prison industry continues, going back to the Obama Administration, which along with ICE came under fire for skipping a standard public bidding process in order to build a detention facility for women and children, many from Central America, seeking asylum.[17] *The Washington Post* reported that a four-year $1 billion contract was issued to CCA for a Dilley, Texas, 2,400 bed facility and another one for a 532-bed family detention center in Karnes City, Texas. Elzea states that the contractual arrangements are unique because they provide a "fixed monthly fee for use of the entire facility regardless of the number of residents."[18]

The article reports that under the "get tough" on illegal immigrants pressure, the administration began seeking solutions to those flowing in mostly from El Salvador, Guatemala, and Honduras, where drug and gang-related violence was rampant. As a result, ICE patched together a temporary solution, placing the first group of mothers and children in Artesia, New Mexico.[19]

CCA, which had operated family detention centers in the past, along with ICE, found a way around the public bidding process, which would delay construction. Instead, they spoke with officials at Eloy, Arizona, where they already had a facility for undocumented men. If Eloy modified their contract, directing CCA to build a new facility in another state, 1,000 miles away, they would be freed from the bidding process. The deal was cemented with two separate agreements. One between ICE and Eloy and the other between Eloy and CCA, both signed the same day. ICE provides the money to Eloy; Eloy receives a small "administrative fee" for being part of the deal.[20]

The bottom line is that CCA is assured of a predictable payment, around $20 million per month, even when the facility's population drops. A CCA spokesman, Jonathan Burns, said that the company is required by the contract to provide full staffing and other services no matter what the population. But, of course, when 2,400 people are detained, the cost-effectiveness is less than when the facility is nearly empty, which it has been at times.[21]

Although stays at Dilley have shortened due to two court decisions in 2015 that ICE couldn't detain asylum seekers "simply to deter others" and one that the government had to abide by a two-decades old settlement requiring that migrant children be held in the least-restrictive environment possible, CCA still continues to reap the profits.[22]

CCA declined interview requests on this story and also declined to respond to twenty-eight of thirty-one written questions. It issued a five-paragraph statement, noting that "CCA is committed to treating all individuals in our care with the dignity and respect they deserve while they have due process before immigration courts."[23]

In July 2016 CCA investors were warned that they might make less money on the Dilley, Texas facility contact or lose it altogether. In its quarterly earnings release, a CCA spokesman stated that they have submitted a proposal to ICE for the South Texas Family Residential Center to reflect a lower cost to ICE. They stated that the company:

> can provide no assurance that we will be awarded a new contract for family unit detention, will successfully renegotiate our existing contract with ICE, or will be able to maintain the margins we currently generate under the contract.[24]

As I ponder these recent developments by the Justice Department and the *Washington Post's* article on the Dilley $1 billion dollar contract, I am hopeful that the trend toward privatization of prisons will be lessened. Perhaps this will occur due to the decrease in stock values. Perhaps the revelation of the lack of transparency and accountability will drive the public and governments to realize that private prisons do not provide the cost-savings they are lauded to provide. I hope the inmates and staff at Bent County and at other private prisons and jails will receive better treatment in the future. However, with the Trump administration now in power, it appears that the use of private prisons will only expand. In fact it is expected to surge with his promised crackdown on illegal immigration.

President Trump signed a series of executive orders on February 23, 2017, all designed to do exactly that. In addition to ordering the Department of Homeland Security to start building the wall, it was announced that Trump's orders will triple the number of Immigration and customs Enforcement officers, with the focus on locking up more immigrants who illegally cross the border. The Center for American Progress estimated the whole project will cost more than $117 billion over the next ten years, with taxpayers footing the bill. A good share of that money will go into the coffers of private prisons. [25]

ACLU released a statement criticizing the president's plan. Omar Jadwat, director of the group's Immigrants' Rights Project stated, "Locking up asylum seekers who pose no danger or flight risk is unconstitutional and benefits nobody except private prison corporations and politicians looking to score rhetorical points." [26]

In the same order that called for a wall, Trump also instructed ICE to expand immigration detention centers, including leasing space in existing local jails and signing new contacts, most likely with private prison companies. [27] A February document from the White House to Homeland Security called for raising the number of immigrants incarcerations daily, nationwide, to 80,000 people. Last year ICE detained over 352,000 people, typically between 31,000 to 34,000, with a high last fall of 41,000. [28]

The ICE detention expansion presents a tremendous business opportunity to the private prison industry. Damon Hininger, CoreCivic President and CEO stated, "When coupled with the average rates of crossings along the southwest border, these executive orders appear likely to increase the need for safe, humane, and appropriate detention bed capacity that we have available." [29]

As of November 2016, 65 percent of ICE detainees were held in private prisons. Carl Takei, staff attorney for ACLU's National Prison Project says that ICE relies on private prisons each time detention system expands. He adds, "There's little doubt in my mind that they will continue to rely on the private prison industry in what's going to be the biggest expansion of the agency in history." [30]

I had hope for change to occur during those last five years I worked at Bent County Correctional Facility. Instead, I saw the further deterioration of programs and resources until I lost faith that offenders would receive the skills they needed to compete and be successful when released. I felt a sense of loss as I moved forward. I am not leaving unfinished business there, but I am a realist and recognize that I can do more elsewhere. I cannot fight a system that is so entrenched in profit that it has little, if any, regard for integrity.

Although I know that I have, in many respects, been able to intervene with some offenders, overall, I have NOT been able to provide the therapy and treatment that could truly make a difference. I have stood by while offenders had their psychotropic medications renewed time and again, but with no organized program of therapy or counseling. Forces outside the responsibility of the mental health department have aligned to make such efforts difficult at best. I realize that while in this position, with the limitations imposed by both supervisors and the CCA system itself, I could not in good conscience continue in this position. However, my concerns for the unethical manner in which mental health offenders are being thrust behind concertina wire and warehoused with no true concern for treatment or healthy reintegration into their communities—that is the most unforgiveable and damnable indictment of the whole system.

Since I left, incoming offender numbers have been reduced. Some duties, such as scheduling, have been moved over to other staff members. Processes continually need to be tweaked and refined to better accommodate case loads and the needs of both staff and offenders. Still, the overall concern exists for the private prison system, which time and again has demonstrated that it is willing to cut corners to save a few bucks here and there. These dollars can be realigned into huge salaries and bonuses for the chief administrative officers.

As an illustration of the continual realignment to insure profit in the private prison industry, on October 28, 2016, CCA announced that it was "rebranding" its corporate enterprise. Now known as CoreCivic, the company announced that will offer three different business arenas. They include: CoreCivic Safety, a focus on corrections and detention management; CoreCivic Properties, which is "innovative, cost-saving government real estate solutions"; and CoreCivic Community, a network of residential reentry centers to "help tackle American's recidivism crises."[31]

This rebranding came on the heels of the Justice Department announcement, which led to decline in then CCA's stock. With the actual charter change on August 11, 2016, the company also changed its logo to a 13-stripe American flag designed to represent a building and stated that it does not anticipate any impact on its "contractual relationships with government partners." The Company notes that the change has been in the works for several years and, according to President and Chief Executive Officer Damon T. Hininger, the new name "speaks to our ability to solve the tough challenges facing government at all levels and to the deep sense of service that we feel every day to help people."[32] I wonder whom Mr. Hininger means to help—the stockholders seem to be the only ones helped by privatization, in whatever guise it takes.

Even with the optimistic announcement, the company also provided a list of nine items which could impact their expectations of moving forward. Among those are occupancy levels, governmental budges, utilization, ability to obtain and maintain correctional, detention and reentry contracts, changes in the privatization of the corrections and detention industry, detention capacity as per U.S. Department of Justice and Department of Homeland Security.[33]

Of course all of that occurred before the Donald Trump was sworn in as President. It occurred before his executive orders opened the door for further expansion and profit for the private prison industry. With the company names and business divisions, along with the cooperation of the current administration and its approach to immigration and the dehumanizing of immigrants, CoreCivic, Geo and Management and Training Corporation stand to further expand and increase their profits—all at the expense of taxpayers.

For those of us who have been a part of the CCA (now CoreCivic) this rebranding represents nothing more than another method of shaking up the corporation in order to locate further means of profit. In spite of its statements that this change results in "high quality", "cost-savings" and tackling "recidivism" methods, the reality is that the organization continues to juggle its corporate make-up in order to locate and focus on other methods of raking in tax-payer dollars in the guise of helping people.

I still have colleagues working within Bent County Correctional Facility. They are in a position to continue making changes within the system with the assistance of the Department of Corrections' Private Prison Monitor. They can continue bringing issues and concerns for their facility, as well as for the private prisons system, as a whole. They can also stand up for the areas where they feel injustices and inappropriate staffing and programming are affecting their clients. And, of course, my concern is primarily to advocate for those offenders who have mental health needs.

For others who read this book, those who are taxpayers, it is important to critically evaluate the processes, programs, and procedures within the private prison system. It is my hope that the focus extends to understaffing issues. Those directly affect safety and security. In addition, I believe it is imperative to evaluate the salaries, bonuses, and benefits, which are extended to the top executives. In effect, they are giving CCA the reputation of being greedy and concerned with profit only and not the welfare of the offenders. While much positive publicity can extol the benefits of the private prison enterprise, it is the fallout, lawsuits, and empty promises that ultimately lead to a negative picture of the entire company.

As for the general public, my hope is that this book will encourage them to demand continual oversight and greater transparency for the private prison system and to advocate for the closing of all private prisons. Because private prisons are not a public enterprise, they have been permitted to seal records from lawsuits, refuse to share valuable financial information, and engage in activities that often appear to influence legislation in the favor of keeping and retaining more inmates in the system. All of this requires ongoing public monitoring.

Bodies in Beds—that philosophy—is what keeps the private prison system operating. Granted, the industry does provide jobs and benefits to thousands of workers, many of them residing in rural communities with poor opportunities for employment. However, despite all the propaganda that insists upon CCA's devotion to customers and staff, that we are all "family," the evidence shows otherwise. My own experience shows otherwise. The company has no real concern for the reintegration and rehabilitation of offenders. And as far as staff, there is not family—unless you belong to a family that shortchanges you and lies to you. As long as there is capital to be generated by incarcerating people, many of whom are not even Americans, CCA will continue to be dominated by one goal only—BODIES IN BEDS.

I am done, but my fervent hope is that the private prison industry, including CCA or now CoreCivic, may also be done.

# ENDNOTES

## Introduction

[1] Razavi, Layla, Director, Human Migration and Mobility. "Eliminate the Immigration Detention Quota," August 26, 2016. American Friends Service Committee. email correspondence.

## Chapter 1

[1] Melissa Blasius, KUSA, News Broadcast, "Most Colorado Sex Offenders Don't Get Treated in Prison," May 6, 2014. www.9news.com/story/news/local / investigations/2014/05/06/most-Colorado-sex-offenders-don't-get-treatment-in-prison/8753419.

[2] Ibid.

[3] Peter Wagner and Leah Sakala. "Mass Incarceration: The Whole Pie-A Prison Policy Initiative Briefing." Prison Policy. Last modified December 8, 2015. http://www.prisonpolicy.org/reports/pie2015.html.

[4] Source Watch. Corrections Corporation of America, Form 10-K, SEC Filing, Fiscal Year Ended December 31, 2013." http://www.sourcewatch.org/index.php/Corrections_Corporation_of_America.

[5] Doug J. Swanson, Dallas Morning News. "Fired TYC Monitors had Worked for Facility Operator: Group Fired for Failing to Report Conditions at West Texas Facility was Employed Earlier by GEO Group." October 12, 2007. www.callcenterinfo.tmcnet/news/2007/10/12/3009957.html.

[6] Craig Harris, "Arizona Cuts Ties with Private Prison Operator over Kingman Riot," Arizona Republic. August 27, 2015. www.azcentral.com/story/news/arizona/politics.

[7] Alan Prendergast, "After the Murder of Tom Clements, Can Colorado's Prison System Rehabilitate Itself?," Westword. August 21, 2014. www.westword.com/news/after-the-murder-of-tom-clements-can-colorados-prison-system-rehabilitate-itself-5125050.


## Chapter 2

[1] Alan Prendergast, "After the Murder of Tom Clements, Can Colorado's Prison System Rehabilitate Itself?," Westword. August 21, 2014. www.westword.com/news/after-the-murder-of-tom-clements-can-colorados-prison-system-rehabilitate-itself-5125050.

[2] Rick Raemisch and Kellie Wasco. "Open the Door—Segregations Reforms in Colorado." December 2015. https://www.colorado.gov/pacific/cdoc/news/open-door-segregation-reforms-colorado.

[3] American Psychiatric Association. "Position Statement on Segregation of Prisoners with Mental Illness." Last modified April 2013. www.dhcs.ca.gov/services/MH/Documents/2013_04_AC_06c_APA_ps2012.

[4] National Commission on Correctional Health Care. "Segregated Inmates." http://www.ncchc.org/spotlight-on-the-standards-26-2.

[5] "Obama to End Solitary Confinement for Juveniles in Federal Prisons." MSNBC, January 25, 2016. http://www.msnbc.com/msnbc/obama-end-solitary-confinement-juveniles-federal-prisons.

[6] Kirk Mitchell, Lynn Bartels, and Kurtis Lee. "2011 Law a Factor in Evan Ebel's Early Release from Prison." The Denver Post. Boulder DailyCamera.com. March 28, 2013. http://www.dailycamera.com/ci_22896714/evan-ebel-out-prison-early-thanks-2011-colorado?source=most_viewed.

[7] D. W Morgan, A. C. Edwards, and L. R. Faulkner, "The Adaptation to Prison by Individuals with Schizophrenia," Bulletin of the American Academy of Psychiatry and the Law 21 (1993): 427-433. http://www.jaapl.org/content/21/4/427.abstract.

[8] Sal Rodriguez, "Solitary Watch Fact Sheet: Psychological Effects of Solitary Confinement." Solitary Watch. 2011. http://solitarywatch.com/wp-content/uploads/2011/06/fact-sheet-psychological-effects-final.pdf.

[9] Kimberly Lupo, "The History of Mental Illness." http://www.toddlertime.com/advocacy/hospitals/Asylum/history-asylum.html.

[10] Fred Osher, D. D'Amora, M. Plotkin, N Jarrett, and A. Eggleston. Adults with Behavioral Health Needs under Correctional Supervision: A Shared Framework for Reducing Recidivism and Promoting Recovery (2012) Criminal Justice Mental Health Consensus Project. Council of State Governments Justice Center, National Institute of Corrections, and Bureau of Justice Statistics.

https://csgjusticecenter.org/mental-health-projects/behavioral-health-framework/

[11] "U.S. Number of Mentally Ill Prisons Quadrupled," Human Rights Watch, September 5, 2006. www.org/news/2006/09/05/us-number-mentally-ill-quadrupled.

[12] E. Fuller Torrey, et al. "The Treatment of Persons with Mental Illness in Prisons and Jails: A State Survey." April 8, 2014. http://tacreports.org/storage/documents/treatment-behind-bars/treatment-behind-bars.pdf

[13] Ibid.

[14] Jamie Fellner, "A Correctional Quandry: Mental Illness and Prison Roles." Harvard Civil Rights-Civil Liberties Law Review. 4 (2006): 391. www.law.harvard.ed/students/orgs/crd/vol41_2/fellner.pdf.

[15] Ibid.

[16] Sharon Dolovich, "Cruelty, Prison Conditions and the Eighth Amendment." New York University Law Review 84, No. 4 (October 2009), 881. www.law.georgetown.edu/cgi/viewcontent.cgi?article=1020&Fac. publ

[17] "Mental Health Courts." California Courts, The Judicial Branch of California. http://www.courts.ca.gov/5982.htm.

[18] "Drug Courts Work," National Association of Drug Court Professionals. http://www.nadcp.org/learn/facts-and-figures.

[19] Fred Osher, D. D'Amora, M. Plotkin, N Jarrett, and A. Eggleston. Adults with Behavioral Health Needs under Correctional Supervision: A Shared Framework for Reducing Recidivism and Promoting Recovery (2012) Criminal Justice Mental Health Consensus Project. Council of State Governments Justice Center, National Institute of Corrections, and Bureau of Justice Statistics. https://csgjusticecenter.org/mental-health-projects/behavioral-health-framework/

[20] Bureau of Justice Statistics, "Prisoners in 2014. Bureau of Justice Statistics Summary." September 2015," NCJ: 218955. Bureau of Justice Statistics. www.bjs.gov/content/pub/pdf/p14_summary.pdf.

[21] Ibid.

[22] Kimberly Lupo, "The History of Mental Illness." www.toddlertime. com/advocacy/hospitals/Asylum/history_asylumwww.toddlertime. com/advocacy/hospitals/Asylum/history_asylum. Retrieved on October 26, 2015.

[23] Ibid.

[24] Ibid.

[25] Thomas Ban, "Fifty Years of Chlorpromazine: A Historical Perspective." Neuropsychiatric Disease and Treatment 3 (4). (2007): 495-500.

[26] Enrique Neader, Drug Discovery: A History. (Chichester: Wiley, 2011).

[27] "Jean Valjean." Wikipedia. https://en.wikipedia.org/wiki/Jean_Valjean. Last modified February 12, 2016.

## Chapter 3

[1] Roberts, John W., Reform and Retribution: An Illustrated History of American Prisons, Lanham, Maryland: American Correctional Association. 1997.

[2] "Private Prison," Wikipedia. "Private Prison." Last modified February 14, 2016. https://en.wikipedia.org/wiki/Private_prison.

[3] "The CCA Story: Our Company History." Corrections Corporation of America website. Last modified 2013. www.cca.com/about/cca-history.

[4] "Corrections Corporation of America: American's Leading Corrections Partner." U.S. Builder's Review, www.usbuildersreview.com/case-studies/corrections-corporation-america-america percentE2 percent-80 percent99s-leading-corrections-partner. Retrieved on December 19, 2015. This site is no longer available.

[5] Shane Bauer. "My Four Months as a Private Prison Guard' A Mother Jones Investigation." June 23, 2016. http://www.motherjones.com//politics/2016/06/cca-private-prisons-corrections-corporation-inmates-investigation-bauer on July 9, 2016.

[6] "The CCA Story: Our Company History." Corrections Corporation of America website. Last modified 2013. www.cca.com/about/cca-history.

[7] Ibid.

[8] Ibid.

[9] Ibid.

[10] Colorado Department of Corrections. www.doc.state.co.us/facility/bccf-bent on September 15, 2015. This website containing history data is no longer valid.

[11] Ibid.

[12] Ibid.

[13] "Las Animas, Colorado." http://en.wikipedia.org/wiki/Las-Animas-Colorado on March 11, 2016.

[14] Kevin E. Courtright, Michael J. Hannon, Susan H. Packard, and Edward T. Brennan, Prisons and Rural Communities: Exploring Impact and Community Satisfaction, (Edinboro University of Pennsylvania, May, 2007). Accessed December 21, 2015. www.rural.palegislature.us/Prisons.pdf

[15] "Bent County Correctional Facility," Corrections Corporation of America. www.cca.com/facilities/bent-county-correctional-facility. Retrieved on December 26, 2015.

[16] "Summary of the HIPAA Privacy Rule,"http://www.hhs.gov/hipaa/for-professionals/privacy/laws-regulations/index.html. Retrieved on March 11, 2016.

[17] "Speed, Inexperience Cited in Prison Van Crash," KKTV website, Last modified December 29, 2011. www.kktv.com//home/headlines/Inmate_And_Officer_Killed_In_Crash_On_I-70_135878708.html.

[18] Colorado Public News and Ann Imse, "Colorado Paying Millions for Unneeded Private Prisons," KUNC. March 11, 2013. www.kunc.org/post/colorado-paying-millions-unneeded-private-prisons#stream/0.

[19] Ibid.

[20] Kirk Mitchell, "Coming Prison Closing Adding to Walsenberg's Woes," Denver Post, March 23, 2010. www.Denverpost.com/ci.14735948.

[21] Colorado Public News and Ann Imse, Ibid.

[22] Ibid.

[23] Ibid.

[24] Ibid.

[25] Ibid.

[26] Ibid.

[27] Ibid.

[28] Ibid.

[29] Andrea Rael, "Fort Lyon Prison, Closed by Budget Cuts, Reopens to House Homeless," Huffington Post, September 5, 2013. http://www.huffingtonpost.com/2013/09/05/fort-lyon-homeless-preven_n_3875883.html.

[30] Rachel Alexander, "Department of Corrections Explains Closing CSP II," Canon City Daily Record, March 21, 2012.

[31] "Idaho moves 130 inmates to Colorado," August 21, 2012. https://www.idoc.idaho.gov/content/story/front_news/idaho_moves_130_inmates_to_colorado. Accessed March 10, 2016.

[32] Office of Planning and Analysis. "Annual Report Concerning the Status of Private Prison Contract Prisons," December 1, 2015. http://www.doc.state.co/us/sites/default/files/opa/PPMU percent20Annual percent202013.pdf. Accessed March 11, 2016.

[33] Jennifer Brown and Kirk Mitchell. "Kit Carson Prison in Burlington to Close; 142 Jobs Lost," Denver Post, June 30, 2016. http://www.denverpost.com/2016/06/30/kit-carson-burlington-prison-closing/

[34] Ibid.

[35] Ibid.

[36] Ibid.

[37] Ibid.

[38] Sue Binder, I'll Never Make Parole, E-Book, available through Amazon for Kindle or Barnes-Noble for Nook, or Smashwords for other e-machines, March 2013.

[39] Stephen Raher, "Private Prisons and Public Money: Hidden Costs Borne by Colorado's Taxpayers," CCJRC Briefing Report, Colorado Criminal Justice Reform Coalition, September 2002. http://www.ccjrc.org/pdf/CostDataReport2002.pdf

[40] Ibid.

[41] "Corrections Corp of America CXW," Morningstar website, December 9, 2015. www.insiders.morningstar.com/trading/executive-compensation.action?t=cxw.

[42] "CXW Annual Income Statement," Market Watch website, retrieved December 26, 2015 at www. marketwatch.com/investing/stock/CXW/financials.

[43] Ibid.

[44] "Corrections Corporation of America," Source Watch, May 2013. http://www.sourcewatch.org/index.php?title=Corrections_Corporation_of_America.

[45] Investopedia Online, "Real Estate Investment Trust-REIT." Retrieved December 26, 2015. www.Investopedia.com/terms/r/reit.asp.

[46] Paul Ashton, "Gaming the System: How the Political Strategies of Private Prison Companies Promote Ineffective Incarceration Policies," Justice Policy Institute, June 22, 2011. www.justicepolicy. org/research/2614www. justicepolicy. org/research/2614.

[47] Wyden, Ron. "Breaking: OR Sen. Ron Wyden Introduces Bill to End Prison Tax Breaks." July 14, 2016. https://prisondivest.com/2016/07/14/or-sen-ron-wyden-introduces-bill-to-end-prison-tax-breaks/

[48] Ibid.

[49] Ibid.

[50] Beau Hodai, "Corporate Con Game: How the Private Prison Industry Helped Shape Arizona's Anti-Immigrant Laws," In These Times, June 21, 2010. www. inthesetimes.com/article/6084/corporate_con_game.

[51] Ibid.

[52] Paula M. Ditton and Doris James Wilson, "Truth in Sentencing in State Prisons," Bureau of Justice Statistics Special Report, January 10, 1999, www. bjs.gov/xonrwnr/puv/pewaa/raap.pe.

[53] Ibid.

[54] Khalek Rania, "The Shocking Ways the Corporate Prison Industry Games the System," AlterNet. November 29, 2011. www.truth-out.org/news/item/5283:the-shocking-ways-the-corporate-prison-industry-games-the-system.

[55] Chris Kirkham, "War on Undocumented Immigrants Threatens to Swell U.S. Population," Huffington Post, Last modified August 23, 2013. www.huffingtonpost.com/2013/08/23/undocumented-immigrants-prison_n_3792187.html.

[56] Ibid.

[57] Corrections Corporation of America. 2014 Annual Report, Form 10-K, retrieved at www.cca. com/investors/financial/annual-reportswww.cca. com/investors/financial/annual-reports.

[58] Lee Fang, How Private Prisons Game the Immigration System"How Private Prisons Game the Immigration System," The Nation, February 27, 2013. www. thenation.com/article/how-private-prisons-game-immigration-system.

[59] Francis Reynolds and Lee Fang, "What Does Millions in Lobbying Buy," The Nation, February 27, 2013. www.thenation.com/article/what-does-millions-lobbying-buy.

[60] The CCA Story: Our Company History.www.cca.com/our-history. Retrieved on December 27, 2015.

[61] David Simon, The Big Interview with Dan Rather, April 1, 2014 on AXSTV. Also available at www. youtube.com.

**Chapter 4: No Endnotes**

# Chapter 5

[1] "CCA Named One of the 100 Best Corporate Citizens in the U.S.," Corporate Press Release. March 3, 2008. www.Reuters.com/article/idUS230450+03-Mar-2008+MW20080303.

[2] "CCA Named Top Military Friendly Employer," Corporate Press Release, November 9, 2011. www.cca. com/press-releases/cca-named-top-military-friendly-employer*www.cca. com/press-releases/cca-named-top-military-friendly-employer*.

[3] "Forbes Magazine Names CCA's Damon Hininger as one of Nation's Top 20 CEOs," Corporate Press Release, February 24, 2011. www.correctionscorp.com/newsroom/news-releases/42.

[4] Corrections Corporation of America. "Investor Relations." www.cca.com/investors.

[5] Inside CCA: Tackling Recidivism.

[6] CNBC. Billions Behind Bars: Inside America's Prison Industry. www.cnbc.com

[7] Tracy Harmon, "Whole Foods Ends Prison Farm Sales," Pueblo Chieftain, October 2, 2015. http://www.chieftain.com/news/region/3987197-120/correctional-industries-colorado-prison.

[8] Ibid.

[9] "Kite? Where did that come from," Jail Medicine, January 29, 2012. http://www.jailmedicine.com/kite-where-did-that-come-from.

[10] "Incarceration," U.S. Prison Population Trends 1999-2014. February 16, 2016. The Sentencing Project, www.sentencingproject.org/template/page.cfm?id=107.

[11] Katy Hall, "CCA Letters Reveal Private Prison Tactics," Huffington Post, April 11, 2013 and updated on March 7, 2014. www.huffingtonpost.com/2013/04/11/cca-prison-industry_n_3061115.html

[12] Dana Goldstein, "How to Cut the Prison Population by 50 Percent," The Marshall Project, March 4, 2015. www.themarshallproject.org. /2015/03/04/how-to-cut-the-prison-population-by-50-percent#.KVWCPGlm7www.themarshallproject.org. /2015/03/04/how-to-cut-the-prison-population-by-50-percent#.KVWCPGlm7.

[13] Ryan King, Bryce Peterson, Brian Elderbroom, and Elizabeth Pelletier. "Reducing Mass Incarceration Requires Far-Reaching Reforms." Retrieved on December 31, 2015. http://webapp.urban.org/reducing-mass-incarceration/

[14] Goldstein, Dana, "How to Cut the Prison Population by 50 Percent," The Marshall Project, Retrieved on December 31, 2015. www.themarshallproject.org./2015/03/04/how-to-cut-the-prison-population-by-50-percent#.KVWCPGlm7www.themarshallproject.org./2015/03/04/how-to-cut-the-prison-population-by-50-percent#.KVWCPGlm7.

[15] "Obama Cuts Prison Time for 46: Change Urged in Sentencing of Nonviolent Drug Cases," Associated Press, July 14, 2015. www.journalgazette.net/news/us/Obama-cuts-prison-time-for-46-7714246.

[16] Ibid.

[17] Dan Pens, "Prison Realty/CCA Verges on Bankruptcy," Prison Legal News," July 15, 2000. www.prisonlegalnews.org/news/2000/jul/15/prison-realtycca/verges-on-bankruptcy.

[18] American Civil Liberties Union (ACLU),"Banking on Bondage: Private Prisons and Mass Incarceration," May 10, 2012. www.aclu.org/banking-bondage-private-prisons-and-mass-incarceration.

[19] Judith Green, "Banking on the Prison Boom," In Prison Profiteers: Who Makes Money from Mass Incarceration. Tara Herivel and Paul Wright, Eds. (New York: The New Press, 2005).

[20] Katy, Hall, "CCA Letters Reveal Private Prison Tactic," Huffington Post, April 11, 2013. Last modified March 7, 2014. www.huffingtonpost.com/2013/04/11/cca-prison-industry_n_3061115.html.

[21] Damascus Road Law Group, "What is the 'Three Strikes' Law in Colorado?,"August 2015. www.broadlaw.com/Blog/2015/August/what-is-the-Three-Strikes-law-in-Colorado-.asp.

[22] Dina Rasor, "America's Top Prison Corporation: A Study in Predatory Capitalism and Cronyism," May 3, 2012. www.truth-out.org/news/item/8875-corrections-corporation-of-america-a-study-in-predatory-capitalism-and-cronyism/tmpl=component&print=1.

[23] Elizabeth Marlow, and Catherine Chesla, "Prison Experiences and the Reintegration of Male Parolees," U.S. National Library of Medicine, National Institute of Health, June 2009. In Advanced Nursing Science 2009 April-June 32 (2). http://www.ncbi.nlm.nih.gov/pmc/articles/PMC2886197/ Retrieved March 12, 2016.

[24] Kevin E. Courtright, Michael J. Hannan, Susan H. Packard, and Edward T. Brennan. "Prisons and Rural Communities: Exploring Impact and Community Satisfaction." The Center for Rural Pennsylvania. May 2007. http://www.rural.palegislature.us/Prisons.pdf.

[25] "Corrections Corporation of America Salaries." www.glassdoor.com/Salary/Corrections-Corporation-of-America-Salaries-E6826.htm. Retrieved March 12, 2016.

[26] "Colorado Department of Corrections Salaries." www.glassdoor.com/Salary/Colorado-Department-of-Corrections-E42800.htm. Retrieved March 12, 2016.

[27] Private Corrections Institute, Inc., "Quick Facts About Prison Privatization." http://www.privateci.org/private_pics/Private percent20prison percent20fact percent20sheet percent202009.pdf. Retrieve March 10, 2016.

[28] Jesse Lava, and Sarah Solon, "The Biggest, Baddest Prison Profiteer of Them All," American Civil Liberties Union (ACLU), April 19, 2014. www.aclu.org/blog/biggest-baddest-prison-profiteer-them-all.

[29] Rebecca Boone, "Idaho Governor Orders Police to Investigate CCA Prison," Huffington Post, February 18, 2014. www.huffingtonpost.com/2014/02/18/butch-otter-CCA-prison_n_4812598.html.

[30] Jesse Lava, and Sarah Solon, "The Biggest, Baddest Prison Profiteer of Them All," American Civil Liberties Union (ACLU), April 19, 2014. www.aclu.org/blog/biggest-baddest-prison-profiteer-them-all.

[31] Piper Madison. "Meet The Private Prison Industry's Lobbyists Who Could Shape Immigration Reform," Grassroots Leadership, February 2013. www.grassrootsleadership.org/blog/2013/02/meet-private-prison-industry-s-lobbyists-who-could-shape-immigration-reform.

[32] Corrections Corporation of America "Investor Relations," Retrieved January 2, 2015. www.cca.com/investors/financial-information/annual-CCA 2014AR Final reports web.pdf.

[33] Ibid.

[34] Jesse Lava, and Sarah Solon. "The Biggest, Baddest Prison Profiteer of Them All," American Civil Liberties Union (ACLU), April 19, 2014. www.aclu.org/blog/biggest-baddest-prison-profiteer-them-all.

[35] Rebecca. Boone, "Private Prison Taken Over by State after Years of Horrifying Allegations," Huffington Post, January 3, 2014. www.huffingtonpost.com/2014/01/03/cca-taken-over_n_4537366.html.

[36] Rebecca Boone, "Idaho Governor Orders Police to Investigate CCA Prison," Huffington Post, February 18, 2014. www.huffingtonpost.com/2014/02/18/butch-otter-cca-prison_n_4812598.html.

[37] Rebecca Boone, "American Civil Liberties Union Suing Corrections Corp. of America," Associated Press, March 11, 2010. www.correctionsone.com/treatment/articles/2017869-ACLU-suing-Corrections-Corp-of-America.

[38] Charlie Litchfield, "Federal Judge Orders CCA to Pay Attorney Fees to American Civil Liberties Union," Idaho Press-Tribune, February 22, 2014. www.idahopress.com/news/state/federal-judge-orders-cca-to-pay-attorney-fees-to-aclu/article_d9cdcfd6-9b2c-11e3-9498-001a4bcf887a.html.

[39] Rebecca Boone, "Idaho Inmates Chain Gangs Run Prison," Associated Press, November 13, 2012. www.news.yahoo.com/apnewsbreak-idaho-inmates.claim-gangs-run-prison-082049301.html.

[40] Rebecca Boone, "Judge: CCA in Contempt for Prison Understaffing," Associated Press, September 16, 2013. www.finance.yahoo.com/news/judge-cca-contempt-prison-understaffing-19205490.html.

[41] Rebecca Boone, "Prison Company Leaving Idaho," Associated Press, October 3, 2013. www.finance.yahoo.com/news/ap-newsbreak-prison-company-ke-avubg-162639829,html.

[42] Chris Kirkham, "Lake Erie Prison Plagued by Violence and Drugs after Corporate Takeover," Huffington Post, March 22, 2013. www.huffingtonpost.com/2013/03/22/lake-erie-prison-violence_n_2925151.html .

[43] Colorado Department of Corrections, "Annual Report Concerning the Status of Private Contract Prisons," December 2015. Accessed March 10, 2016. http://www.doc.state.co.us/sites/default/files/opa/PPMU percent20Annual percent202013.pdf.

[44] Associated Press, "Yard Brawl Rages into Fiery Prison Riot in Colorado," July 21, 2004. www.usatoday30.usatoday.com/news/nation/2004-07-21-inmate-riot_x.html on November 15, 2015.

[45] U.S. Equal Employment Opportunity Commission. "Private Prison Pays $1.3 Million to Settle Sexual Harassment, Retaliation Claims for Class of Women," Press Release, October 13, 2009. www.eeoc.gov/eeoc/newsroom/release/10-13-09.cfm.

[46] Associated Press, "Yard Brawl Rages into Fiery Prison Riot in Colorado," July 21, 2004. www.usatoday30.usatoday.com/news/nations/2004-07-21-inmate-riot_x.htm.

[47] Ibid.

[48] Scott Harrison and Joe Dominguez, "Settlement Reached in 2004 Crowley County Prison Riot," KRDO, April 24, 2013. www.krdo.com/news/settlement-reached-in-2004-crowley-county-prison-riot/19878880.

[49] Ibid.

[50] Ibid.

[51] Alan Prendergast, "Crowley County Riot: New Details of Unheeded Warnings Emerge in Epic Lawsuit," Westword, December 21, 2011. www.westword.com/news/crowley-prison-riot-new-details-of-unheeded-warnings-emerge-in-epic-lawsuit-5863180.

[52] Ibid.

[53] Ibid.

## Chapter 6

[1] Chris. Kirkham. "Lake Erie Prison Plagued by Violence and Drugs After Corporate Takeover," Huffington Post, February 2, 2013. www.huffingtonpost.com/2013/03/22/lake-ere-prison-violence_n_2925151.html.

[2] "Family of a Second Hawaii Prisoner Murdered in Mainland Prison Files Suit Against State of Hawaii and Corrections Corporation of America," American Civil Liberties Union (ACLU), February 15, 2012.. www.aclu/org/news/family-hawaii-prisoner-murdered-in-mainland-prison-files-lawsuit-against-state-hawaii-corrections-corporation-America.

[3] Nina Bernstein, "Officials Hid Truths about Immigrant Deaths in Jail, New York Times, January 10, 2010. www.nytimes.com/2010/01/10/us/10detain.html.

⁴ Jula, Megan and Daniel Gonzalez, "Eloy Detention Center: Why so Many Suicides?," The Republic. July 29, 2015. http://www.azcentral.com/story/news/arizona/investigations/2015/07/28/eloy-detention-center-immigrant-suicides/30760545.

⁵ Holbrook Mohr, "Mississippi Prison Riot Started by Gang, Sheriff Says," Huffington Post, May 21, 2012. www.huffingtonpost.com/2012/05/21/mississippi-prison-riot_n_1533936.html.

⁶ Ibid.

⁷ "PLN Managing Editor Quoted Re CCA Annual Meeting and Death of CCA Employee," Clarion Ledger, January 1, 2013. http://www.clarionledger.com/20130517/N...

⁸ Ibid.

⁹ Ibid.

¹⁰ Ibid.

¹¹ Ibid.

¹² Holbrook Mohr, "Mississippi Prison Riot Started by Gang, Sheriff Says," Huffington Post, May 21, 2012. www.huffingtonpost.com/2012/05/21/mississippi-prison-riot_n_1533936.html.

¹³ Shane Bauer, "My Four months as a Private Prison Guard: A Mother Jones Investigation." June 30, 2016. http://www.motherearth.com/politics/2016/06/cca-private-prisons-corrections-corporation-inmates-investigation-bauer.

¹⁴ Ibid.

¹⁵ Ibid.

¹⁶ Scott Harrison and Jose Dominguez, "Settlement Reached in 2004 Crowley County Prison Riot," KRDO, April 24, 2013. http://www.krdo.com/news/settlement-reached-in-2004-crowley-county-prison-riot/19878880.

## Chapter 7

¹ Shane Bauer, "My Four months as a Private Prison Guard: A Mother Jones Investigation." June 30, 2016. http://www.motherearth.com/politics/2016/06/cca-private-prisons-corrections-corporation-inmates-investigation-bauer.

² Ann Imse, and Colorado Public News, "Colorado Paying Millions for Unneeded Private Prisons," KUNC, March 11, 2013. www.kunc.org/post/colorado-paying-millions-unneeded-private-prisons.

³ In the Public Interest, "Criminal: How Lockup Quotas and 'Low-Crime Taxes' Guarantee Profits for Private Prison Corporations," September 2013. www.inthepublicinterest.org/criminal-how-lockup-quotas-and-low-crime-taxes-guarantee-profits-for-private-prison-corporations.

⁴ Ibid.

⁵ Chris Kirkham, "Private Prison Corporation Offers Cash in Exchange for State Prisons," Huffington Post, February 14, 2012. www.huffingtonpost.com/2012/02/14/private-prisons-buying-state-prisons_n_1272143.

[6] In the Public Interest, "Criminal: How Lockup Quotas and 'Low-Crime Taxes' Guarantee Profits for Private Prison Corporations," September 2013. www. inthepublicinterest.org/criminal-how-lockup-quotas-and-low-crime-taxes-guarantee-profits-for-private-prison-corporations

[7] Ibid.

[8] Timothy R. Markham, "Imprisoned by Profit: Breaking Colorado's Dependency on For-Profit Prison," Colorado WINS. February 27, 2013. http://dailycaller. com/wp-content/uploads/2013/03/DOC+white+paper+ISSUU.pdf.

[9] Colorado Department of Corrections, "Annual Report Concerning the Status of Private Contract Prisons," December 2015. Accessed March 10, 2016. http://www.doc.state.co.us/sites/default/files/opa/PPMU    percent20Annual percent202013.pdf.

## Chapter 8

[1] Binder, Sue. *I'll Never Make Parole.* (March 2013). Available at Amazon.com for Kindle or Barnes and Noble for Nook or at Smashwords for other e-machines.

## Chapter 9

[1] ACA Statement on Accreditation. Retrieved on October 11, 2015. www.cca. com/ Media/Default/documents/Misc/ACA_Statement_on_Accreditation.pdfwww. cca. com/Media/Default/documents/Misc/ACA_Statement_on_Accreditation. pdf.

[2] Silja J. A. Talvi, "Inside the American Correctional Association," Prison Legal News, September 15, 2004, www.prisonlegalnews.org/news/2005/sep/15/ inside-the-american-corrections-association.

[3] American Correctional Association. "Our History." Retrieved on March 13, 2016. http://www.aca.org/ACA_Prod_IMIS/ACA_Member/About_Us/Our_History/ ACA_Member/AboutUs/AboutUs_Home.aspx?hkey=0c9cb058-e3d5-4bb0-ba7c-be29f9b34380.

[4] Ibid.

[5] "Our History: Hospital Corporation of America." Retrieved on October 4, 2015. . www.hcalhealthcare.com/about/our-history.dot6Ibid.

[7] Hutto v Finney, 437 U. A. 678 (1978). https://www.oyez.org/cases/1977/76-1660.

[8] Dana Priest, "Sheriff Gondles Settles Suit on Harassment for $25,000," The Washington Post, April, 28, 2001. www.highbeam.com/doc/1P2-1253519.html on October 4, 2015.

[9] Albert Samaha, "The Prison Reform Blues," December 5, 2014. http://www. buzzfeed.com/albertsamaha/the-rise-and-fall-of-mississippis-top-prison-reformer#.swnZQ2vVmhttp://www.buzzfeed.com/albertsamaha/the-rise-and-fall-of-mississippis-top-prison-reformer#.swnZQ2vVm.

[10] Elizabeth Alexander, "What's Wrong with ACA?" September 15, 2005. Prison Legal News, www.prisonlegalnews. org/search/?=What percent27s+wrong+with+acawww.prisonlegalnews. org/search/?=What percent27s+wrong+with+aca.

[11] Ibid.

[12] Ibid.

[13] Ibid.

[14] Ibid.

[15] Francie Latour, "Suffolk Jail Audit Group is Faulted: Critics to Demand New Review Panel," Boston Globe, June 20, 2001. www.prisonpolicy.org/scans/stoptheaca/stoptheaca062001/html.

[16] Elizabeth Alexander, "What's Wrong with ACA?" September 15, 2005. Prison Legal News, www.prisonlegalnews. org/search/?=What percent27s+wrong+with+acawww.prisonlegalnews. org/search/?=What percent27s+wrong+with+aca.

[17] Shane Bauer, "My Four months as a Private Prison Guard: A Mother Jones Investigation." June 30, 2016. http://www.motherearth.com/politics/2016/06/cca-private-prisons-corrections-corporation-inmates-investigation-bauer

[18] Ibid.

[19] Elizabeth Alexander, "What's Wrong with ACA?" September 15, 2005. Prison Legal News, www.prisonlegalnews. org/search/?=What percent27s+wrong+with+acawww.prisonlegalnews. org/search/?=What percent27s+wrong+with+aca.

[18] Ibid.

[19] Silja J. A. Talvi, "Inside the American Correctional Association," Prison Legal News, September 15, 2004, www.prisonlegalnews.org/news/2005/sep/15/inside-the-american-corrections-association

[20] Ibid.

[21] Ibid.

[22] Ibid.

[23] Ibid.

[24] Ibid.

[25] Ibid.

[26] Ibid.

[27] Ibid.

[28] Clif LeBlanc, "Prisons Might Lose Accreditation," April 14, 2003. www.prisonpolicy.org/scans/stoptheaca/thestate5628651.html.

[29] Ibid.

[30] ACA Statement on Accreditation. www.cca. com/Media/Default/documents/Misc/ACA_Statement_on_Accreditation.pdfwww.cca. com/Media/Default/documents/Misc/ACA_Statement_on_Accreditation.pdf .

[31] Silja J. A. Talvi, "Inside the American Correctional Association," Prison Legal News, September 15, 2004, www.prisonlegalnews.org/news/2005/sep/15/inside-the-american-corrections-association

## Chapter 10

[1] Detention Watch Network and the Center for Constitutional Rights. "Banking on Detention: Local Lockup Quotas and the Immigrant Dragnet," Detention Watch Network and the Center for Constitutional Rights. (2015). www.detentionwatchnetwork.org/sites/default/files/Banking_on_Detention_DWN.pdf.

[2] Dan Pens, "Prison Realty/CCA Verges on Bankruptcy," Prison Legal News, July 15, 2000. https://www.prisonlegalnews.org/news/2000/jul/15/prison-realtycca-verges-on-bankruptcy/.

[3] Public Law 108-458, Sec. 5204(a). "Intelligence Reform and Terrorism Prevention Act of 2004," December 17, 2004. https://www.nctc.gov/docs/pll08_458.pdf.

[4] Eric Lipton, "In Kentucky Hills, a Homeland Security Bonanza," New York Times, May 14, 2006. https://www.quiery.nytimes.com/gst/fullpage.html.

[5] "Department of Homeland Security Annual Report: Immigration Enforcement Actions: 2012," December 2013. https://dhs.gov/sites/default/files/publications/ois_enforcement_ar_2012_1.pdf.

[6] U.S. Immigration and Customs Enforcement, "DHS Releases End of Fiscal Year 2015 Statistics," December 22, 2015. https://www. ice. gov/news/releases/dhs-releases-end-fiscal-year-2015-statistics.

[7] Bethany Carson and Eleana Diaz. "Payoff: How Congress Ensures Private Prison Profit with an Immigrant Detention Quota," Grassroots Leadership, April 2015. http://grassrootsleadership. org/sites/default/files/reports/quota_report_final_digital.pdf http://grassrootsleadership. org/sites/default/files/reports/quota_report_final_digital.pdf

[8] "The Immigration Detention Transparency and Human Rights Project." National Immigrant Justice Center, August 2015.http://immigrantjustic.org/immigration-detention-transparency-and-human-rights-project-august-2015-report.

[9] Ibid.

[10] "Banking on Detention: Local Lockup Quotas & the Immigrant Dragnet," Detention Watch Network, 2015. www.detentionwatchnetwork.org/sites/default/files/Banking_on_Detention_DWN.pdf.

[11] "Immigration and Customs Enforcement," Detention Watch Network at Center for Constitutional Rights, November 2013. http://ccrjustice.org/bed-quota-foia.

[12] "Banking on Detention: Local Lockup Quotas & the Immigrant Dragnet," Ibid.

[13] Ibid.

[14] Ibid.

[15] "Immigrants Rights Project: Practice Advisory," American Civil Liberties Union (ACLU), February 23, 2015. http://www.aclu.org/sites/default/files/assets/rilr_advisory_final.pdf.

[16] Josh Gerstein, "Johnson: Feds Looking At Family Immigration Detention Changes," Politico, Under the Radar, August 4, 2016. http://www.politico.

com/blogs/under-the-radar/2016/08/johnson-dhs-looking-at-family-detention-changes-in-wake-of-court-ruling-226694#ixzz4LINxWd4z.

[17] Ibid.

[18] Ibid.

[19] John F Simanski and Lesley M. Sapp, "Immigration Enforcement Actions 2012, Department of Homeland Security Annual Report," December 2013. http://preview.dhs. gov/sites/default/files/publications/ois_enforcement_ar_2012_1.pdfhttp://preview.dhs. gov/sites/default/files/publications/ois_enforcement_ar_2012_1.pdf.

[20] Alistair Graham Robertson, Rachel Beaty, Jane Atkinson, and Bob Libal. "Operation Streamline: Costs and Consequences," Grassroots Leadership, September 2012. http://grassrootsleadership. org/sites/default/files/uploads/GRL_Sept2012_Report-finalpdf.

[21] Ibid.

[22] Associated Press, "Private prisons profit from illegal immigrants," Associated Press, August 2, 2012. http://www.cbsnews.com/8301-201_162-57485392/ap-private-prisons-profit-from-illegal-immigrants/?pageNum=2.

[23] Piper Madison, "Meet the Private Prison Industry's Lobbyists Who Could Shape Immigration Reform," Grassroots Leadership, February 6, 2013. http://grassrootsleadership.org/blog/2013/02/meet-the-private-prison-industry's-lobbyists-who-could-shape-immigration-reform.

[24] Ibid.

[25] "Donald Trump Doubles Down on Mexican Immigrant Remarks," CBS/AP, July 6, 2015. www.cbsnews.com/news/election-2016-donald-trump-doubles-down-on-Mexican-immigrant-remarks.

[26] Madison Pauly, "The Private Prison Industry is Licking Its Chops Over Trump's Deportation Plans," Mother Jones, February 21, 2017. http://www.motherjones.com/politics/2017/02/trumps-immigration-detention-center-expansion[26].

[27] Ibid.

[28] Ibid.

[29] Ibid.

[30] "ACLU of Texas Sues ICE Officials, Williamson County and CCA for Sexual Assault of Immigrant Women," American Civil Liberties Union (ACLU), October 19, 2011. http://www.aclutx. org/2011/10/19/aclu-of-texas-sues-ice-officials-williamson-county-and-cca-for-sexual-assault0of-immigrant-womenhttp://www.aclutx.

[31] Ibid.

[32] Ibid.

[33] Harrison Jacobs, "Why Minorities Are Even More Overrepresented in Private Prisons," Business Insider, February 15, 2014. http://www.businessinsider.com/christopher-petrella-private-prison-study-2014-2.

[34] David Hudson, "President Obama: 'Our Criminal Justice System Isn't as Smart as It Should Be,'" Coverage of Speech of NAACP's 106th national convention,

July 15, 2015. http://www. whitehouse.gov/blog/2015/7/15/president-obama-our-criminal-justice-system-isnt-smart-it-should-be

[35] Christopher Petrella, "The Color of Radical Criminology, Part II: Contractual Exemptions and the Overrepresentation of People of Color in Private Prisons." Journal of Radical Criminology 3, (January 2014). http://journal. radicalcriminology. org/index. php/rc/article/view/44/

[36] Ibid.

[37] "At America's Expense: The Mass Incarceration of the Elderly, American Civil Liberties (ACLU), June 2012. http://www.aclu.org/files/assets/elderlyprisonreport_20120613_1.pdf.

[38] Harrison Jacobs, "Why Minorities are Even More Overrepresented in Private Prisons," Business Insider, February 15, 2014. www.businessinsider.com/christopher-petrella-private-prison-study-2014-2.

[39] Ibid.

[40] Beau Hodai, "Corporate Con Game: How the Private Prison Industry Helped Shape Arizona's Anti-Immigrant Laws," In These Times, June 21, 2010. http://inthesetimes.com/article/6084/corporate_con_game.

[41] Ibid.

[42] Ibid.

[43] Ibid.

[44] Ibid.

[45] Ibid.

## Chapter 11

[1] Associated Press. "Yard Brawl Rages into Fiery Prison Riot in Colorado," USA Today, July 21, 2004. www.usatoday30.usatoday.com/news/nations/2004-07-21-inmate-riot_x. htm.

## Chapter 12

[1] Mike McGraw, "Private Prison Firm to Give Back Pay to Guards," Kansas City Star, September 1, 2009. www.donelonpc.com/pdfs/Private_prison_firm_to_give_back_pay_to_guards.pdf .

[2] Ibid.

[3] CCA has history of wage violations, poor treatment of employees," Human Rights Defense Center, August 22, 2014. www.humanrightscenter.org/action/news/2014/cca-has-history-wage-violations-poor-treatment-employees.

[4] Ibid.

[5] Ibid.

## Chapter 13

[1] Ruiz v. Estelle, 503 F. Supp 1265 (S. D. Tx. 1980). https://tarlton.law.utexas. edu/exhibits/wwjustice/documents-3/Ruiz_opinion_1_1980.pdfhttps://tarlton. law.utexas. edu/exhibits/wwjustice/documents-3/Ruiz_opinion_1_1980.pdf.

[2] Elaine Hirsch,"ACLU Files New Lawsuit Against CCA," November 30, 2011. http://whyihatecca.blogspot. com/2011/11/aclu-files-new-lawsuit-against-cca.htmlhttp://whyihatecca.blogspot. com/2011/11/aclu-files-new-lawsuit-against-cca.html.

## Chapter 14  No Endnotes.

## Chapter 15

[1] Chris Kirkham,"With States Facing Shortfalls, Private Corporation Offers Cash for Prisons," Huffington Post, February 14, 2012. http://www.huffingtonpost. com/2012/02/14/private- prisons-buying-state-prisons_n_1272143.html.

[2] Eoghan Keenan, "Case Profile. In Re: Northeast Ohio Correctional Center," June 10, 2005. www.clearinghouse.net/detail.php?id=901&search.

[3] Grassroots Leadership. "The Dirty Thirty: Nothing to Celebrate About 30 Years of Corrections Corporation of America. Subsection: Mismanagement and Violence at the Kit Carson Correctional Facility," Grassroots Leadership, Accessed on January 11, 2016. http://grassrootsleadership.org/cca-dirty-30#25http://grassrootsleadership.org/cca-dirty-30#25.

[4] Bob Libal, "Victory in Texas--the Dawson State Jail Will Close!" Grassroots Leadership, June 11, 2013, www.grassrootsleadership.org/blog/2013/06/victory-texas-dawson-state-jail-will-close.

[5] Ginger Allen, "Another Family Blames Dawson State Jail for Inmate Death," CBS, June 14, 2012, http://dfw.cbslocal.com/2012/06/14/another-family-blames-dawson-state-jail-for-inmate-death.

[6] Ginger Allen, "CBS 11 Investigates: Woman Dies After Being Held Sick at Dawson State Jail for Days," November 30, 2012. http://dfw.cbslocal. com/2012/11/30/cbs-11-investigates-woman-dies-after-being-held-sick-at-dawson-state-jail-for-days.

[7] Ginger Allen, "Mysterious Jail Death Raises Question," CBS, April 26, 2012. http://cbslocal.com/2012/04/26/mysterious-jail-death-raises-questions.

[8] Emily DePrang, "Death at Dawson: Why Is Texas' Worst State Jail Still Open?" Texas Observer, February 26, 2013. www.texasobserver.org/death-at-dawson-why-is-texas-worst-state-jail-still-open.

[9] Ibid.

## Chapter 16

[1] "CCA has History of Wage Violations, Poor Treatment of Employees," Human Rights Defense Center, August 22, 2014. www.humanrightscenter.org/action/news/2014/cca-has-history-wage-violations-poor-treatment-employees.

[2] Shane Bauer, "My Four months as a Private Prison Guard: A Mother Jones Investigation." June 30, 2016. http://www.motherearth.com/politics/2016/06/cca-private-prisons-corrections-corporation-inmates-investigation-bauer.

[3] Ibid.

[4] Ibid.

[5] Ibid.

## Chapter 17

[1] "What are the Characteristics of an Effective Counselor?," Career Igniter. www.careerigniter.com/questions/what-are-the-characteristics-of-an-effective-counselor/.

[2] Ibid.

## Chapter 18

[1] Molly Jackson, "Bernie Sanders on Private Prisons: 'Justice Is Not for Sale'," Christian Science Monitor, September 17, 2015. https://www.questia.com/newspaper/1P2-38751912/bernie-sanders-on-private-prisons-justice-is-not

[2] Ibid.

[3] Congress. Gov. S.2054-Justice is Not for Sale Act of 2015. http://www.sanders.senate.gov/download/justice-is-not-for-sale-act?inline=file.

[4] Congress. Gov. S.2054-Justice is Not for Sale Act of 2015. www.congress.gov/bill/114th-congress/senate-bill/2054/titles.

[5] Elise Foley, "Hillary Clinton Says She'll End Private Prisons, Stop Accepting Their Money," Huffington Post, October 23, 2015. www.huffingtonpost.com/hillary-clinton-private-prisons_562a3e3ee4b0ec0a389418ed.

[6] Atkins, C.J. "Obama Administration to End Prisons-for-Profits Contracts," People's World, August 18, 2016. http://peoplesworld.org/obama-administrations-to-end-prisons-for-profits-contracts/

[7] "Denver Reception and Diagnostic Center," Prison Path. http://www.prisonpath.com/state_doc/denver-reception-diagnostic-center/.

## Chapter 19 No Endnotes.

## Chapter 20

[1] Atkins, C. J. "Obama Administration to End Prisons-for-Profits Contracts," People's World, August 18, 2016. http://peoplesworld.org/obama-administrations-to-end-prisons-for-profits-contracts/

[2] Ibid.

[3] Ibid.

[4] Ibid.

[5] "Obama Administration to End Use of Private Prisons," Fox News, August 18, 2016. http://www.foxnews.com/politics/2016/08/18/obama-administration-to-end-use-private-prisons.html.

[6] Ibid.

[7] Barnett, Devlin and Austen Hufford. "GEO: Justice Department Says It Will Stop Using Private Prisons," August 18, 2016. http:www.4-traders.com/THE-GEO-GROUP-INC-16970422/news/GEO-Justice-Department-Says-It-Will-Stop-Using-Private-Prisons-229224061/

[8] Ibid.

[9] Ibid.

[10] Ibid.

[11] Ibid.

[12] Lills, Mike, "Sanders, Liberals Press Obama to Expand Closure of Private Prisons," August 18, 2016. http://thehill.com/homenews/administration/291925-sanders-liberals-press-obama-to-expand-closure-of-private-prisons.

[13] Ibid.

[14] Ibid.

[15] Wilber, Del Quentin, "Justice Department Rescinds Order Phasing Out Use of Private Prisons, LA Times, February 23, 2017. www.latimes.com/politics/washington/la-na-essential-washington-updates-justice-department-rescinds-order-1487893081-htmlstory.html[15]

[16] Market Watch News, "Private Prison Stocks Jump After Trump Official Says Feds Will Continue Using Facilities," February 23, 2017. http://www.marketwatch.com/investing/stock/CXW?countrycode=US

[17] Harlan, Chico, "$1 Billion, But Holds Few Immigrants," Washington Post, August 15, 2016. https://www.washingtonpost.com/business/economy/inside-the-administrations-1-billion-deal-to-detain-central-american-asylum-seekers/2016/08/14/e47f1960-5819-11e6-9aee-8075993d73a2_story.html.

[16] Ibid.

[17] Ibid.

[18] Ibid.

[19] Ibid.

[20] Ibid.

[21] Ibid.

[22] Josh Gerstein, "Johnson: Feds Looking At Family Immigration Detention Changes," Politico, Under the Radar, August 4, 2016. http://www.politico.com/blogs/under-the-radar/2016/08/johnson-dhs-looking-at-family-detention-changes-in-wake-of-court-ruling-226694#ixzz4LINxWd4zhttp://www.politico.com/blogs/under-the-radar/2016/08/johnson-dhs-looking-at-family-detention-changes-in-wake-of-court-ruling-226694#ixzz4LINxWd4z.

[25] Woodruff, Betsy. "Private Prisons Cheer Trump's Immigration Crackdown," The Daily Beast, January 25, 2017. http://www.thedailybeast.com/articles/2017/01/25/private-prisons-cheer-trump-s-immigration-crackdown.html[23]GlobeNewswire.

[26] Ibid.

[27] Pauly, Madison, "The Private Prison Industry is Liking Its Chops Over Trump's Deportation Plans," Mother Jones, February 21, 2017. http://www.motherjones.com/politics/2017/02/trumps-immigration-detention-center-expansion.

[28] Ibid.

[29] Ibid.

[30] Ibid.

[31] GlobeNewswire, "Corrections Corporation of America Rebrands as CoreCivic," October 28, 2016. http://www.einnews.com/pr_news/351464751/corrections-corporation-of-american-rebrands-as-CoreCivic.

[24] Ibid.

[25] Ibid.

# REFERENCES

Alexander, Elizabeth. "What's wrong with ACA?." *Prison Legal News.* 2005. Accessed October 14, 2015. www.prisonlegalnews.org/search/?=What percent27s+wrong+with+aca.

Alexander, Rachel. "Department of Corrections Explains Closing CSP II." *Canon City Daily Record.* March 21, 2012.

Allen, Ginger. "Mysterious jail death raises question." CBS. (April 26, 2012a.). Accessed January 12, 2016. http://cbslocal.com/2012/04/26/mysterious-jail-death-raises-questions.

___. "Another family blames Dawson State for inmate death." CBS. (June 14, 2012b). Accessed January 12, 2016. http://dfw.cbslocal.com/2012/06/14/another-family-blames-dawson-state-jail-for-inmate-death.

___. "CBS 11 Investigates, Woman Dies After Being Held Sick at Dawson State Jail for Days." CBS. (November 30, 2012c.). Accessed January 12, 2016. http://dfw.cbslocal.com/2012/11/30/cbs-11-investigates-woman-dies-after-being-held-sick-at-dawson-state-jail-dor-days.

American Civil Liberties Union (ACLU). "ACLU of Texas Sues ICE Officials, Williamson County and CCA for Sexual Assault Of Immigrant Women." (October 19, 2011). Accessed January 30, 2016. http://www,aclux.org/2011/10/19/aclu-of-texas-sues-ice-officials-williamson-county-and-cca-for-sexual-assault-of-immigrant-women.

___. "At America's Expense: The Mass Incarceration of the Elderly." (June 2012). Accessed January 30, 2015. http://www.aclu.org/files/assets/elderlyprisonreport_20120613_1.pdf.

___. 2013. "Family of a second Hawaii prisoner murdered in mainland prison files suit against State of Hawaii and Corrections Corporation of America." (May 23). Accessed November 15, 2015. www.aclu/org/news/family-hawaii-prisoner-murdered-in-mainland-prison-files-lawsuit-against-state-hawaii-corrections-corporation-America.

___. "Banking on Bondage: Private Prisons and Mass Incarceration." (2015a) Accessed November 14, 2015. www.aclu.org/banking-bondage-private-prisons-and-mass-incarceration.

___. "Immigrants Rights Project: Practice Advisory." (February 23, 2015b.). Accessed January 10, 2016. http://www.aclu.org/sites/degault/files/assets/rilr_advisory_final.pdf.

American Correctional Association. "ACA statement on accreditation." (2015). Accessed October 11, 2015. www.cca.com/Media/Default/documents/Misc?ACA_Statement_on_Accreditation.pdf.

American Psychiatric Association. "Position Paper on Segregation of Prisoners with Mental Illness." Last modified April, 2013. Accessed January 2, 2016. www.dhcs.ca.gov/services/MH/Documents/2013_04_AC_06c_APA_ps2012.

Ashton, Paul. "Gaming the System: How the Political Strategies of Private Prison Companies Promote Ineffective Incarceration Policies." *Justice Policy Institute.* (June 22, 2011). Accessed December 26, 2015. www.justicpolicy.org/research/2614.

Associated Press. "Yard brawl rages into fiery prison riot in Colorado." *USA Today.* (July 21, 2004). Accessed November 15, 2015. www.usatoday30.usatoday.comnews/nations/2004-07-21-inmate-riot_x.html.

___. "Private Prisons Profit from Illegal Immigrants." CBS News. (August 2, 2012). Accessed January 29, 2016. http://www.cbsnews.com/8301-201_162-57485392/ap-private-prisons-profit-from-illegal-immigrants/?pageNum-2.

___. "Idaho to Take Over Privately Run State Prison." *USA Today.* (January 3, 2014). Retrieved February 26, 2016. http://www.usatoday.com/story/news/nation/2014/01/03/idaho-prison/4304689/.

___. "Obama Cuts Prison Time for 46: Change Urged In Sentencing of Nonviolent Drug Cases." *Journal Gazette.* (July 14, 2015a). Accessed January 1, 2016. www.journalgazette. net/news/us/Obama-cuts-prison-time-for-46-7714246www.journalgazette. net/news/us/Obama-cuts-prison-time-for-46-7714246.

___. "Donald Trump Doubles Down on Mexican Immigrant Remarks." CBS News. (July 6, 2015b). Accessed January 21, 2016. www.cbsnews.com/news/election-2016-donald-trump-doubles-down-on-Mexican-immigrant-remarks.

Atkins, C.J. "Obama Administration to End Prisons-for-Profits Contracts." *People's World.* (August 18, 2016). Accessed August 19, 2016. http://peoplesworld.org/obama-administration-to-end-prions-for-profits-contract/.

Aulderheide, Dean H. and Patrick H. Brown. "Crises in Corrections: The Mentally Ill in American's Prisons." *Corrections Today* (February 2005): 67, 2, 30-33.

Ban, Thomas. "Fifty Years Chlorpromazine: A Historical Perspective." *Neuropsychiatric Disease and Treatment* 3 No. 4 (2007):495-500.

Barnett, Devlin and Austen Hufford. "GEO: Justice Department Says It Will Stop Using Private Prisons." (August 18, 2016). Accessed August 18, 2016. . http:www.4-traders.com/THE-GEO-GROUP-INC-16970422/news/GEO-Justice-Department-Says-It-Will-Stop-Using-Private-Prisons-229224061/

Bauer, Shane. "My Four Months as a Private Prison Guard: A Mother Jones Investigation." (June 23, 2016). Accessed July 9, 2016. http://www.motherjones.com/politics/2016/06/cca-private-prisons-corrections-corporation-inmates-investigation-bauer.

Bernstein, Nina. "Officials Hid Truths about Immigrant Deaths in Jail." *New York Times.* (January 10, 2010). Accessed November 15, 2015. www.nytimes.com/2010/01/10/us/10detain.html.

Binder, Sue. *Hands Down: A Domestic Violence Treatment Workbook.* 2007.Annapolis, Maryland. American Correctional Association.

____. *I'll Never Make Parole.* (March 2013). Available at Amazon.com for Kindle or Barnes and Noble for Nook or Smashwords.com.

____. "Foxholes." *Meltdown (October 2011).* Available at Amazon.com for Kindle or Smashwords.com.

Blasius, Melissa. "Most Colorado Sex Offenders Don't Get Treated in Prison." *KUSA News Broadcast.* (May 6, 2014). Accessed December 5, 2015. http://www.9news.    com/story/news/local/investigations/2014/05/06/most-Colorado-sex-offenders-don't-get-treatment-in-prison/8753419http://www.9news.    com/story/news/local/investigations/2014/05/06/most-Colorado-sex-offenders-don't-get-treatment-in-prison/8753419

Boone, Rebecca. "American Civil Liberties Union Suing Corrections Corp. of America." (March 11, 2010.). CorrectionsOne.com. Accessed December 10, 2015. www.correctionsone.com/treatment/articles/2017869-ACLU-suing-Corrections-Corp-of-America.

____ "Idaho Inmates Chain Gangs Run Prison." Associated Press. (November 13, 2012). Accessed November 10, 2015. www.news.yahoo.com/apnewsbreak-idaho-inmates.claim-gangs-run-prison-understaffing-19205490.html.

___ "Judge: CCA in Contempt for Prison Understaffing." Associated Press. (September 16, 2013a). Accessed November 10, 2015. www.finance.yahoo. com/news/judge-cca-contempt-prison-understaffing-19205490.html.

___ "Prison Company Leaving Idaho." Associated Press. (October 3, 2013b). Accessed November 10, 2015. www.finance.yahoo.com/news/ap-newsbreak-prison-company-leaving-162639829.html.

___. "Private Prison Taken Over by State after Years of Horrifying Allegations." *Huffington Post.* (January 3, 2014a). Accessed November 15, 2014. www. huffingtonpost.com/2014/01/03/cca-taken-over_n_4537366.html.

___. "Idaho Governor Orders Police to Investigate CCA Prison." *Huffington Post.* (February 18, 2014b). Accessed January 2, 2016. www.huffingtonpost. com/2014/02/18/butch-otter-CCA-prison_n_4812598.html.

Brown, Jennifer and Kirk Mitchell. "Kit Carson Prison in Burlington to Close: 142 Jobs Lost." *Denver Post.* (June 30, 2016). Accessed July 5, 2016. http:// www.denverpost.com/2016/06/30/kit-carson-burlington-prison-closing/

Bureau of Justice Statistics. "Prisoners in 2014. Bureau of Justice Statistics Summary." September 2015," NCJ: 218955. Bureau of Justice Statistics. www.bjs.gov/content/pub/pdf/p14_summary.pdf .

Byron, Robert. "Criminals Need Mental Health Care," *Scientific American MIND.* March 1, 2014. http://www.scientificamerican.com/article/criminals-need-mental-health-care//.

Career Igniter. 2016. "What are the Characteristics of an Effective Counselor?" Accessed January 16, 2016. www.careerigniter.com/questions/what-are-the-characteristics-of-an-effective-counselor.

Carson, Bethany and Eleana Diaz. "Payoff: How Congress Ensures Private Prison Profit with an Immigrant Detention Quota." *Grassroots Leadership.* (April 2015.). Accessed January 21, 2016. http://grassrootsleadership.org/ sites/default/files/reports/quota_report_final_digital.pdf.

City of Las Animas, Colorado website. City Data. Accessed September 15, 2015. www.city-data. com/city/Las-Animas-Coloradowww.city-data. com/ city/Las-Animas-Colorado.

Clarion Ledger. "PLN Managing Editor Quoted Re CCA Annual Meeting and Death of CCA Employee" January 1, 2013. http://www.clarionledger.com/ article/20130517/

Clear, Todd R. *Imprisoning Communities: How Mass Incarceration Makes Disadvantaged Neighborhood Worse: Studies in Crime and Public Policy.* Oxford: Oxford University Press. 2007.

Clear, Todd R. and Natasha A. Frost. *The Punishment Imperative: The Rise and Failure of Mass Incarceration in America.* New York: New York University Press. 2013.

CNBC. *Billions Behind Bars: Inside America's Prison Industry.* www.cnbc.com

Colorado Department of Corrections. *Annual Report Concerning the Status of Private Contract Prisons.* Accessed March 10, 2016. http://www.doc.state. co.us/sites/default/files/opa/PPMU percent20Annual percent202013.pdf.

Colorado Department of Corrections. *Bent County History.* Accessed September 15, 2015. www.doc.state.co.us/facility/bccf-bent.

___. *Open the Door—Segregation Reforms in Colorado.* https://www.colorado.gov/.../ open-door-segregation-reforms-colorado. Accessed March 1, 2016.

"Colorado Department of Corrections Salaries." Accessed March 12, 2016. www. glassdoor.com/Salary/Colorado-Department-of-Corrections-E42800.

Colorado WINS. "Imprisoned by Profit: Breaking Colorado's Dependency on For-Profit Prisons." (February 27, 2013). Accessed November 18, 2015. www.coloradowins.org/2013/02/27/imprisoned-by-profit-breaking-Colorados-dependency-on-for-profit-prisons.

"Corrections Corporation of America Salaries." Accessed March 12, 2016. www.glassdoor.com/Salary/Corrections-Corporation-of-American-Salaries-E6826.htm.

Corrections Corporation of America. "CCA Named One of the 100 Best Corporate Citizens in the U.S." (March 3, 2008). Accessed November 15, 2015. www. Reuters.com/article/idUS230450+03-Mar-2008+MW20080303.

___. "CCA Names Top Military Friendly Employer." (November 9, 2011). Accessed November 15, 2015. www.cca.com/press-releases/cca-named-top-military-friendly-employer

___. "Forbes Magazine Names CCA's Damon Hininger as one of Nation's Top 20 CEOs." (February. 24,

2011). Accessed November 15, 2015. www.correctionscorp.com/newsroom/ news-releases/42.

___. "The CCA Story: Our Company History." (2015a). Accessed September 15, 2015. www.cca.com/about/cca-history. .

___. "Investor Relations," Accessed January 2, 2015.

www.cca.com/investors/financial- information/annual-CCA 2014AR Final reports web.pdf.

___. Bent County Correctional History. (2015c). Accessed December 26, 2015. Retrieved from

www.cca.com/facilities/bent-bounty-correctional-facility

"Corrections Corporation of America Compensation: Corrections Corporation of America CXW." . *Morningstar.* (2015). Accessed December 9, 2015. www. insiders.morningstar.com/trading/executive-compensation.action?t_cwx.

Council of State Governments. . "Criminal Justice/Mental Health Consensus Project." (June 2002). Accessed October 24, 2015. http://www.consensusproject.org.

Courtright, Kevin E., Michael J. Hannon, Susan H. Packard, and Edward T. Brennan. *Prisons and Rural Communities: Exploring Impact and Community Satisfaction.* (May 2007). Edinboro: University of Pennsylvania. Accessed www.rural.palegislature.us/Prisons.pdf.

CXW Income. "CXW Annual Income Statement: Market Watch website. 2015. Accessed December 26, 2015. www.marketwatch.com/investing/stock/CXW/financials.

Damascus Road Law Group. "What is the 'Three Strikes' Law in Colorado?" (August 2015). Accessed January 2, 2016. www.broadlaw.com/Blog/2015/August/what-is-the-Three-Strikes-law-in-Colorado.

DeMoss, Dustin. "The Nightmare of Prisons for Individuals with Mental Illness." *Huffington Post.* (March 25, 2015). Accessed December 17, 2015. www.huffingtonpost.com/dustin-demoss/prison-mental-illness-b_6867988.html

Denver Reception and Diagnostic Center. *Prison Path.* (2016). Accessed February 2, 2016. www.prisonpath. com/state_doc/denver-reception-diagnosicwww.prisonpath. com/state_doc/denver-reception-diagnosic.

DePrang, Emily. "Death at Dawson: Why is Texas' Worst State Jail Still Open?" *Texas Observer.* (February 26, 2013). Accessed January 12, 2016. www.texasobserver.org/death-at-dawson-why-is-texass-worst-state-jail-still-open.

Detention Watch Network. "Immigration and Customs Enforcement." (November 2013). Accessed January 21, 2016. http://ccrjustic.org/bd-quota-foia.

__. "Banking on Detention: Local Lockup Quotas & the Immigrant Dragnet." (2015). Accessed January 27, 2016. www.detentionwatchnetwork.org/sites/default/files/Banking_on_Detention_DWN. pdf.

Ditton, Paula M. and Doris James Wilson. "Truth in Sentencing in State Prisons." *Bureau of Justice Special Report.* (January 10, 1999). Accessed December 29, 2015. www.bjs. gov/xonrwnr/puv/pewaa/raap.pewww.bjs.gov/xonrwnr/puv/pewaa/raap.pe.

Dolovich, Sharon. "Cruelty, Prison Conditions and the Eighth Amendment." *New York University Law Review* 84, No. 4 (October 2009.): 881. Accessed November 1, 2015. www.law.georgetown. ed/cgi/viewcontent.cgi?article=1020&Fac. publwww.law.georgetown. ed/cgi/viewcontent.cgi?article=1020&Fac. publ.

Drucker, Ernest. 2011. *A Plague of Prisons: The Epidemiology of Mass Incarceration in America.* New York: The New Press.

Dyer, Joel. *The Perpetual Prisoner Machine: How America Profits from Crime.* Boulder: Westview Press. 2000.

Fang, Lee. "How Private Prisons Game the Immigration System." *The Nation.* (February 27, 2013.). Accessed December 27, 2015. www.thenation.com/ article/how-private-prisons-game-immigration-system.

Fellner, Jamie. "A Correctional Quandry: Mental Illness and Prison Roles." *Harvard Civil Rights-Civil Liberties Law Review,* 4 (2006):391. Accessed November 1, 2015. www.law.harvard. ed/students/orgs/crd/vol41_2/ fellner.pdfwww.law.harvard. ed/students/orgs/crd/vol41_2/fellner.pdf.

Foley, Elise. "Hillary Clinton Says She'll End Private Prisons, Stop Accepting Their Money." *Huffington Post.* (October 23, 2015). Accessed December 12, 2015. www.huffingtonpost.com/hillary-clinton-private-prisons-562a3e3ee4b0ec0389418ed.

Fox News. "Obama Administration to End Use of Private Prisons." (August 18, 2016). Accessed August 20, 2016. http://www.foxnews.com/ politics/2016/08/18/obama-administration-to-end-use-private-prisons. html.

Gerstein, Josh. "Johnson: Feds Looking at Family Immigration Detention Changes." *Politico, Under the Radar.* (August 4, 2016). Accessed October 1, 2016. http://www.politico.com/blogs/under-the-radar-2016/08/johnson-dhs-looking-at-family-detention-changes-in-wake-of-court-ruling-226694#ixzz4LINxWD4Zhttp://www.politico.com/blogs/under-the-radar-2016/08/johnson-dhs-looking-at-family-detention-changes-in-wake-of-court-ruling-226694#ixzz4LINxWD4Z.

GlobeNewswire."Corrections Corporation of America Rebrands as CoreCivic." (October 28, 2016). Accessed November 4, 2016. http://www.einnews. com/pr_news/351464751/correcitons-corporation-of-american-rebrands-as-corecivic.

Goldstein, Dana. "How to Cut the Prison Population by 50 Percent." *The Marshall Project.* (2015). Accessed December 31, 2015. www.themarshallproject. org/2015/03/04/how-to-cut-the-prison-population-by-50-percent@. KVWCPGlm7.

Grassroots Leadership. "The Dirty Thirty: Nothing to Celebrate About 30 Years of Corrections Corporation of America." Subsection: "Mismanagement and Violence at the Kit Carson Correctional Facility." (2016). Accessed January 11, 2016. www.grassrootsleadership.org/cca-dirty-30.

Green, Judith. "Banking on the Prison Boom." In *Prison Profiteers: Who Makes Money from Mass Incarceration.* Tara Herivel and Paul Wright, eds. New York: The New Press. 2005.

Hall, Katy. "CCA Letters Reveal Private Prison Tactics." *Huffington Post.* (April 11, 2013). Updated March 7, 2014. Accessed December 15, 2015. www. huffingtonpost.com/2013/04/11/cca-prison-industry_n_306115.html.

Harlan, Chico. "$1 Billion, But Holds Few Immigrants." *Washington Post.* (August 15, 2016). Accessed August 19, 2016. https://www.washingtonpost.com/business/economy/inside-the-administrations-1-billion-deal-to-detain-central-american-asylum-seekers/2016/08/14/e47f1960-5819-11e6-9aee-8075993d73a2_story.html.

Harmon, Tracy. "Report: Less Segregation Working Well." *Pueblo Chieftain and Star Journal,* December 27, 2015. http://www.chieftain.com/news/region/4263220-120/report-inmates-prisons-colorado

Harris, Craig. "Arizona Cuts Ties with Private Prison Operator over Kingman Riot." *Arizona Republic.* (August 27, 2015). Accessed December 12, 2015. http://www. azcentral. com/story/news/arizona/politics.

Harrison, Scott and Joe Dominguez."Settlement Reached in 2004 Crowley County Prison Riot." KRDO News. (April 24, 2013). Accessed October 30, 2015. www.krdo.com/news/settlement-reached-in-2004-crowley-county-prison-riot.

Herivel, Tara and Paul Wright.. *Prison Profiteers: Who Makes Money from Mass Incarceration.* New York: The New Press. 2007

Herivel, Tara and Paul Wright, eds. *Prison Nation: The Warehousing of American's Poor.* New York: Routledge Press. 2003.

HIPPA Privacy. "What Does HIPPA Stand For?" (2015). Accessed December 26, 2015. www. hipaaoralprivacy.com/hipaa.html.

Hirsch, Elaine. "ACLU Files New Lawsuit Against CCA." (November 30, 2011). Accessed January 13, 2016. http://whyihatecca.blogspot.com/2011/11/aclu-files-new-lawsuit-against-cca.html.

Hodai, Beau. "Corporate Con Game: How the Private Prison Industry Helped Shape Arizona's Anti-Immigrant Laws." *In These Times.* (June 21, 2010). Accessed December 26, 2015. www.inthesetimes.com/article/6084/corporate_con_game.

Hospital Corporation of America. "Our History." (2015). Accessed October 4, 2015.www. hcahealthcare. com/about/our-history.dot.

Hudson, David. "President Obama: Our Criminal Justice System Isn't as Smart as It Should Be." Coverage of Speech of NAACP's 106th National Convention. (July 15, 2015.). Accessed February 4, 2015.

https://www.whitehouse.gov/blog/2015/07/15/president-obama-our-criminal-justice-system-isnt-smart-it-should-be.

Human Rights Defense Center. "CCA has History of Wage Violations, Poor Treatment of Employees." (August 22, 2014). www.humanrightscenter.

org/actions/news/2014/cca-has-history-wage-violations-poor-treatment-employees.

Human Rights Watch. "Ill Equipped: U.S. Prisons and Offenders with Mental Illness." (2003). Accessed December 15, 2015. http://www.hrw.org/reports/2003/usal003.

___ . "U.S. Number of Mentally Ill Prisons Quadrupled." (September 2006.). Accessed December 16, 2015. http://www.org.news/2006/09/05/us-number-mentally-ill-quadupled

Imse, Ann and Colorado Public News. "Colorado Paying Millions for Unneeded Private Prisons." KUNC website (March 11, 2013). Accessed September 15, 2015. www.kunch.org/post/colorado-paying-millions-unneeded-private-prisons#stream/0www.kunch.org/post/colorado-paying-millions-unneeded-private-prisons#stream/0.

In the Public Interest. "Criminal: How Lockup Quotas and 'Low-Crime Taxes' Guarantee Profits for Private Prison Corporations." (September 2013). Accessed November 19, 2015. www. inthepublicinterest.org/criminal-how-lockup-quotas-and-low-crime-taxes-guarantee-profits-for-private-prison-corporations.

Jackson, Molly. "Bernie Sanders on private prisons: 'Justice is not for sale'." *Christian Science Monitor.* (September 17, 2015). Accessed December 15, 2015. http://www.csmonitor. con/USA/Justic/2015/0917;Bernie-Sanders-on-private-prisons-Justic-is-not-for-sale-videohttp://www.csmonitor. con/USA/Justic/2015/0917;Bernie-Sanders-on-private-prisons-Justic-is-not-for-sale-video.

Jacobs, Harrison. "Why Minorities Are Even More Overrepresented in Private Prisons." *Business Insider.* (February 15, 2014). Accessed January 30, 2016. www.businessinsider.com/christopher-poetrella-private-prison-study-2014-2.

Joad, Gary. "The Health Care Crises in the U.S. Prison System." *Internet Committee of the 4th International (ICFI).* (February 20, 2013). Accessed October 26, 2015. www.wsws. rog/en/articles/2013/02/20/ .

Jula Megan and Daniel Gonzalez. "Eloy Detention Center: Why so Many Suicides?" *The Republic* (July 29, 2015). Accessed March 1, 2016. www. azcentral.com/story/news/arizona/investigations/2015/07/28/eloy-detention-center-immigrant-suicides/30760545.

Keenan, Eogham. "Case Profile. *In Re: Northeast Ohio Correctional Center.*" (June 10, 2005). Accessed January 11, 2016. www.clearinghouse.net/detail/php?id=901&search.

King, Ryan, Bryce Peterson, Brian Elderbroom, and Elizabeth Pelletier. "Reducing Mass Incarceration Requires Far-Reaching Reforms." (2015).

Accessed December 31, 2015. www.http://webapp. urban.org/reducing-mass-incarceration/

Kirkham, Chris. "Private Prison Corporation Offers Cash in Exchange for State Prisons." *Huffington Post.* (February 14, 2012a). Accessed November 18, 2015. www.huffingtonpost.com/2012/02/14/private-prisons-buying-state-prisons_n_1272143.

___ . "With States Facing Shortfalls, Private Corporation Offers Cash for Prisons." *Huffington Post.* (2012b). Accessed November 22, 2015. www.huffingtonpost.com/2012/02/14/private-prisons-buying-state-prisons_n_1272143.html

___ . "Lake Erie Prison Plagued by Violence and Drugs after Corporate Takeover." *Huffington Post.* (March 22, 2013). Accessed November 10, 2015. www.huffingtonpost.com/2013/03/22/lake-erie-prison-violence_n_2925151.html

"Kite? Where did that come from," *Jail Medicine,* January 29, 2012. Retrieved March 2, 2016. http://www.jailmedicine.com/kite-where-did-that-come-from

Latour, Francie. "Suffolk Jail Audit Group is Faulted: Critics to Demand New Review Panel." *Boston Globe.* (June 20, 2001). Accessed October 14, 2015. www.prisonpolicy. org/scans/stoptheaca/stoptheaca062001/htmlwww.prisonpolicy. org/scans/stoptheaca/stoptheaca062001/html.

Lava, Jesse and Sarah Solon. "The Biggest, Baddest Prison Profiteer of Them All." American Civil Liberties Union (ACLU). (April 19, 2014). Accessed October 15, 2015. www.aclu.org/blog/biggest-baddest-prison-prifiteer-them-all.

LeBlanc. Clif. "Prisons Might Lose Accreditation." (April 14, 2003). Accessed October 11, 2015. www.prisonpolicy.org/scans/stoptheaca/thestate5628651.html.

Lewis, Rene. "U.S. Prisons Have 10 Times as Many Mentally Ill as in State Hospitals." (April 8, 2014). Accessed December 16, 2015. http://america.aljazeera.com/articles/2014/4/8/mental-illness-prison.html

Libal, Bob. "Victory in Texas-the Dawson State Jail Will Close!" (June 11, 2013). Accessed January 11, 2016. www.grassrootsleadership.org/blog/2013/06/victory-texas-dawson-state-jail-will-close.

Lills, Mike. "Sanders, Liberals Press Obama to Expand Closure of Private Prisons." (August 18, 2016). Accessed August 20, 2016. http://thehill.com/homenews/administration/291925-sanders-liberals-press-obama-to-expand-closure-of-private-prisons.

Lipton, Eric. "In Kentucky Hills, a Homeland Security Bonanza." *New York Times.* (May 14, 2006). Accessed January 2, 2016. https://www.quiery.nytimes.com/gst/fullpage.html.

Litchfeld, Charlie. "Federal Judge Orders CCA to Pay Attorney Fees to American Civil Liberties Union." *Idaho Press Tribune.* (February 22, 2014). Accessed November 10, 2015. www.idahopress. com/news/state/federal-judge-orders-cca-to-pay-attorney-fees-to-aclu/article_d9cdcfd6-9b2c-lle3-9498-001a4bcf887a.htmlwww.idahopress. com/news/state/federal-judge-orders-cca-to-pay-attorney-fees-to-aclu/article_d9cdcfd6-9b2c-lle3-9498-001a4bcf887a.html.

Lupo, Kimberly. "The History of Mental Illness." (2015). Accessed October 26, 2015.

http://www.toddlertime. com/advocacy/hospitals/Asylum/history_asylumhttp://www.toddlertime. com/advocacy/hospitals/Asylum/history_asylum.

Madison, Piper. "Meet the Private Prison Industry's Lobbyists Who Could Shape Immigration Reform." *Grassroots Leadership.* (February 2013). Accessed December 15, 2015. www. grassrootsleadership.org/blog/2013/02/meet-private-prison-industry-s-lobbyists-who-could-shape-immigration-reform.

Market Watch News. "Private Prison Stocks Jump After Trump Official Says Feds Will Continue Using Facilities." (February 23, 2017). Accessed February 23, 2017. http://www.marketwatch.com/investing/stock/CXW?countrycode=US

Markham, Timothy R. "Imprisoned by Profit: Breaking Colorado's Dependency on For-Profit Prison," Colorado WINS. (February 27, 2013). http://dailycaller.com/wp-content/uploads/2013/03/DOC+white+paper+ISSUU.pdf.

Marlow, Elizabeth and Catherine Chesla. *Prison Experiences and the Reintegration of Male Parolees.* U.S. National Library of Medicine, National Institute of Health. In ADS Adv Nurs Sci 2009 April-June 32 (2). http://www.ncbi.nlm.ni.gov/pmc/articles/PMC2886197/ Accessed March 10, 2106.

Mattera, Phillip and Mafruza Khan. *Corrections Corporation of America: A Critical Look at its First Twenty Years.* Corporate Research Project of Good Jobs First and Prison Privatization Report International. Grassroots Leadership: Washington, DC. (2003). Retrieved February 26, 2016 from http://www.goodjobsfirst.org/sites/default/files/docs/pdf/CCA percent20Anniversary percent20Report.pdf

McGraw, Mike.. "Private prison firm to give back pay to guards." *Kansas City Star.* (r 1, 2009). AcceSeptember 1, 2009). Accessed January 14, 2016. www.donelonpc. com/pdfs/Private_prison_to_give_back_pay_to_guards. pdf.

"Mental Health Courts." California Courts, The Judicial Branch of California. Retrieved March 1, 2016. http://www.courts.ca.gov/5982.htm.

Mitchell, Kirk. "Coming Prison Closing Adding to Walsenberg's Woes." *Denver Post.* (March 23, 2010). Accessed September 15, 2015. www.Denverpost. com/ci.14735948.

Mitchell, Kirk, Lynn Bartels, and Kurtis Lee. "2011 law a factor in Evan Ebel's early release from prison." The Denver Post. Boulder DailyCamera.com. March 28, 2013. http://www.dailycamera.com/ci_22896714/evan-ebel-out-prison-early-thanks-2011-colorado?source=most_viewed

Mohr, Holbrook. "Mississippi Prison Riot Started by Gang, Sheriff Says." *Huffington Post.* (May 21, 2012). Accessed February 15, 2016. www. huffingtonpost.com/2012/05/21/mississippi-prison riot_n_1533936.html.

Morgan, D. W., A. C Edwards, and L. R. Faulkner. "The Adaptation to Prison by Individuals with Schizophrenia." *Bulletin of the American Academy of Psychiatry and the Law.* 21: (1993): 427-433. Accessed December 12, 2016. http://www.jaapl.org/content/21/4/427.abstract

*National Association of Drug Court Professionals.* "Drug Courts Work." Accessed March 1, 2016. http://www.nadcp.org/learn/facts-and-figures.

National Commission on Correctional Health Care. "Segregated Inmates." Accessed March 1, 2016. http://www.ncchc.org/spotlight-on-the-standards-26-2.

National Criminal Justice Reference Service. "In the Spotlight Drug Courts—Facts and Figures." June 30, 2013. https://www.ncjrs.gov/spotlight/drug_courts/facts.html.

Neader, Enrique. *Drug Discovery: A History.* Chichester: Wiley, 2011.

National Immigrant Justice Center. "The Immigration Detention Transparency and Human Rights Project." (August 2015.). Accessed January 21, 2016. http://immigrantjustice.          org/immigration-detention-transparency-and-human-rights-project-august-2015-reportRetrieved from http:// immigrantjustice.  org/immigration-detention-transparency-and-human-rights-project-august-2015-report.

Osher, Fred, D. D'Amora, M. Plotkin, N Jarrett, and A. Eggleston. *Adults with Behavioral Health Needs under Correctional Supervision: A Shared Framework for Reducing Recidivism and Promoting Recovery .* Criminal Justice Mental Health Consensus Project. Council of State Governments Justice Center, National Institute of Corrections, and Bureau of Justice Statistics. (2012) https://csgjusticecenter.org/mental-health-projects/behavioral-health-framework/

Pauly, Madison. "The Private Prison Industry is Licking Its Chops Over Trump's Deportation Plans." *Mother Jones.* (February 21, 2017). Accessed February 24, 2017. http://www.motherjones.com/politics/2017/02/trumps-immigration-detention-center-expansion

Pens, Dan. "Prison Realty/CCA Verges on Bankruptcy." *Prison Legal News.* (July 15, 2000). Accessed January 2, 2016. www.prisonlegalnews.org/ news/2000/jul/15/prison-realtycca/verges-on-bankruptcy.

Petrella, Christopher. "The Color of Radical Criminology, Part II: Contractual Exemptions and the Overrepresentation of People of Color in Private Prions." *Journal of Radical Criminology,* 3 (January 2014). Accessed January 30, 2016. http://journal.radicalcriminology. org/indexphp/rc/article/ view/44/pdfhttp://journal.radicalcriminology. org/indexphp/rc/article/ view/44/pdf.

Prendergast, Alan. "After the Murder of Tom Clements Can Colorado's Prison System Rehabilitate Itself?" *Westword.* (August 21, 2014a.). Accessed on December 12, 2015. http://www.westword. com/news/after-the-murder-of-tom-clements-cab-colorados-prison-system-rehabilitate-itself-5125050http://www.westword. com/news/after-the-murder-of-tom-clements-cab-colorados-prison-system-rehabilitate-itself-5125050.

___. "Crowley County Riot: New Details of Unheeded Warnings Emerge in Epic Lawsuit." *Westword.* (2014b.). Accessed November 20, 2015. http://www. westword.com/news/crowley-prison-riot-new-details-of-unheeded-warnings=emerge-in-epic-lawsuit-5863180

Priest, Dana. "Sheriff Gondles Settles Suit on Harassment for $25,000." *Washington Post.* (April 28, 2001). Accessed October 4, 2015. www. highbeam.com/doc/1P2-1253519. html.

Prison Van Crash. "Speed, Inexperience Cited in Prison Van Crash." KKTV. (December 29, 2011). Accessed September 15, 2015. www.kktv. com/home/ headlines/Inmate_And_Officer_Killed_In_Crash_On_I-70_135878708. htmlwww.kktv. com/home/headlines/Inmate_And_Officer_Killed_In_ Crash_On_I-70_135878708.html.

"Private Prison," Wikipedia. Retrieved February 27, 2016 from https:// en.wikipedia.org/wiki/Private_prison.

Private Corrections Institute, Inc. "Quick Facts About Prison Privatization." http://www.privateci.org/private_pics/Private percent20prison percent20fact percent20sheet percent202009.pdf.

Public Law 108-458, Sec. 5204(a). "Intelligence Reform and Terrorism Prevention Act of 2004." (Dec. 17, 2004). Accessed January 10, 2016. https://www.nctc.gov/docs/pl108_458.pdg.

Puryear, Eugene. *Shackled and Chained: Mass Incarceration in Capitalist America.* San Francisco: PSL Publications, 2013.

Rael, Andrea. "Fort Lyon Prison, Closed By Budget Cuts, Reopens to House Homeless." *Huffington Post.* (September 5, 2013). Accessed November 15, 2015. www.huffingtonpost.com/2013/09/05/fort-lyon-homeless-preven_n_387588.html.

Raemisch, Rick and Kellie Wasko, *Open the Door—Segregation Reforms in Colorado.* Colorado Department of Corrections. https://drive.google.com/file/d/0B30yLl0IlyBRY2h2UDBCZ0Q5WlE/view. Accessed March 2, 2016.

Raher, Stephen. "Private Prisons and Public Money: Hidden Costs Borne by Colorado's Taxpayers." *CCJRC Briefing Report* from Colorado Criminal Justice Reform Coalition. (September 2002). Accessed December 15, 2015. www.ccjrc.org/pdf/CostDateReport2002.pdf.

Rania, Khalek. "The Shocking Ways the Corporate Prison Industry Games the System." *Truth Out.* (November 29, 2011). Accessed November 15, 2015. www.truth-out.org/news/item/5283:the-shocking-ways-the-corporate-prison-industry-games-the-system.

Rasor, Dina. "American's Top Prison Corporation: A Study in Predatory Capitalism and Cronyism." (May 3, 2012). Accessed January 2, 2016. www.truth-out-org/news/item/8875-corrections-corporation-of-american-a-study-in-predatory-capitalism-and-cronyism/tmpl=component&print=1.

Razavi, Layla, Director, Human Migration and Mobility. "Eliminate the Immigration Detention Quota." American Friends Service Committee. (August 26, 2016). *Email correspondence.*

Real Estate Investment Trust. "Real Estate Investment Trust-REIT." *Investopedia Online.* (2015). Accessed December 26, 2015. www.Investophedia.com/terms/r/reit. asp.

Reiman, Jeffrey and Paul Leighton. *The Rich Get Richer and the Poor Get Prison,* 9th Ed. Boston: Allyn and Bacon, 2010.

Reynolds, Francis and Lee Fang. "What Does Millions in Lobbying Buy/" *The Nation.* (February 27, 2013). Accessed December 27, 2015. www.thenation.com/article/what-does-millions-lobbying-buy.

Roberts, John W. *Reform and Retribution: An Illustrated History of American Prisons.* American Correctional Association: Lanham, Maryland. 1997.

Robertson, Alistair Graham, Rachel Beaty, Jane Atkinson, and Bob Libal. "Operation Streamline: Costs and Consequences." *Grassroots Leadership.* (2012). Accessed January 29, 2016. http://grassrootsleadership.org/sites/default/files/uploads/GRL_Sept2012_report-finalpdf.

Rodriguez, Sal. "Solitary Watch Fact Sheet: Psychological Effects of Solitary Confinement." Solitary Watch. http://solitarywatch.com/wp-content/uploads/2011/06/fact-sheet-psychological-effects-final.pdf.

*Ruiz v Estelle,* 503 F. Supp 1265 (S. D. Tx.). (December 12, 1980). Accessed February 26, 2016. .

FindLaw. Retrieved from http://caselaw.findlaw.com/us-5th-circuit/1381589.html.

Samaha, Albert. "The Prison Reform Blues." *Buzz Feed.* (December 5, 2014) Accessed October 3, 2015. www.buzzfeed. com/albertsamaha/the-rise-and-fall-of-Mississippis-top-prison-reformer#.1pQ88GIiQYewww. buzzfeed. com/albertsamaha/the-rise-and-fall-of-Mississippis-top-prison-reformer#.1pQ88GIiQYe.

Sanders, Bernie. "S. 2054-Justice is Not for Sale Act of 2015." 2015. Accessed December 15, 2015. www.congress.gov/bill/114th-congress/senate-bill/2054/all-actions?overview=closed.

Schlosser, Eric. "The Prison-Industrial Complex," *Atlantic Monthly* (December 1998) 282: 51-77.

Sclar, Elliott D. *You Don't Always Get What You Pay For: The Economics of Privatization.* Ithaca, New York: Cornell University Press, 2000.

Selman, Donna and Paul Leighton. *Punishment for Sale: Private Prisons, Big Business, and the Incarceration Binge.* Lanham, Maryland: Rowman & Littlefield Publishers, Inc., 2010.

Sentencing Project, The. "Why Minorities Are Even More Overrepresented in Private Prisons." *Sentencing Project.* (February 18, 2014). Accessed on January 30, 2016. www.sentencingproject. org/detail/news/ctim?news_id=1770www.sentencingproject. org/detail/news/ctim?news_id=1770.

___. "Incarceration: U.S. Prison Population Trends: 1999-2014." *Sentencing Project.* February 16, 2016.. www.sentencingproject.org/template/page.cfm?id=107.

Simanski, John F. and Lesley M. Sapp. "Immigration Enforcement Actions 2012." Department of Homeland Security Annual Report (December 2013). Accessed January 10, 2016. http://preview.dhs. gov/sites/default/files/publications/ois_enforcement_ar_2012_1.pdfhttp://preview.dhs. gov/sites/default/files/publications/ois_enforcement_ar_2012_1.pdf.

Simon, David. *The Big Interview with Dan Rather.* (April 1, 2014.). AXSTV. Also available at www. youtube.com.

Solomon, Alisha. "Detainees Equal Dollars: The Rise of Immigrant Incarceration Drives a Prison Boom." *Village Voice.* (August 13, 2002). Accessed December 15, 2015. http://www.villagevoice. com/issues/02-33/solomon. phphttp://www.villagevoice. com/issues/02-33/solomon. php.

Source Watch. "Corrections Corporation of America." (May 2013a.). Accessed October 8, 2015.

www.SourceWatch. org/index.php/corrections_corporation_of_americawww. SourceWatch. org/index.php/corrections_corporation_of_america.

___. "Corrections Corporation of America, Form 10-K, SEC filing, fiscal year ended December 31, 2013." (May2013b.). Accessed December 12, 2015.

http://www.SourceWatch.org/index/php?title=Corrections_Corporation_of_ America.

Stelloh, Tim. "Obama to End Solitary Confinement for Juveniles in Federal Prisons." MSNBC. Last modified January 25, 2016. www.msnbc.com/msnbc/obama-end-solitary-confinement-juveniles-federal-prisons.

Swanson, Doug J. "Fired TYC Monitors had Worked for Facility Operator: Group Fired For Failing to Report Conditions at West Texas facility was Employed Earlier by GEO Group." *Dallas Morning News.* (October 12, 2007). Accessed December 12, 2015. http://callcenterinfo. tmcnet/news/2007/10/12/3009957.htmlhttp://callcenterinfo. tmcnet/news/2007/10/12/3009957.html

Taibbi, Matt. *The Divide: American Injustice in the Age of the Wealth Gap.* New York: Spiegel & Grau imprint of Random House, 2014.

Talvi, Silja J. A. "Inside the American Correctional Association." *Prison Legal News.* (September 15, 2004). Accessed October 4, 2015. https://www.prisonlegalnews.org/news/2005/sep/15/inside-the-american-correctional-association/.

Torrey, E. Fuller, Mary T. Zdanowicz, Aaron D. Kennard, H. Richard Lamb, Donald F. Eslinger, Michael C. Biasotti, and Doris A. Fuller. "The Treatment of Persons with Mental Illness in Prisons and Jails:

A State Survey." April 8, 2014. http://tacreports.org/storage/documents/treatment-behind-bars/treatment-behind-bars.pdf. .

U.S. Builder's Review. "Corrections Corporation of America: American's Leading Corrections Partner." (2015). Accessed December 19, 2015. www.usbuildersreview.com/case-studies/corrections-corportion-america-america percentE2 percent-80 percent99s-leading-corrections-partner.

U.S. Department of Homeland Security. Annual Report. "Immigration Enforcement Actions: 2012." (December 2013.). Accessed December 26, 2015. https://dhs. gov/sites/default/files/publications/ois_enforcement_ar_2012_1.pdf https://dhs. gov/sites/default/files/publications/ois_enforcement_ar_2012_1.pdf

U.S. Equal Employment Opportunity Commission. "Private Prison Pays $1.3 Million to Settle Sexual Harassment Retaliation Claims for Class of Women." Government Commission Press Release (October 13, 2009). Accessed ss Release (October 13, 2009). Accessed January 3, 2015. www.eeoc.gov/eeoc/newsroom/release/10-13-09.cfmU.

U.S. Immigration and Customs Enforcement. "DHS Releases End of Fiscal Year 2015 Statistics." (December 22, 2015). Accessed February 4, 2016. https://www.ice.gov/news/releases/dhs-releases-end-fiscal-year-2015-statistics.

U. S. Supreme Court. "*Hutto v Finney.*" 437 U.A. 678 (1978). Justica U.S. Supreme Court Center. Accessed October 4, 2015. www.supreme.justica.com/cases/federal/us/437/678.

Wagner, Peter and Bernadette Rabuy. Mass Incarceration: The Whole Pie-A Prison Policy Initiative Briefing". *Prison Policy.* (December 8, 2015). Accessed February 26, 2016. http://www.prisonpolicy. org/reports/pie/ htmlhttp://www.prisonpolicy. org/reports/pie/html.

Wagner, Peter and Leah Sakala. "Mass Incarceration: The Whole Pie-A Prison Policy Initiative Briefing." *Prison Policy.* (March 12, 2014). Accessed December 5, 2015. http://www.prisonpolicy. org/reports/pie/html.

http://www.prisonpolicy. org/reports/pie/html.

Wilber, Del Quentin, "Justice Department Rescinds Order Phasing Out Use of Private Prisons." (February 23, 2017). Accessed February 23, 2017.www. latimes.com/politics/Washington/la-na-essential-washington-updates- justice-department-re scinds-order-1487893081-htmlstory.html

Woodruff, Betsy. "Private Prisons Cheer Trump's Immigration Crackdown." *The Daily Beast.* (January 25, 2017). Accessed February 25, 2017. http:// www.thedailybeast.com/articles/2017/01/25/private-prisons-cheer- trump-s-immigration-crackdown.htmlWyden, Ron. "Breaking: OR Sen Ron Wyden Introduces Bill to End Prison Tax Breaks." (July 14, 2016). Accessed August 26, 2016. https://prisondivest.com/2016/07/14/or-sen- ron-wyden-introduces-bill-to-end-prison-tax-breaks/

Printed in the United States
By Bookmasters